THE WORLD'S CLASSICS

600

MATTHEW ARNOLD

SELECTED ESSAYS

Oxford University Press, Amen House, London E.C. 4

GLASGOW   NEW YORK   TORONTO   MELBOURNE   WELLINGTON
BOMBAY   CALCUTTA   MADRAS   KARACHI   LAHORE   DACCA
CAPE TOWN   SALISBURY   NAIROBI   IBADAN   ACCRA
KUALA LUMPUR   HONG KONG

MATTHEW ARNOLD

SELECTED ESSAYS

Chosen with an Introduction
by

NOEL ANNAN

LONDON
OXFORD UNIVERSITY PRESS
NEW YORK TORONTO
1964

MATTHEW ARNOLD

Born: Laleham, near Staines, 24 December 1822
Died: Liverpool, 15 April 1888

This selection from the essays was first included in
The World's Classics *in 1964*

Selection and Introduction
© *Oxford University Press, 1964*

PRINTED IN GREAT BRITAIN

CONTENTS

INTRODUCTION

MATTHEW ARNOLD was the first modern critic.[1] He was the first to declare that people could be consoled, healed, and changed by reading literature and therefore that their awakening depended on understanding which was the finest literature. He was the first to argue that the spiritual health of a society such as England depended on there being a sufficient number of civilized human beings devoted to the ideal of spreading Culture. He was the first to claim for criticism the role of civilizing the nation's mind. T. S. Eliot, F. R. Leavis, and Arnold's own fine interpreter, Lionel Trilling, differ immensely as critics from each other and from him, but they continue the argument that he began.

Arnold saw the critic quite differently from anyone before him. He did not see him as a scholar who deduced Aristotelian rules and applied to them literature; or as an arbiter of cultivated taste; or as a student of psychology categorizing mental faculties such as imagination, fancy, or appetencies through which men respond to different kinds of poetry. He did not treat criticism as a branch of philosophy. He had no theory of the sublime nor did he divide works of art into the sentimental and the naive, into classical and romantic, Apollonian and Dionysian as the great German critics did. Criticism was not a branch of anything—it was a self-organizing activity. It

[1] Anyone who wants to study Arnold as a critic should read Lionel Trilling, *Matthew Arnold* (1949); T. S. Eliot, 'Arnold and Pater' in *Selected Essays* (1932) and 'Matthew Arnold' in *The Use of Poetry and the Use of Criticism* (1933); F. R. Leavis, 'Arnold as Critic', *Scrutiny*, vii (1938); Vincent Buckley, *Poetry and Morality* (1959).

was not a craft—it was an art, the act of judgement. It was not an essay in the last issue of a quarterly magazine —it was a calling that demanded the same dedication of mind, temperament, and spirit as art itself.

It was a calling because the quality of life itself must be the concern of the critic. What was the function of poetry? 'Poetry is at bottom a criticism of life' was Arnold's famous answer. When the critic considered a poem he must set it against his ideal of what life should be. He should judge at once the poem and the poet and the quality of the civilization that both embodied. To be a critic is above all to be a moralist. The critic is the judge not of the past so much as of his own times. Every judgement he makes is in some sense a reflection upon the society in which he lives. That is why Arnold, however academic the titles of his essays may be, is always writing about contemporary sensibility or standards. Why Homer is translated as he is, why there is no Academy of Letters in Britain, why a woman called Wragg has been committed to prison, all illuminate the state of our society and the terrible inadequacy of our culture. That is why the essays in this volume range from literary criticism to education, to social structure, to an analysis of the essence of culture, and end by examining what was to the Victorians the supreme and ever-recurring problem—man's relation to God.

Arnold, then, was a sage, but he differed from the other Victorian sages by asking a more complicated and subtle question. Carlyle, Ruskin, Newman, and behind them the great preachers and Evangelical revivalists, asked in that religious age: how should a man live and what must he do to be saved? The answer to this question must always contain the same elements: man must be converted and society submit to what is virtually a revolution in structure and morals. Arnold was less ambitious. He asked: what things should we consider important and what things trivial if we are to learn how to live? What is the quality of life and how are we to discriminate between the valuable and the less valuable and the worthless? He asked the conservative to consider whether the education that Lord Lumpington got at Eton and Christ Church was really adequate. He suggested to the liberal that freedom and the determination to do as one likes were inadequate at a time when only State intervention could give England a system of public education. He told the radicals and freethinkers that a diet of science and utilitarianism and a contempt for tradition was inadequate nourishment for the mind. He intimated to churchmen and dissenters that their stubbornness in trying to preserve certain dogmas in the sense that they had been understood in the last hundred years was hastening the disintegration of Christianity itself. Whatever subject he handled he tried to expose some popular error or prejudice and persuade his countrymen to be less rigid, less provincial, more open-minded, more willing to learn from the experience of other countries or from antiquity and to liberate themselves from partisan polemics.

But how was a critic to range so wide and not become an opinionated wind-bag? Arnold declared that the critic needed two especial qualities: disinterestedness and a sense of what is relevant. He must be dispassionate and stand above the battle. He must belong to no party, whether political, intellectual, or religious. Parties are needed by men who want to get things done and change affairs: the critic must beware of what is practical and efficient, because he is pursuing something finer than discovering the highest common factor of agreement between opposing opinions. He judges all this practical activity by ideal standards. This he can do only if he learns to think objectively. To do so he must learn to distinguish what is relevant. Sifting the relevant from the unimportant is hard because a man must not only see through the dust that the combatants kick up when disputing some great issue to the centre of the issue itself, but must also discipline his own mind and rid it of quirks, conceits, and idiosyncrasies that might lead him away from the issue to flatter his own vanity. At the end of his controversy with Francis Newman on how Homer should be translated Arnold wrote:

To handle these matters properly there is needed a poise so perfect that the least overweight in any direction tends to destroy the balance. Temper destroys it, a crochet destroys it, even erudition may destroy it. To press to the sense of the thing itself with which one is dealing, not to go off on some collateral issue about the thing, is the hardest matter in the world. . . .

Yet however much the critic must display delicacy of perception and sensitivity of ear and eye and apprehension—however much he must hesitate and qualify and refine—Arnold never let his reader forget what the ultimate duty of the critic was. It was to discriminate—to demonstrate that this was better than that. At the high tide of romantic poetry Arnold told Englishmen that their idol Tennyson was not to be spoken of in the same breath as Homer; and as for Macaulay—in such company the *Lays of Ancient Rome* should never be mentioned. He told them that Shelley was eccentric and that most of their native geniuses were provincial. Arnold claimed that the greatest poetry was always sustained by high seriousness and a luminous serenity. He thought of poetry as a religious act, a kind of knowledge that is acquired through sympathy rather than reasoning; and he believed conversely that the essence of religion was a kind of poetic grace that kindled morality. Moral profundity is his criterion of excellence—for in what other way, he asks, is man to be fortified and elevated? But profundity alone will not inspire—it needs to be exhibited in the grand style. Style whether in expression or in the art of living is the elixir that renders a work of art or a human action imperishable. These are the touchstones by which we are to judge life and that which makes life intelligible—literature.

Today, a century since Arnold was writing the best of his criticism, no one any longer would accept Arnold's concepts, criteria, or methods of discriminating between different works of art. Criticism has now, as Arnold hoped it would, passed into the academies as a recognized discipline, and the simple distinctions that Arnold made have been swept away in the torrent of analysis that has flowed from the hard-working movement in literary criticism that has been established in the last few decades, and which has had to take account of not only the romanticism that Arnold tried to place in the poetic procession but also the revolution in art that began shortly after Arnold's death and which his criteria were totally inadequate to deal with. But his stature as a critic is undiminished. He cannot be ignored by anyone who wants to understand what it is that literature does; and he must be read by anyone who wants to understand the Victorian age.

The essays in this book can reflect only a few of the facets of his mind. They begin with analyses of poetry and the critic's relation to it. Arnold lived too early to realize just how great an art form the novel was, but his essay on *Anna Karenina* shows that he understood that Tolstoy was in a different class from any novelist that had appeared in England or in France. He wrote little on drama—the theatre in his time was in an abysmal state: but the little-known fragment on *Hamlet* is included because Arnold, swimming as ever against the popular stream, calls the play 'ineffective' and anticipates a line that has been developed in criticism today. Then follow essays on culture which show how broad Arnold's conception of conditions that either civilize or brutalize was. The noble essay on Equality shows how he realized that the critic cannot ignore the structure of the society in which he lives; and the opening chapters of *Culture and Anarchy* reveal his dismay at the lack in England of an informed and highly cultivated intelligentsia whose refinement of mind and taste and conduct set standards for the nation at large. Then there is Arnold's reply to T. H. Huxley in which he vindicates the study of the humanities for their own sake and questions the claims of science to provide a satisfactory education: this essay—and Huxley's admirable provocation—should have been read by C. P. Snow before he reopened the issue in his shallow lecture on the Two Cultures. Lastly come two essays on religion. They cannot by themselves give more than a hint of the fervour and controlled passion with which Arnold sought to urge his countrymen to retain their hold on the Bible and the saving truths of Christianity which still had the unique power of making men prefer righteousness to evil while at the same time being prepared to jettison dogmas, including even the divinity of Christ, that had become meaningless impediments. God as a First Cause or the evidence for miracles, and the resurrection are as nothing to the insistent message of the Gospels to practise self-renunciation and inwardness: for there, Arnold maintains, in the day-to-day practice of Christian conduct, lies the true resurrection of the spirit.

Just as in reading literature Arnold asked for delicacy of perception, so in religion he besought people to abandon the blind, combative, literal-mindedness with which they were so accustomed to interpret Scripture.

The great critics are those who provoke our intense disagreement and in so doing disturb us. Arnold nearly always succeeds in getting under our skin. If poetry is to stay and console—if it is to speak to our experience and deepen and extend it—why restrict its scope and insist that only a few pages of it demand our attention? Religion without dogma can still be religion; but it cannot be Christianity. The metaphysics that Arnold laid so lightly aside are age-long answers to questions that men have put about their predicament in this world and their relation to God and the universe and a world to come. A great inspector of schools, such as Arnold was, ought not to have been so bestially ignorant of how scientists reason and how scientific methods can be applied to social problems: Huxley the agnostic insisting that the Bible be read in schools and generous in his appreciation of the place of literature was far more impressive than Arnold whose essay, so far from going against the grain, reinforced for two generations the prevailing complacency and disdain for science and technology. Arnold's conception of culture is too neat and circumscribed—even though he ranged from Homer and Dante to the *Gita*. It hardly began to take account of non-European works and behind it stands the notion that art is experience recollected in tranquillity and given suitable gnomic utterance; and art is something other than this. And yet it is also worth noting how some of Arnold's dreams have in a sense materialized. For quite a number of people literature and its exegesis (criticism) have replaced church-going and the perusal of sermons and theology as aids to the spiritual life; two generations of Arnoldians through institutions including the State itself have tried to spread sweetness and light by insisting that the arts are part of national life; some even in their hearts interpret Christianity in his fashion. For he possessed possibly the most persuasive voice of all the Victorian sages.

Persuasive . . . *that* is one of the most enduring qualities of Arnold's prose. If the sole purpose of this edition were to give as concise and wide an account of Arnold's thought as possible it would have been a collection of extracts from his essays. But this would have meant losing something that can be got only by reprinting a few of the essays in full. That is the play of his mind, his method of developing an argument, the eloquence and delicacy of his advocacy—above all his irony and his humour. He was assured. His assurance was not that of the man with the big battalions on his side: on the contrary he writes as a lonely figure. Nor was it the assurance of the smug: on the contrary he knew his limitations as a thinker and the limits of what can be asserted in criticism. It is the assurance of a man who is at ease with his audience, at ease with himself, and even at ease with his opponents. He can banter and mock them but with equanimity, in good temper, knowing his own place in the comedy that he presents as well as theirs.

Today the tone of many literary critics is deplorably different. They whine or display savage ill-temper, they write in the voice that Arnold knew so well and sighed at hearing—the self-righteous, narrow, querulous, vindictive tone of the Evangelical organ the *Record*, or the slashing, self-approbatory, loud-mouthed voice of the *Saturday Review*: both deficient in charity or compassion. When Arnold stalks his prey he never forgets that the Barbarian and the Philistine, Mr. Bottles and Francis Newman, even the Bishops of Winchester and Gloucester, are human beings to be treated with the courtesy and dignity that human beings deserve. There are no completely unregenerate or elect in his world. We may disagree with his notions of culture but cannot doubt that we are listening to a cultured man: his concepts are embodied in his style. For the critic, perhaps even more than the artist, appears to his reader as a living acquaintance. What he wrote the day before yesterday is so contemporaneous, so urgent, so bound up with our own situation, interests, and desires that we can overlook at that moment of first reading the character—and the *authority* embodied in the character—that lie behind his comment. But a century later the dead critic's character is his prime hope of immortality. It is that which speaks to us when the issues that he raised have long since changed their shape, and what reassures us is the consistency between what is advocated and the voice that advocates it. When Arnold urges the spread of sweetness and light the words he chooses are suffused with these qualities. What is still today irresistible is Arnold's gaiety, his wry astonishment at stupidity, his delighted amusement at folly, his instant recognition of distinction, and the urbane, self-deprecating, faintly weary inflexion that does not for an instant conceal the hopeful and intense seriousness with which he approached the life that he saw about him.

NOEL ANNAN

the Bishops of Winchester and Gloucester, are human
beings to be treated with the courtesy and dignity that
human beings deserve. There are no completely unregenerate or clear in the world. We may disagree with
the notions of culture but cannot doubt that we are
listening to a cultured man. His opinions are embodied
in his style. But the tones perhaps even more than the
artist, appears to his reader as a living acquaintance.
What he wrote the day before yesterday is so contemporaneous, so unusual, so bound up with our own situation,
interests, and themes that we can overlook in that moment
of that reading the hatred—and the others, unlicensed
in the characters—at he behind his centuries. But a
century later the dead critic's character seems to us what the
of immortality. It is that which speaks to us, when the
issues that he raised have long since changed their shape,
and what reassures us is the consistency between what is
advocated and the voice that advocates it. When Arnold
urges the spread of sweetness and light, the words he
chooses are suffused with these qualities. What is still
today irresistible is Arnold's gaiety, his wry astonishment
at stupidity, his delighted amusement at folly, his instant
recognition of distinction, and the winning, self-depreciat-
ing, faintly weary inflexion that does not for an instant
conceal the hopeful and intense seriousness with which he
apprehended the life that he saw about him.

NOEL ANNAN

PREFACE TO THE FIRST EDITION
OF *ESSAYS IN CRITICISM*
[*FIRST SERIES*]

(1865)

SEVERAL of the Essays which are here collected and reprinted have had the good or the bad fortune to be much criticised at the time of their first appearance. I am not now going to inflict upon the reader a reply to those criticisms; for one or two explanations which are desirable I shall elsewhere, perhaps, be able some day to find an opportunity; but indeed, it is not in my nature,—some of my critics would rather say, not in my power,—to dispute on behalf of any opinion, even my own, very obstinately. To try and approach Truth on one side after another, not to strive or cry, not to persist in pressing forward, on any one side, with violence and self-will,— it is only thus, it seems to me, that mortals may hope to gain any vision of the mysterious Goddess, whom we shall never see except in outline, but only thus even in outline. He who will do nothing but fight impetuously towards her on his own, one, favourite, particular line, is inevitably destined to run his head into the folds of the black robe in which she is wrapped.

I am very sensible that this way of thinking leaves me under great disadvantages in addressing a public composed from a people 'the most logical', says the *Saturday Review*, 'in the whole world'. But the truth is, I have never been able to hit it off happily with the logicians, and it would be mere affectation in me to give myself the airs of doing so. They imagine truth something to be proved, I something to be seen; they something to be manufactured, I as something to be found. I have a profound respect for intuitions, and a very lukewarm respect for the elaborate machine-work of my friends the logicians. I have always thought that all which was worth much in this elaborate machine-work of theirs came from an intuition, to which they gave a grand name of their own. How did they come by this intuition? Ah, if they could tell us that. But no; they set their machine in motion, and build up a fine showy edifice, glittering and unsubstantial like a pyramid of eggs; and then they say: 'Come and look at our pyramid.' And what does one find it? Of all that heap of eggs, the one poor little fresh egg, the original intuition, has got hidden away far out of sight and forgotten. And all the other eggs are addled.

So it is not to build rival pyramids against my logical enemies that I write this preface, but to prevent a misunderstanding, of which certain phrases that some of them use make me apprehensive. Mr. Wright, one of the many translators of Homer, has just published a Letter to the Dean of Canterbury, complaining of some remarks of mine, uttered now a long while ago, on his version of the Iliad. One cannot be always studying one's own works, and I was really under the impression, till I saw Mr. Wright's complaint, that I had spoken of him with all respect. The reader may judge of my astonishment, therefore, at finding, from Mr. Wright's pamphlet, that I had 'declared with much solemnity that there is not any proper reason for his existing'. That I never said; but, on looking back at my Lectures on translating Homer, I find that I did say, not that Mr. Wright, but that Mr. Wright's version of the Iliad, repeating in the main the merits and defects of Cowper's version, as Mr. Sotheby's repeated those of Pope's version, had, if I might be pardoned for saying so, no proper reason for existing. Elsewhere I expressly spoke of the merit of his version; but I confess that the phrase, qualified as I have shown, about its want of a proper reason for existing, I used. Well, the phrase had, perhaps, too much vivacity: alas! vivacity is one of those faults which advancing years will only too certainly cure; that, however, is no real excuse; we have all of us a right to exist, we and our works; an unpopular author should be the last person to call in question this right. So I gladly withdraw the offending phrase, and I am sorry for having used it; Mr. Wright, however, will allow me to observe that he has taken an ample revenge. He has held me up before the public as 'condemned by my own umpire'; as 'rebutted', and 'with an extinguisher put upon me' by Mr. Tennyson's remarkable pentameter:

When did a frog coarser croak upon our Helicon?

(till I read Mr. Wright I had no notion, I protest, that this exquisite stroke of pleasantry was aimed at me); he has exhibited me as 'condemned by myself, refuted by myself', and, finally, my hexameters having been rejected by all the world, 'somewhat crest-fallen'. And he has himself made game of me, in this forlorn condition, by parodying those unlucky hexameters. So that now, I should think, he must be quite happy.

Partly, no doubt, from being crest-fallen, but partly, too, from sincere contrition for that fault of over-vivacity which I have acknowledged, I will not raise a finger in self-defence against Mr. Wright's blows. I will not even ask him,—what it almost irresistibly rises to my lips to ask him when I see he writes from Mapperly,—if he can tell me what has become of that poor girl, Wragg? She has been tried, I suppose: I know how merciful a view judges and juries are apt to take of these cases, so I cannot but hope she has got off. But what I should so like to ask is, whether the impression the poor thing made was, in general, satisfactory: did she come up to the right standard as a member of 'the best breed in the whole world?' were her life-experiences an edifying testimony to 'our unrivalled happiness?' did she find Mr. Roebuck's speech a comfort to her in her prison? But I must stop; or my kind monitor, the *Guardian*, whose own gravity is so profound that the frivolous are sometimes apt to give it a heavier name, will be putting a harsh construction upon my innocent thirst for knowledge, and again taxing me with the unpardonable crime of being amusing.

Amusing—good heavens! We shall none of us be amusing much longer. Mr. Wright would perhaps be more indulgent to my vivacity if he considered this. It is but the last sparkle of flame before we are all in the dark; the last glimpse of colour before we all go into drab. Who that reads the *Examiner* does not know that representative man, that Ajax of liberalism, one of our modern leaders of thought, who signs himself 'Presbyter Anglicanus'? For my part, I have good cause to know him; terribly severe he was with me two years ago, when he thought I had spoken with levity of that favourite pontiff of the Philistines, the Bishop of Natal. But his masterpiece was the other day. Mr. Disraeli, in the course of his lively speech at Oxford, talked of 'nebulous professors, who, if they could only succeed in obtaining a perpetual study of their writings, would go far to realise that eternity of punishment which they object to'. Presbyter Anglicanus says 'it would be childish to affect ignorance' that this was aimed at Mr. Maurice. If it was, who can doubt that Mr. Maurice himself, full of culture and urbanity as he is, would be the first to pronounce it a very smart saying, and to laugh at it good-humouredly? But only listen to Mr. Maurice's champion:

This passage must fill all sober-minded men with astonishment and dismay; they will regard it as one of the most ominous signs of the time. This contemptible joke, which betrays a spirit of ribald profanity not easily surpassed, excited from the Bishop, the clergy, and laity present, not an indignant rebuke, but 'continued laughter'. Such was the assembly of Englishmen and Christians, who could listen in uproarious merriment to a Parliamentary leader while he asserted that the vilest iniquity would be well compensated by a forced perusal of the writings of Frederick Denison Maurice!

And, for fear this trumpet-blast should not be carried far enough by the *Examiner*, its author, if I am not greatly mistaken, blew it also, under a different name, in half a dozen of the daily newspapers. As Wordsworth asks:

> . . . the happiest mood
> Of that man's mind, what can it be?

was he really born of human parents, or of Hyrcanian tigers? If the former, surely to some of his remote ancestors, at any rate,—in far distant ages, I mean, long before the birth of Puritanism,—some conception of a joke must, at one moment or other of their lives, have been conveyed. But there is the coming east wind! there is the tone of the future!—I hope it is grave enough for even the *Guardian*;—the earnest prosaic, practical, austerely literal future! Yes, the world will soon be the Philistines'; and then, with every voice, not of thunder, silenced, and the whole earth filled and ennobled every morning by the magnificent roaring of the young lions of the *Daily Telegraph*, we shall all yawn in one another's faces with the dismallest, the most unimpeachable gravity. No more vivacity then! my hexameters, and dogmatism, and scoffs at the Divorce Court, will all have been put down; I shall be quite crest-fallen. But does Mr. Wright imagine that there will be any more place, in that world, for his heroic blank verse Homer than for my paradoxes? If he does, he deceives himself, and knows little of the Palatine Library of the future. A plain edifice, like the British College of Health enlarged: inside, a light, bleak room, with a few statues; Dagon in the centre, with our English Caabah, or Palladium of enlightenment, the hare's stomach; around, a few leading friends of humanity or fathers of British philosophy;—Goliath, the great Bentham, Presbyter Anglicanus, our intellectual deliverer Mr. James Clay and . . . yes! with the embarrassed air of a late convert, the editor of the *Saturday Review*. Many a shrewd nip has he in the old days given to the Philistines, this editor; many a bad half-hour has he made them pass; but in his old age he has mended his courses, and declares that his heart has always been in the right place, and that he is at bottom, however appearances may have been against him, staunch for Goliath and 'the most logical nation in the whole world'. Then, for the book-shelves. There will be found on them a monograph by Mr. Lowe on the literature of the ancient Scythians, to revenge them for the iniquitous neglect with which the Greeks treated them; there will be Demosthenes, because he was like Mr. Spurgeon; but, else, from all the lumber of antiquity they will be free. Everything they contain will be modern, intelligible, improving; *Joyce's Scientific Dialogues, Old Humphrey, Bentham's Deontology,*

Little Dorrit, Mangnall's Questions, The Wide Wide World, D'Iffanger's Speeches, Beecher's Sermons;—a library, in short, the fruit of a happy marriage between the profound philosophic reflection of Mr. Clay, and the healthy natural taste of Inspector Tanner.

But I return to my design in writing this Preface. That design was, after apologizing to Mr. Wright for my vivacity of five years ago, to beg him and others to let me bear my own burdens, without saddling the great and famous University, to which I have the honour to belong, with any portion of them. What I mean to deprecate is such phrases as, 'his professional assault', 'his assertions issued *ex cathedrâ*', 'the sanction of his name as the representative of poetry', and so on. Proud as I am of my connection with the University of Oxford, I can truly say, that, knowing how unpopular a task one is undertaking when one tries to pull out a few more stops in that powerful, but at present somewhat narrow-toned organ, the modern Englishman, I have always sought to stand by myself, and to compromise others as little as possible. Besides this, my native modesty is such, that I have always been shy of assuming the honourable style of Professor, because this is a title I share with so many distinguished men,—Professor Pepper, Professor Anderson, Professor Frickel, and others,—who adorn it, I feel, much more than I do. These eminent men, however, belonging to a hierarchy of which Urania, the Goddess of Science herself, is the sole head, cannot well by any vivacity or unpopularity of theirs compromise themselves with their superiors; because with their Goddess they are not likely, until they are translated to the stars, to come into contact. I, on the other hand, have my humble place in a hierarchy whose seat is on earth; and I serve under an illustrious Chancellor who translates Homer, and calls his Professor's leaning towards hexameters 'a pestilent heresy'. Nevertheless, that cannot keep me from admiring the performance of my severe chief; I admire its freshness, its manliness, its simplicity; although, perhaps if one looks for the charm of Homer, for his play of a divine light ... Professor Pepper must go on, I cannot.

My position is, therefore, one of great delicacy; but it is not from any selfish motives that I prefer to stand alone, and to concentrate on myself, as a plain citizen of the republic of letters, and not as an office-bearer in a hierarchy, the whole responsibility for all I write; it is much more out of genuine devotion to the University of Oxford, for which I feel, and always must feel, the fondest, the most reverential attachment. In an epoch of dissolution and transformation, such as that on which we are now entered, habits, ties, and associations are inevitably broken up, the action of individuals becomes more distinct, the short-comings, errors, heats, disputes, which necessarily attend individual action, are brought into greater prominence. Who would not gladly keep clear, from all these passing clouds, an august institution which was there before they arose, and which will be there when they have blown over?

It is true, the *Saturday Review* maintains that our epoch of transformation is finished; that we have found our philosophy; that the British nation has searched all anchorages for the spirit, and has finally anchored itself, in the fulness of perfected knowledge, to Benthamism. This idea at first made a great impression on me; not only because it is so consoling in itself, but also because it explained a phenomenon which in the summer of last year had, I confess, a good deal troubled me. At that time my avocations led me to travel almost daily on one of the Great Eastern lines,—the Woodford Branch. Every one knows that Müller perpetrated his destestable act on the North London Railway, close by. The English middle class, of which I am myself a feeble unit, travel on the Woodford Branch in large numbers. Well, the demoralisation of our class,—which (the newspapers are constantly saying it, so I may repeat it without vanity) has done all the great things which have ever been done in England,— the demoralisation, I say, of our class, caused by the Bow tragedy, was something bewildering. Myself a transcendentalist (as the *Saturday Review* knows), I escaped the infection; and, day after day, I used to ply my agitated fellow-travellers with all the consolations which my transcendentalism, and my turn for the French, would naturally suggest to me. I reminded them how Caesar refused to take precautions against assassination, because life was not worth having at the price of an ignoble solicitude for it. I reminded them what insignificant atoms we all are in the life of the world. 'Suppose the worst to happen', I said, addressing a portly jeweler from Cheapside; 'Suppose even yourself to be the victim; *il n'y a pas d'homme nécessaire.* We should miss you for a day or two upon the Woodford Branch; but the great mundane movement would still go on: the gravel walks of your villa would still be rolled; dividends would still be paid at the Bank; omnibuses would still run; there would still be the old crush at the corner of Fenchurch Street.' All was of no avail. Nothing could moderate, in the bosom of the great English middle class, their passionate, absorbing, almost blood-thirsty clinging to life. At the moment I thought this over-concern a little unworthy; but the *Saturday Review* suggests a touching explanation of it. What I took for the ignoble clinging to life of a comfortable worldling, was, perhaps, only the ardent longing of a faithful Benthamite, traversing an age still dimmed by the last mists of transcendentalism, to be spared long enough to see his religion in the full and final blaze of its triumph. This respectable man,—whom I imagined to be going up to London to buy shares, or to attend an Exeter Hall meeting, or to hear Mr. D'Iffanger speak, or to see Mr. Spurgeon, with his well-known reverence for every authentic *Thus saith the Lord*, turn his other cheek to the amiable Dean of Ripon,—was, perhaps, in real truth on a pious pilgrimage, to obtain, from Mr. Bentham's executors, a sacred bone of his great, dissected Master.

And yet, after all, I cannot but think that the *Saturday Review* has here, for once, fallen a victim to an idea,—a beautiful but deluding idea,—and that the British nation has not yet, so entirely as the reviewer seems to imagine, found the last work of its philosophy. No; we are all seekers still; seekers often make mistakes, and I wish mine to redound to my own discredit only, and not to touch Oxford. Beautiful city! so venerable, so lovely, so unravaged by the fierce intellectual life of our century, so serene!

There are our young barbarians, all at play.

And yet, steeped in sentiment as she lies, spreading her gardens to the moonlight, and whispering from her towers the last enchantments of the Middle Age, who will deny that Oxford, by her ineffable charm, keeps ever calling us near to the true goal of all of us, to the ideal, to perfection,—to beauty, in a word, which is only truth seen from another side?—nearer, perhaps, than all the science of Tübingen. Adorable dreamer, whose heart has been so romantic! who hast given thyself so prodigally, given thyself to sides and to heroes not mine, only never to the Philistines! home of lost causes, and forsaken beliefs, and unpopular names, and impossible loyalties! what example could ever so inspire us to keep down the Philistine in ourselves, what teacher could ever so save us from that bondage to which we are all prone, that bondage which Goethe, in those incomparable lines on the death of Schiller, makes it his friend's highest praise (and nobly did Schiller deserve the praise) to have left miles out of sight behind him;—the bondage of *was uns alle bändigt*, DAS GEMEINE! She will forgive me, even if I have unwittingly drawn upon her a shot or two aimed at her unworthy son, for she is generous, and the cause in which I fight is, after all, hers. Apparitions of a day, what is our puny warfare against the Philistines, compared with the warfare which this Queen of Romance has been waging against them for centuries, and will wage after we are gone?

THE FUNCTION OF CRITICISM
AT THE PRESENT TIME

(1864)

MANY objections have been made to a proposition which, in some remarks of mine on translating Homer, I ventured to put forth; a proposition about criticism, and its importance at the present day. I said: 'Of the literature of France and Germany, as of the intellect of Europe in general, the main effort, for now many years, has been a critical effort; the endeavour, in all branches of knowledge, theology, philosophy, history, art, science, to see the object as in itself it really is.' I added, that owing to the operation in English literature of certain causes, 'almost the last thing for which one would come to English literature is just that very thing which now Europe most desires,—criticism'; and that the power and value of English literature was thereby impaired. More than one rejoinder declared that the importance I here assigned to criticism was excessive, and asserted the inherent superiority of the creative effort of the human spirit over its critical effort. And the other day, having been led by a Mr. Shairp's excellent notice of Wordsworth[1] to turn

---

[1] I cannot help thinking that a practice, common in England during the last century, and still followed in France, of printing a notice of this kind,—a notice by a competent critic,—to serve as an introduction to an eminent author's works, might be revived among us with advantage. To introduce all succeeding editions of Wordsworth, Mr. Shairp's notice might, it seems to me, excellently serve; it is written from the point of view of an admirer, nay, of a disciple, and that is right; but then the disciple must be also, as in this case he is, a critic, a man of letters, not, as too often happens, some relation or friend with no qualification for his task except affection for his author.

again to his biography, I found, in the words of this great man, whom I, for one, must always listen to with the profoundest respect, a sentence passed on the critic's business, which seems to justify every possible disparagement of it. Wordsworth says in one of his letters:

The writers in these publications [the Reviews], while they prosecute their inglorious employment, can not be supposed to be in a state of mind very favourable for being affected by the finer influences of a thing so pure as genuine poetry.

And a trustworthy reporter of his conversation quotes a more elaborate judgment to the same effect:

Wordsworth holds the critical power very low, infinitely lower than the inventive; and he said to-day that if the quantity of time consumed in writing critiques on the works of others were given to original composition, of whatever kind it might be, it would be much better employed; it would make a man find out sooner his own level, and it would do infinitely less mischief. A false or malicious criticism may do much injury to the minds of others, a stupid invention, either in prose or verse, is quite harmless.

It is almost too much to expect of poor human nature, that a man capable of producing some effect in one line of literature, should, for the greater good of society, voluntarily doom himself to impotence and obscurity in another. Still less is this to be expected from men addicted to the composition of the 'false or malicious criticism' of which Wordsworth speaks. However, everybody would admit that a false or malicious criticism had better never have been written. Everybody, too, would be willing to admit, as a general proposition, that the critical faculty is lower than the inventive. But is it true that criticism is really, in itself, a baneful and injurious employment; is it true that all time given to writing critiques on the works of others would be much better employed if it were given to original composition, of whatever kind this may be? Is it true that Johnson had better have gone on producing more *Irenes* instead of writing his *Lives of the Poets*; nay, is it certain that Wordsworth himself was better employed in making his Ecclesiastical Sonnets than when he made his celebrated Preface, so full of criticism, and criticism of the works of others? Wordsworth was himself a great critic, and it is to be sincerely regretted that he has not left us more criticism; Goethe was one of the greatest of critics, and we may sincerely congratulate ourselves that he has left us so much criticism. Without wasting time over the exaggeration which Wordsworth's judgment on criticism clearly contains, or over an attempt to trace the causes,—not difficult, I think, to be traced,—which may have led Wordsworth to this exaggeration, a critic may with advantage seize an occasion for trying his own conscience, and for asking himself of what real service at any given moment the practice of criticism either is or may be made to his own mind and spirit, and to the minds and spirits of others.

The critical power is of lower rank than the creative. True; but in assenting to this proposition, one or two things are to be kept in mind. It is undeniable that the exercise of a creative power, that a free creative activity, is the highest function of man; it is proved to be so by man's finding in it his true happiness. But it is undeniable, also, that men may have the sense of exercising this free creative activity in other ways than in producing great works of literature or art; if it were not so, all but a very few men would be shut out from the true happiness of all men. They may have it in well-doing, they may have it in learning, they may have it even in criticising. This is one thing to be kept in mind. Another is, that the exercise

of the creative power in the production of great works
of literature or art, however high this exercise of it may
rank, is not at all epochs and under all conditions possible; and that therefore labour may be vainly spent in
attempting it, which might with more fruit be used in
preparing for it, in rendering it possible. This creative
power works with elements, with materials; what if it
has not those materials, those elements, ready for its use?
In that case it must surely wait till they are ready. Now,
in literature,—I will limit myself to literature, for it is
about literature that the question arises,—the elements
with which the creative power works are ideas; the best
ideas on every matter which literature touches, current
at the time. At any rate we may lay it down as certain
that in modern literature no manifestation of the creative
power not working with these can be very important or
fruitful. And I say *current* at the time, not merely accessible at the time; for creative literary genius does not
principally show itself in discovering new ideas, that is
rather the business of the philosopher. The grand work
of literary genius is a work of synthesis and exposition,
not of analysis and discovery; its gift lies in the faculty of
being happily inspired by a certain intellectual and
spiritual atmosphere, by a certain order of ideas, when it
finds itself in them; of dealing divinely with these ideas,
presenting them in the most effective and attractive
combinations,—making beautiful works with them, in
short. But it must have the atmosphere, it must find itself
amidst the order of ideas, in order to work freely; and
these it is not so easy to command. This is why great
creative epochs in literature are so rare, this is why
there is so much that is unsatisfactory in the productions
of many men of real genius; because, for the creation of
a master-work of literature two powers must concur, the

power of the man and the power of the moment, and the man is not enough without the moment; the creative power has, for its happy exercise, appointed elements, and those elements are not in its own control.

Nay, they are more within the control of the critical power. It is the business of the critical power, as I said in the words already quoted, 'in all branches of knowledge, theology, philosophy, history, art, science, to see the object as in itself it really is'. Thus it tends, at last, to make an intellectual situation of which the creative power can profitably avail itself. It tends to establish an order of ideas, if not absolutely true, yet true by comparison with that which it displaces; to make the best ideas prevail. Presently these new ideas reach society, the touch of truth is the touch of life, and there is a stir and growth everywhere; out of this stir and growth come the creative epochs of literature.

Or, to narrow our range, and quit these considerations of the general march of genius and of society,—considerations which are apt to become too abstract and impalpable,—every one can see that a poet, for instance, ought to know life and the world before dealing with them in poetry; and life and the world being in modern times very complex things, the creation of a modern poet, to be worth much, implies a great critical effort behind it; else it must be a comparatively poor, barren, and short-lived affair. This is why Byron's poetry had so little endurance in it, and Goethe's so much; both Byron and Goethe had a great productive power, but Goethe's was nourished by a great critical effort providing the true materials for it, and Byron's was not; Goethe knew life and the world, the poet's necessary subjects, much more comprehensively and thoroughly than Byron. He knew a great deal more of them, and he knew them much more as they really are.

It has long seemed to me that the burst of creative activity in our literature, through the first quarter of this century, had about it in fact something premature; and that from this cause its productions are doomed, most of them, in spite of the sanguine hopes which accompanied and do still accompany them, to prove hardly more lasting than the productions of far less splendid epochs. And this prematureness comes from its having proceeded without having its proper data, without sufficient materials to work with. In other words, the English poetry of the first quarter of this century, with plenty of energy, plenty of creative force, did not know enough. This makes Byron so empty of matter, Shelley so incoherent, Wordsworth even, profound as he is, yet so wanting in completeness and variety. Wordsworth cared little for books, and disparaged Goethe. I admire Wordsworth, as he is, so much that I cannot wish him different; and it is vain, no doubt, to imagine such a man different from what he is, to suppose that he *could* have been different. But surely the one thing wanting to make Wordsworth an even greater poet than he is,—his thought richer, and his influence of wider application,—was that he should have read more books, among them, no doubt, those of that Goethe whom he disparaged without reading him.

But to speak of books and reading may easily lead to a misunderstanding here. It was not really books and reading that lacked to our poetry at this epoch; Shelley had plenty of reading, Coleridge had immense reading. Pindar and Sophocles—as we all say so glibly, and often with so little discernment of the real import of what we are saying—had not many books; Shakespeare was no deep reader. True; but in the Greece of Pindar and Sophocles, in the England of Shakespeare, the poet lived in a current of ideas in the highest degree animating and nourishing to the creative power; society was, in the fullest measure, permeated by fresh thought, intelligent and alive. And this state of things is the true basis for the creative power's exercise, in this it finds its data, its materials, truly ready for its hand; all the books and reading in the world are only valuable as they are helps to this. Even when this does not actually exist, books and reading may enable a man to construct a kind of semblance of it in his own mind, a world of knowledge and intelligence in which he may live and work. This is by no means an equivalent to the artist for the nationally diffused life and thought of the epochs of Sophocles or Shakespeare; but, besides that it may be a means of preparation for such epochs, it does really constitute, if many share in it, a quickening and sustaining atmosphere of great value. Such an atmosphere the many-sided learning and the long and widely-combined critical effort of Germany formed for Goethe, when he lived and worked. There was no national glow of life and thought there as in the Athens of Pericles or the England of Elizabeth. That was the poet's weakness. But there was a sort of equivalent for it in the complete culture and unfettered thinking of a large body of Germans. That was his strength. In the England of the first quarter of this century there was neither a national glow of life and thought, such as we had in the age of Elizabeth, nor yet a culture and a force of learning and criticism such as were to be found in Germany. Therefore the creative power of poetry wanted, for success in the highest sense, materials and a basis; a thorough interpretation of the world was necessarily denied to it.

At first sight it seems strange that out of the immense stir of the French Revolution and its age should not have come a crop of works of genius equal to that which came out of the stir of the great productive time of Greece, or out of that of the Renascence, with its powerful episode the Reformation. But the truth is that the stir of the French Revolution took a character which essentially distinguished it from such movements as these. These were, in the main, disinterestedly intellectual and spiritual movements; movements in which the human spirit looked for its satisfaction in itself and in the increased play of its own activity. The French Revolution took a political, practical character. The movement which went on in France under the old *régime*, from 1700 to 1789, was far more really akin than that of the Revolution itself to the movement of the Renascence; the France of Voltaire and Rousseau told far more powerfully upon the mind of Europe than the France of the Revolution. Goethe reproached this last expressly with having 'thrown quiet culture back'. Nay, and the true key to how much in our Byron, even in our Wordsworth, is this!—that they had their source in a great movement of feeling, not in a great movement of mind. The French Revolution, however,— that object of so much blind love and so much blind hatred,—found undoubtedly its motive-power in the intelligence of men, and not in their practical sense; this is what distinguishes it from the English Revolution of Charles the First's time. This is what makes it a more spiritual event than our Revolution, an event of much more powerful and world-wide interest, though practically less successful; it appeals to an order of ideas which are universal, certain, permanent. 1789 asked of a thing, Is it rational? 1642 asked of a thing, Is it legal? or, when it went furthest, Is it according to conscience? This is the English fashion, a fashion to be treated, within its own sphere, with the highest respect; for its success, within its own sphere, has been prodigious. But what is law in one place is not law in another, what is law here today is not law even here tomorrow; and, as for conscience, what is binding on one man's conscience is not binding on another's. The old woman who threw her stool at the head of the surpliced minister in St. Giles's Church at Edinburgh obeyed an impulse to which millions of the human race may be permitted to remain strangers. But the prescriptions of reason are absolute, unchanging, of universal validity; *to count by tens is the easiest way of counting*—that is a proposition of which every one, from here to the Antipodes, feels the force; at least I should say so if we did not live in a country where it is not impossible that any morning we may find a letter in the *Times* declaring that a decima l coinage is an absurdity. That a whole nation should have been penetrated with an enthusiasm for pure reason, and with a ardent zeal for making its prescriptions triumph, is a very remarkable thing, when we consider how little of mind, or anything so worthy and quickening as mind, comes into the natives which alone, in general, impel great masses of men. In spite of the extravagant direction given to this enthusiasm, in spite of the crimes and follies in which it lost itself, the French Revolution derives from the force, truth, and universality of the ideas which it took for its law, and from the passion with which it could inspire a multitude for these ideas, a unique and still living power; it is—it will probably long remain—the greatest, the most animating event in history. And as no sincere passion for the things of the mind, even though it turn out in many respects an unfortunate passion, is ever quite thrown away and quite barren of good, France has reaped from hers one fruit—the natural and legitimate fruit, though not precisely the grand fruit she expected: she is the country in Europe where *the people* is most alive.

But the mania for giving an immediate political and practical application to all these fine ideas of the reason was fatal. Here an Englishman is in his element: on this theme we can all go on for hours. And all we are in the habit of saying on it has undoubtedly a great deal of truth. Ideas cannot be too much prized in and for themselves, cannot be too much lived with; but to transport them abruptly into the world of politics and practice, violently to revolutionise this world to their bidding,— that is quite another thing. There is the world of ideas and there is the world of practice; the French are often for suppressing the one and the English the other; but neither is to be suppressed. A member of the House of Commons said to me the other day: 'That a thing is an anomaly, I consider to be no objection to it whatever'. I venture to think he was wrong; that a thing in an anomaly *is* an objection to it, but absolutely and in the sphere of ideas: it is not necessarily, under such and such circumstances, or at such and such a moment, an objection to it in the sphere of politics and practice. Joubert has said beautifully: 'C'est la force et le droit qui règlent toutes choses dans le monde; la force en attendant le droit.' (Force and right are the governors of this world; force till right is ready.) *Force till right is ready*; and till right is ready, force, the existing order of things, is justified, is the legitimate ruler. But right is something moral, and implies inward recognition, free assent of the will; we are not ready for right,—*right*, so far as we are concerned, *is not ready*,— until we have attained this sense of seeing it and willing it. The way in which for us it may change and transform force, the existing order of things, and become, in its turn, the legitimate ruler of the world, should depend on the way in which, when our time comes, we see it and will it. Therefore for other people enamoured of their own newly discerned right, to attempt to impose it upon us as ours, and violently to substitute their right for our force, is an act of tyranny, and to be resisted. It sets at nought the second great half of our maxim, *force till right is ready.* This was the grand error of the French Revolution; and its movement of ideas, by quitting the intellectual sphere and rushing furiously into the political sphere, ran, indeed, a prodigious and memorable course, but produced no such intellectual fruit as the movement of ideas of the Renascence, and created, in opposition to itself, what I may call an *epoch of concentration.* The great force of that epoch of concentration was England; and the great voice of that epoch of concentration was Burke. It is the fashion to treat Burke's writings on the French Revolution as superannuated and conquered by the event; as the eloquent but unphilosophical tirades of bigotry and prejudice. I will not deny that they are often disfigured by the violence and passion of the moment, and that in some directions Burke's view was bounded, and his observation therefore at fault. But on the whole, and for those who can make the needful corrections, what distinguishes these writings is their profound, permanent, fruitful, philosophical truth. They contain the true philosophy of an epoch of concentration, dissipate the heavy atmosphere which its own nature is apt to engender round it, and make its resistance rational instead of mechanical.

But Burke is so great because, almost alone in England, he brings thought to bear upon politics, he saturates politics with thought. It is his accident that his ideas were at the service of an epoch of concentration, not of an epoch of expansion; it is his characteristic that he so lived by ideas, and had such a source of them welling up within him, that he could float even an epoch of concentration and English Tory politics with them. It does not hurt him that Dr. Price and the Liberals were enraged with him; it does not even hurt him that George the Third and the Tories were enchanted with him. His greatness is that he lived in a world which neither English Liberalism nor English Toryism is apt to enter;—the world of ideas, not the world of catchwords and party habits. So far is it from being really true of him that he 'to party gave up what was meant for mankind', that at the very end of his fierce struggle with the French Revolution, after all his invectives against its false pretensions, hollowness, and madness, with his sincere conviction of its mischievousness, he can close a memorandum on the best means of combating it, some of the last pages he ever wrote,—the *Thoughts on French Affairs*, in December 1791, —with these striking words:

The evil is stated, in my opinion, as it exists. The remedy must be where power, wisdom, and information, I hope, are more united with good intentions than they can be with me. I have done with this subject, I believe, for ever. It has given me many anxious moments for the last two years. *If a great change is to be made in human affairs, the minds of men will be fitted to it; the general opinions and feelings will draw that way. Every fear, every hope will forward it; and then they who persist in opposing this mighty current in human affairs, will appear rather to resist the decrees of Providence itself, than the mere designs of men. They will not be resolute and firm, but perverse and obstinate.*

That return of Burke upon himself has always seemed to me one of the finest things in English literature, or indeed in any literature. That is what I call living by ideas: when one side of a question has long had your earnest support, when all your feelings are engaged, when you hear all round you no language but one, when your party talks this language like a steam-engine and can imagine no other,—still to be able to think, still to be irresistibly carried, if so it be, by the current of thought to the opposite side of the question, and, like Balaam, to be unable to speak anything *but what the Lord has put in your mouth.* I know nothing more striking, and I must add that I know nothing more un-English.

For the Englishman in general is like my friend the Member of Parliament, and believes, point-blank, that for a thing to be an anomaly is absolutely no objection to it whatever. He is like the Lord Auckland of Burke's day, who, in a memorandum on the French Revolution, talks of 'certain miscreants, assuming the name of philosophers, who have presumed themselves capable of establishing a new system of society'. The Englishman has been called a political animal, and he values what is political and practical so much that ideas easily become objects of dislike in his eyes, and thinkers 'miscreants', because ideas and thinkers have rashly meddled with politics and practice. This would be all very well if the dislike and neglect confined themselves to ideas transported out of their own sphere, and meddling rashly with practice; but they are inevitably extended to ideas as such, and to the whole life of intelligence; practice is everything, a free play of the mind is nothing. The notion of the free play of the mind upon all subjects being a pleasure in itself, being an object of desire, being an essential provider of elements without which a nation's spirit, whatever compensations it may have for them, must, in the long run, die of inanition, hardly enters into an Englishman's thoughts. It is noticeable that the word *curiosity*, which in other languages is used in a good sense, to mean, as a high and fine quality of man's nature, just this disinterested love of a free play of the mind on all subjects, for its own sake,—it is noticeable, I say, that this word has in our language no sense of the kind, no sense but a rather bad and disparaging one. But criticism, real criticism, is essentially the exercise of this very quality. It obeys an instinct prompting it to try to know the best that is known and thought in the world, irrespectively of practice, politics, and everything of the kind; and to value knowledge and thought as they approach this best, without the intrusion of any other considerations whatever. This is an instinct for which there is, I think, little original sympathy in the practical English nature, and what there was of it has undergone a long benumbing period of blight and suppression in the epoch of concentration which followed the French Revolution.

But epochs of concentration cannot well endure for ever; epochs of expansion, in the due course of things, follow them. Such an epoch of expansion seems to be opening in this country. In the first place all danger of a hostile forcible pressure of foreign ideas upon our practice has long disappeared; like the traveller in the fable, therefore, we begin to wear our cloak a little more loosely. Then, with a long peace, the ideas of Europe steal gradually and amicably in, and mingle, though in infinitesimally small quantities at a time, with our own notions. Then, too, in spite of all that is said about the absorbing and brutalising influence of our passionate material progress, it seems to me indisputable that this progress is likely, though not certain, to lead in the end to an apparition of intellectual life; and that man, after he has made himself perfectly comfortable and has now to determine what to do with himself next, may begin to remember that he has a mind, and that the mind may be made the source of great pleasure. I grant it is mainly the privilege of faith, at present, to discern this end to our railways, our business, and our fortune-making; but we shall see if, here as elsewhere, faith is not in the end the true prophet. Our ease, our travelling, and our unbounded liberty to hold just as hard and securely as we please to the practice to which our notions have given birth, all tend to beget an inclination to deal a little more freely with these notions themselves, to canvass them a little, to penetrate a little into their real nature. Flutterings of curiosity, in the foreign sense of the word, appear amongst us, and it is in these that criticism must look to find its account. Criticism first; a time of true creative activity, perhaps,—which, as I have said, must inevitably be preceded amongst us by a time of criticism,—hereafter, when criticism has done its work.

It is of the last importance that English criticism should clearly discern what rule for its course, in order to avail itself of the field now opening to it, and to produce fruit for the future, it ought to take. The rule may be summed up in one word,—*disinterestedness*. And how is criticism to show disinterestedness? By keeping aloof from what is called 'the practical view of things'; by resolutely following the law of its own nature, which is to be a free play of the mind on all subjects which it touches. By steadily refusing to lend itself to any of those ulterior, political, practical considerations about ideas, which plenty of people will be sure to attach to them, which perhaps ought often to be attached to them, which in this country at any rate are certain to be attached to them quite sufficiently, but which criticism has really nothing to do with. Its business is, as I have said, simply to know the best that is known and thought in the world, and by in its turn making this known, to create a current of true and fresh ideas. Its business is to do this with inflexible honesty, with due ability; but its business is to do no more, and to leave alone all questions of practical consequences and applications, questions which will never fail to have due prominence given to them. Else criticism, besides being really false to its own nature, merely continues in the old rut which it has hitherto followed in this country, and will certainly miss the chance now given to it. For what is at present the bane of criticism in this country? It is that practical considerations cling to it and stifle it. It subserves interests not its own. Our organs of criticism are organs of men and parties having practical ends to serve, and with them those practical ends are the first thing and the play of mind the second; so much play of mind as is compatible with the prosecution of those practical ends is all that is wanted. An organ like the *Revue des Deux Mondes*, having for its main function to understand and utter the best that is known and thought in the world, existing, it may be said, as just an organ for a free play of the mind, we have not. But we have the *Edinburgh Review*, existing as an organ of the old Whigs, and for as much play of the mind as may suit its being that; we have the *Quarterly Review*, existing as an organ of the Tories, and for as much play of mind as may suit its being that; we have the *British Quarterly Review*, existing as an organ of the political Dissenters, and for as much play of mind as may suit its being that; we have the *Times*, existing as an organ of the common, satisfied, well-to-do English man, and for as much play of mind as may suit its being that. And so on through all the various factions, political and religious, of our society; every faction has, as such, its organ of criticism, but the notion of combining all factions in the common pleasure of a free disinterested play of mind meets with no favour. Directly this play of mind wants to have more scope, and to forget the pressure of practical considerations a little, it is checked, it is made to feel the chain. We saw this the other day in the extinction, so much to be regretted, of the *Home and Foreign Review*. Perhaps in no organ of criticism in this country was there so much knowledge, so much play of mind; but these could not save it. The *Dublin Review* subordinates play of mind to the practical business of English and Irish Catholicism, and lives. It must needs be that men should act in sects and parties, that each of these sects and parties should have its organ, and should make this organ subserve the interests of its action; but it would be well, too, that there should be a criticism, not the minister of these interests, not their enemy, but absolutely and entirely independent of them. No other criticism will ever attain any real authority or make any real way towards its end,—the creating a current of true and fresh ideas.

It is because criticism has so little kept in the pure intellectual sphere, has so little detached itself from practice, has been so directly polemical and controversial, that it has so ill accomplished, in this country, its best spiritual work; which is to keep man from a self-satisfaction which is retarding and vulgarising, to lead him towards perfection, by making his mind dwell upon what is excellent in itself, and the absolute beauty and fitness of things. A polemical practical criticism makes men blind even to the ideal imperfection of their practice, makes them willingly assert its ideal perfection, in order the better to secure it against attack; and clearly this is narrowing and baneful for them. If they were reassured on the practical side, speculative considerations of ideal perfection they might be brought to entertain, and their spiritual horizon would thus gradually widen. Sir Charles Adderley says to the Warwickshire farmers:

Talk of the improvement of breed! Why, the race we ourselves represent, the men and women, the old Anglo-Saxon race, are the best breed in the whole world. . . . The absence of a too enervating climate, too unclouded skies, and a too luxurious nature, has produced so vigorous a race of people, and has rendered us so superior to all the world.

Mr. Roebuck says to the Sheffield cutlers:

I look around me and ask what is the state of England? Is not property safe? Is not every man able to say what he likes? Can you not walk from one end of England to the other in perfect security? I ask you whether, the world over or in past history, there is anything like it? Nothing. I pray that our unrivalled happiness may last.

Now obviously there is a peril for poor human nature in words and thoughts of such exuberant self-satisfaction, until we find ourselves safe in the streets of the Celestial City.

> Das wenige verschwindet leicht dem Blicke
> Der vorwärts sieht, wie viel noch übrig bleibt—

says Goethe; 'the little that is done seems nothing when we look forward and see how much we have yet to do'. Clearly this is a better line of reflection for weak humanity, so long as it remains on this earthly field of labour and trial.

But neither Sir Charles Adderley nor Mr. Roebuck is by nature inaccessible to considerations of this sort. They only lose sight of them owing to the controversial life we all lead, and the practical form which all speculation takes with us. They have in view opponents whose aim is not ideal, but practical; and in their zeal to uphold their own practice against these innovators, they go so far as even to attribute to this practice an ideal perfection. Somebody has been wanting to introduce a six-pound franchise, or to abolish church-rates, or to collect agricultural statistics by force, or to diminish local self-government.

How natural, in reply to such proposals, very likely improper or ill-timed, to go a little beyond the mark and to say stoutly, 'Such a race of people as we stand, so superior to all the world! The old Anglo-Saxon race, the best breed in the whole world! I pray that our unrivalled happiness may last! I ask you whether, the world over or in past history, there is anything like it?' And so long as criticism answers this dithyramb by insisting that the old Anglo-Saxon race would be still more superior to all others if it had no church-rates, or that our unrivalled happiness would last yet longer with a six-pound franchise, so long will the strain, 'The best breed in the whole world!' swell louder and louder, everything ideal and refining will be lost out of sight, and both the assailed and their critics will remain in a sphere, to say the truth, perfectly unvital, a sphere in which spiritual progression is impossible. But let criticism leave church-rates and the franchise alone, and in the most candid spirit, without a single lurking thought of practical innovation, confront with our dithyramb this paragraph on which I stumbled in a newspaper immediately after reading Mr. Roebuck:

A shocking child murder has just been committed at Nottingham. A girl named Wragg left the workhouse there on Saturday morning with her young illegitimate child. The child was soon afterwards found dead on Mapperly Hills, having been strangled. Wragg is in custody.

Nothing but that; but, in juxtaposition with the absolute eulogies of Sir Charles Adderley and Mr. Roebuck, how eloquent, how suggestive are those few lines! 'Our old Anglo-Saxon breed, the best in the whole world!'—how much that is harsh and ill-favoured there is in this best! *Wragg!* If we are to talk of ideal perfection, of 'the best in the whole world', has any one reflected what a touch of grossness in our race, what an original short-coming in the more delicate spiritual perceptions, is shown by the natural growth amongst us of such hideous names, as Higginbottom, Stiggins, Bugg! In Ionia and Attica they were luckier in this respect than 'the best race in the world'; by the Ilissus there was no Wragg, poor thing! And 'our unrivalled happiness';—what an element of grimness, bareness, and hideousness mixes with it and blurs it; the workhouse, the dismal Mapperly Hills,—how dismal those who have seen them will remember;—the gloom, the smoke, the cold, the strangled illegitimate child! 'I ask you whether, the world over or in past history, there is anything like it?' Perhaps not, one is inclined to answer; but at any rate, in that case, the world is very much to be pitied. And the final touch,—short, bleak, and inhuman: *Wragg is in custody*. The sex lost in the confusion of our unrivalled happiness; or (shall I say?) the superfluous Christian name lopped off by the straight-forward vigour of our old Anglo-Saxon breed! There is profit for the spirit in such contrasts as this; criticism serves the cause of perfection by establishing them. By eluding sterile conflict, by refusing to remain in the sphere where alone narrow and relative conceptions have any worth and validity, criticism may diminish its momentary importance, but only in this way has it a chance of gaining admittance for those wider and more perfect conceptions to which all its duty is really owed. Mr. Roebuck will have a poor opinion of an adversary who replies to his defiant songs of triumph only by murmuring under his breath, *Wragg is in custody*; but in no other way will these songs of triumph be induced gradually to moderate themselves, to get rid of what in them is excessive and offensive, and to fall into a softer and truer key.

It will be said that it is a very subtle and indirect action which I am thus prescribing for criticism, and that, by embracing in this manner the Indian virtue of detachment and abandoning the sphere of practical life, it condemns itself to a slow and obscure work. Slow and obscure it may be, but it is the only proper work of criticism. The mass of mankind will never have any ardent zeal for seeing things as they are; very inadequate ideas will always satisfy them. On these inadequate ideas reposes, and must repose, the general practice of the world. That is as much as saying that whoever sets himself to see things as they are will find himself one of a very small circle; but it is only by this small circle resolutely doing its own work that adequate ideas will ever get current at all. The rush and roar of practical life will always have a dizzying and attracting effect upon the most collected spectator, and tend to draw him into its vortex; most of all will this be the case where that life is so powerful as it is in England. But it is only by remaining collected, and refusing to lend himself to the point of view of the practical man, that the critic can do the practical man any service; and it is only by the greatest sincerity in pursuing his own course, and by at last convincing even the practical man of his sincerity, that he can escape misunderstandings which perpetually threaten him.

For the practical man is not apt for fine distinctions, and yet in these distinctions truth and the highest culture greatly find their account. But it is not easy to lead a practical man,—unless you reassure him as to your practical intentions, you have no chance of leading him,—to see that a thing which he has always been used to look at from one side only, which he greatly values, and which, looked at from that side, quite deserves, perhaps, all the prizing and admiring which he bestows upon it,—that this thing, looked at from another side, may appear much less beneficent and beautiful, and yet retain all its claims to our practical allegiance. Where shall we find language innocent enough, how shall we make the spotless purity of our intentions evident enough, to enable us to say to the political Englishman that the British Constitution itself, which, seen from the practical side, looks such a magnificent organ of progress and virtue, seen from the speculative side,—with its compromises, its love of facts, its horror of theory, its studied avoidance of clear thoughts, —that, seen from this side, our august Constitution sometimes looks,—forgive me, shade of Lord Somers!—a colossal machine for the manufacture of Philistines! How is Cobbett to say this and not be misunderstood, blackened as he is with the smoke of a lifelong conflict in the field of political practice? how is Mr. Carlyle to say it and not be misunderstood, after his furious raid into this field with his *Latter-day Pamphlets*? how is Mr. Ruskin, after his pugnacious political economy? I say, the critic must keep out of the region of immediate practice in the political, social, humanitarian sphere, if he wants to make a beginning for that more free speculative treatment of things, which may perhaps one day make its benefits felt even in this sphere, but in a natural and thence irresistible manner.

Do what he will, however, the critic will still remain exposed to frequent misunderstandings, and nowhere so much as in this country. For here people are particularly indisposed even to comprehend that without this free disinterested treatment of things, truth and the highest culture are out of the question. So immersed are they in practical life, so accustomed to take all their notions from this life and its processes, that they are apt to think that truth and culture themselves can be reached by the processes of this life, and that it is an impertinent singularity to think of reaching them in any other. 'We are all *terræ filii*', cries their eloquent advocate; 'all Philistines together. Away with the notion of proceeding by any other course than the course dear to the Philistines; let us have a social movement, let us organise and combine a party to pursue truth and new thought, let us call it *the liberal party*, and let us all stick to each other, and back each other up. Let us have no nonsense about independent criticism, and intellectual delicacy, and the few and the many. Don't let us trouble ourselves about foreign thought; we shall invent the whole thing for ourselves as we go along. If one of us speaks well, applaud him; if one of us speaks ill, applaud him too; we are all in the same movement, we are all liberals, we are all in pursuit of truth.' In this way the pursuit of truth becomes really a social, practical, pleasurable affair, almost requiring a chairman, a secretary, and advertisements; with the excitement of an occasional scandal, with a little resistance to give the happy sense of difficulty overcome; but, in general, plenty of bustle and very little thought. To act is so easy, as Goethe says; to think is so hard! It is true that the critic has many temptations to go with the stream, to make one of the party movement, one of these *terræ filii*; it seems ungracious to refuse to be a *terræ filius*, when so many excellent people are; but the critic's duty is to refuse, or, if resistance is vain, at least to cry with Obermann: *Périssons en résistant.*

How serious a matter it is to try and resist, I had ample opportunity of experiencing when I ventured some time ago to criticise the celebrated first volume of Bishop Colenso.[1] The echoes of the storm which was then raised

[1] So sincere is my dislike of all personal attack and controversy, that I abstain from reprinting, at this distance of time from the occasion which

I still, from time to time, hear grumbling round me. That storm arose out of a misunderstanding almost inevitable. It is a result of no little culture to attain to a clear perception that science and religion are two wholly different things. The multitude will for ever confuse them; but happily that is of no great real importance, for while the multitude imagines itself to live by its false science, it does really live by its true religion. Dr. Colenso, however, in his first volume did all he could to strengthen the confusion,[1] and to make it dangerous. He did this with the best intentions, I freely admit, and with the most candid ignorance that this was the natural effect of what he was doing; but, says Joubert, 'Ignorance, which in matters of morals, extenuates the crime, is itself, in intellectual matters, a crime of the first order.' I criticised Bishop Colenso's speculative confusion. Immediately there was a cry raised: 'What is this? here is a liberal attacking a liberal. Do not you belong to the movement? are not you a friend of truth? Is not Bishop Colenso in pursuit of truth? then speak with proper respect of his book. Dr. Stanley is another friend of truth, and you speak with proper respect of his book; why make these invidious differences? both books are excellent, admirable, liberal; Bishop Colenso's perhaps the most so, because it is the boldest, and will have the best practical consequences for the liberal cause. Do you want to encourage to the

called them forth, the essays in which I criticised Dr. Colenso's book; I feel bound, however, after all that has passed, to make here a final declaration of my sincere impenitence for having published them. Nay, I cannot forbear repeating yet once more, for his benefit and that of his readers, this sentence from my original remarks upon him: *There is truth of science and truth of religion; truth of science does not become truth of religion till it is made religious.* And I will add: Let us have all the science there is from the men of science; from the men of religion let us have religion.

[1] It has been said I make it 'a crime against literary criticism and the higher culture to attempt to inform the ignorant'. Need I point out that the ignorant are not informed by being confirmed in a confusion?

attack of a brother liberal his, and your, and our implac-
able enemies, the *Church and State Review* or the *Record*,—
the High Church rhinoceros and the Evangelical hyæna?
Be silent, therefore; or rather speak, speak as loud as ever
you can! and go into ecstasies over the eighty and odd
pigeons.'

But criticism cannot follow this coarse and indis-
criminate method. It is unfortunately possible for a man
in pursuit of truth to write a book which reposes upon
a false conception. Even the practical consequences of
a book are to genuine criticism no recommendation of it,
if the book is, in the highest sense, blundering. I see that
a lady who herself, too, is in pursuit of truth, and who
writes with great ability, but a little too much, perhaps,
under the influence of the practical spirit of the English
liberal movement, classes Bishop Colenso's book and
M. Renan's together, in her survey of the religious state
of Europe, as facts of the same order, works, both of
them, of 'great importance'; 'great ability, power, and
skill'; Bishop Colenso's, perhaps, the most powerful; at
least, Miss Cobbe gives special expression to her gratitude that to Bishop Colenso 'has been given the strength
to grasp, and the courage to teach, truths of such deep
import'. In the same way, more than one popular writer
has compared him to Luther. Now it is just this kind of
false estimate which the critical spirit is, it seems to me,
bound to resist. It is really the strongest possible proof of
the low ebb at which, in England, the critical spirit is,
that while the critical hit in the religious literature of
Germany is Dr. Strauss's book, in that of France M.
Renan's book, the book of Bishop Colenso is the critical
hit in the religious literature of England. Bishop Colenso's book reposes on a total misconception of the
essential elements of the religious problem, as that

problem is now presented for solution. To criticism, therefore, which seeks to have the best that is known and thought on this problem, it is, however well meant, of no importance whatever. M. Renan's book attempts a new synthesis of the elements furnished to us by the Four Gospels. It attempts, in my opinion, a synthesis, perhaps premature, perhaps impossible, certainly not successful. Up to the present time, at any rate, we must acquiesce in Fleury's sentence on such recastings of the Gospel-story: *Quiconque s'imagine la pouvoir mieux écrire, ne l'entend pas.* Mr. Renan had himself passed by anticipation a like sentence on his own work, when he said: 'If a new presentation of the character of Jesus were offered to me, I would not have it; its very clearness would be, in my opinion, the best proof of its insufficiency.' His friends may with perfect justice rejoin that at the sight of the Holy Land, and of the actual scene of the Gospel-story, all the current of M. Renan's thoughts may have naturally changed, and a new casting of that story irresistibly suggested itself to him; and that this is just a case for applying Cicero's maxim: Change of mind is not inconsistency—*nemo doctus unquam mutationem consilii inconstantiam dixit esse.* Nevertheless, for criticism, M. Renan's first thought must still be the truer one, as long as his new casting so fails more fully to commend itself, more fully (to use Coleridge's happy phrase about the Bible) to *find* us. Still M. Renan's attempt is, for criticism, of the most real interest and importance, since, with all its difficulty, a fresh synthesis of the New Testament *data*,—not a making war on them, in Voltaire's fashion, not a leaving them out of mind, in the world's fashion, but the putting a new construction upon them, the taking them from under the old, traditional, conventional point of view and placing them under a new one,—is the very essence of the religious problem, as now presented; and only by efforts in this direction can it receive a solution.

Again, in the same spirit in which she judges Bishop Colenso, Miss Cobbe, like so many earnest liberals of our practical race, both here and in America, herself sets vigorously about a positive reconstruction of religion, about making a religion of the future out of hand, or at least setting about making it. We must not rest, she and they are always thinking and saying, in negative criticism, we must be creative and constructive; hence we have such works as her recent *Religious Duty*, and works still more considerable, perhaps, by others, which will be in every one's mind. These works often have much ability; they often spring out of sincere convictions, and a sincere wish to do good; and they sometimes, perhaps, do good. Their fault is (if I may be permitted to say so) one which they have in common with the British College of Health, in the New Road. Every one knows the British College of Health; it is that building with the lion and the statue of the Goddess Hygeia before it; at least I am sure about the lion, though I am not absolutely certain about the Goddess Hygeia. This building does credit, perhaps, to the resources of Dr. Morrison and his disciples; but it falls a good deal short of one's idea of what a British College of Health ought to be. In England, where we hate public interference and love individual enterprise, we have a whole crop of places like the British College of Health; the grand name without the grand thing. Unluckily, creditable to individual enterprise as they are, they tend to impair our taste by making us forget what more grandiose, noble, or beautiful character properly belongs to a public institution. The same may be said of the religions of the future of Miss Cobbe and others. Creditable, like the British College of Health, to the resources of their authors, they yet tend to make us forget what more grandiose, noble, or beautiful character properly belongs to religious constructions. The historic religions, with all their faults, have had this; it certainly belongs to the religious sentiment, when it truly flowers, to have this; and we impoverish our spirit if we allow a religion of the future without it. What then is the duty of criticism here? To take the practical point of view, to applaud the liberal movement and all its works,—its New Road religions of the future into the bargain,—for their general utility's sake? By no means; but to be perpetually dissatisfied with these works while they perpetually fall short of a high and perfect ideal.

For criticism, these are elementary laws; but they never can be popular, and in this country they have been very little followed, and one meets with immense obstacles in following them. That is a reason for asserting them again and again. Criticism must maintain its independence of the practical spirit and its aims. Even with well-meant efforts of the practical spirit it must express dissatisfaction, if in the sphere of the ideal they seem impoverishing and limiting. It must not hurry on to the goal because of its practical importance. It must be patient, and know how to wait; and flexible, and know how to attach itself to things and how to withdraw from them. It must be apt to study and praise elements that for the fulness of spiritual perfection are wanted, even though they belong to a power which in the practical sphere may be maleficent. It must be apt to discern the spiritual shortcomings or illusions of powers that in the practical sphere may be beneficent. And this without any notion of favouring or injuring, in the practical sphere, one power or the other; without any notion of playing off, in this sphere, one power against the other. When one looks, for instance, at the English Divorce Court,—an institution which perhaps has its practical conveniences, but which in the ideal sphere is so hideous; an institution which neither makes divorce impossible nor makes it decent, which allows a man to get rid of his wife, or a wife of her husband, but makes them drag one another first, for the public edification, through a mire of unutterable infamy, —when one looks at this charming institution, I say, with its crowded trials, its newspaper reports, and its money compensations, this institution in which the gross unregenerate British Philistine has indeed stamped an image of himself,— one may be permitted to find the marriage theory of Catholicism refreshing and elevating. Or when Protestantism, in virtue of its supposed rational and intellectual origin, gives the law to criticism too magisterially, criticism may and must remind it that its pretensions, in this respect, are illusive and do it harm; that the Reformation was a moral rather than an intellectual event; that Luther's theory of grace no more exactly reflects the mind of the spirit than Bossuet's philosophy of history reflects it; and that there is no more antecedent probability of the Bishop of Durham's stock of ideas being agreeable to perfect reason than of Pope Pius the Ninth's. But criticism will not on that account forget the achievements of Protestantism in the practical and moral sphere; nor that, even in the intellectual sphere, Protestantism, though in a blind and stumbling manner, carried forward the Renascence, while Catholicism threw itself violently across its path.

I lately heard a man of thought and energy contrasting the want of ardour and movement which he now found amongst young men in this country with what he remembered in his own youth, twenty years ago. 'What reformers we were then!' he exclaimed; 'what a zeal we had!

how we canvassed every institution in Church and State, and were prepared to remodel them all on first principles!' He was inclined to regret, as a spiritual flagging, the lull which he saw. I am disposed rather to regard it as a pause in which the turn to a new mode of spiritual progress is being accomplished. Everything was long seen, by the young and ardent amongst us, in inseparable connection with politics and practical life. We have pretty well exhausted the benefits of seeing things in this connection, we have got all that can be got by so seeing them. Let us try a more disinterested mode of seeing them; let us betake ourselves more to the serener life of the mind and spirit. This life, too, may have its excesses and dangers; but they are not for us at present. Let us think of quietly enlarging our stock of true and fresh ideas, and not, as soon as we get an idea or half an idea, be running out with it into the street, and trying to make it rule there. Our ideas will, in the end, shape the world all the better for maturing a little. Perhaps in fifty years' time it will in the English House of Commons be an objection to an institution that it is an anomaly, and my friend the Member of Parliament will shudder in his grave. But let us in the meanwhile rather endeavour that in twenty years' time it may, in English literature, be an objection to a proposition that it is absurd. That will be a change so vast, that the imagination almost fails to grasp it. *Ab integro sæclorum nascitur ordo.*

If I have insisted so much on the course which criticism must take where politics and religion are concerned, it is because, where these burning matters are in question, it is most likely to go astray. I have wished, above all, to insist on the attitude which criticism should adopt towards things in general; on its right tone and temper of mind. But then comes another question as to the subject-matter which literary criticism should most seek. Here, in general, its course is determined for it by the idea which is the law of its being; the idea of a disinterested endeavour to learn and propagate the best that is known and thought in the world, and thus to establish a current of fresh and true ideas. By the very nature of things, as England is not all the world, much of the best that is known and thought in the world cannot be of English growth, must be foreign; by the nature of things, again, it is just this that we are least likely to know, while English thought is streaming in upon us from all sides, and takes excellent care that we shall not be ignorant of its existence. The English critic of literature, therefore, must dwell much on foreign thought, and with particular heed on any part of it, which, while significant and fruitful in itself, is for any reason specially likely to escape him. Again, judging is often spoken of as the critic's one business, and so in some sense it is; but the judgment which almost insensibly forms itself in a fair and clear mind, along with fresh knowledge, is the valuable one; and thus knowledge, and ever fresh knowledge, must be the critic's great concern for himself. And it is by communicating fresh knowledge, and letting his own judgment pass along with it,—but insensibly, and in the second place, not the first, as a sort of companion and clue, not as an abstract lawgiver,—that the critic will generally do most good to his readers. Sometimes, no doubt, for the sake of establishing an author's place in literature, and his relation to a central standard (and if this is not done, how are we to get at our *best in the world*?) criticism may have to deal with a subject-matter so familiar that fresh knowledge is out of the question, and then it must be all judgment; an enunciation and detailed application of principles. Here the great safeguard is never to let oneself become abstract, always to retain an intimate and lively consciousness of the truth of what one is saying, and, the moment this fails us, to be sure that something is wrong. Still, under all circumstances, this mere judgment and application of principles is, in itself, not the most satisfactory work to the critic; like mathematics, it is tautological, and cannot well give us, like fresh learning, the sense of creative activity.

But stop, some one will say; all this talk is of no practical use to us whatever; this criticism of yours is not what we have in our minds when we speak of criticism; when we speak of critics and criticism, we mean critics and criticism of the current English literature of the day; when you offer to tell criticism its function, it is to this criticism that we expect you to address yourself. I am sorry for it, for I am afraid I must disappoint these expectations. I am bound by my own definition of criticism: *a disinterested endeavour to learn and propagate the best that is known and thought in the world.* How much of current English literature comes into this 'best that is known and thought in the world?' Not very much, I fear; certainly less, at this moment, than of the current literature of France or Germany. Well, then, am I to alter my definition of criticism, in order to meet the requirements of a number of practising English critics, who, after all, are free in their choice of a business? That would be making criticism lend itself just to one of those alien practical considerations, which, I have said, are so fatal to it. One may say, indeed, to those who have to deal with the mass —so much better disregarded—of current English literature, that they may at all events endeavour, in dealing with this, to try it, so far as they can, by the standard of the best that is known and thought in the world; one may say, that to get anywhere near this standard, every critic should try and possess one great literature, at least, besides his own; and the more unlike his own, the better. But, after all, the criticism I am really concerned with,— the criticism which alone can much help us for the future, the criticism which, throughout Europe, is at the present day meant, when so much stress is laid on the importance of criticism and the critical spirit,—is a criticism which regards Europe as being, for intellectual and spiritual purposes, one great confederation, bound to a joint action and working to a common result; and whose members have, for their proper outfit, a knowledge of Greek, Roman, and Eastern antiquity, and of one another. Special, local, and temporary advantages being put out of account, that modern nation will in the intellectual and spiritual sphere make most progress, which most thoroughly carries out this programme. And what is that but saying that we too, all of us, as individuals, the more thoroughly we carry it out, shall make the more progress?

There is so much inviting us!—what are we to take? what will nourish us in growth towards perfection? That is the question which, with the immense field of life and of literature lying before him, the critic has to answer; for himself first, and afterwards for others. In this idea of the critic's business the essays brought together in the following pages have had their origin; in this idea, widely different as are their subjects, they have, perhaps, their unity.

I conclude with what I said at the beginning: to have the sense of creative activity is the great happiness and the great proof of being alive, and it is not denied to criticism to have it; but then criticism must be sincere, simple, flexible, ardent, ever widening its knowledge. Then it may have, in no contemptible measure, a joyful sense of creative activity; a sense which a man of insight and conscience will prefer to what he might derive from a poor, starved, fragmentary, inadequate creation. And at some epochs no other creation is possible.

Still, in full measure, the sense of creative activity belongs only to genuine creation; in literature we must never forget that. But what true man of letters ever can forget it? It is no such common matter for a gifted nature to come into possession of a current of true and living ideas, and to produce amidst the inspiration of them, that we are likely to underrate it. The epochs of Æschylus and Shakespeare make us feel their pre-eminence. In an epoch like those is, no doubt, the true life of literature; there is the promised land, towards which criticism can only beckon. That promised land it will not be ours to enter, and we shall die in the wilderness: but to have desired to enter it, to have saluted it from afar, is already, perhaps, the best distinction among contemporaries; it will certainly be the best title to esteem with posterity.

THE STUDY OF POETRY [1]
(1880)

'THE future of poetry is immense, because in poetry, where it is worthy of its high destinies, our race, as time goes on, will find an ever surer and surer stay. There is not a creed which is not shaken, not an accredited dogma which is not shown to be questionable, not a received tradition which does not threaten to dissolve. Our religion has materialised itself in the fact, in the supposed fact; it has attached its emotion to the fact and now the fact is failing it. But for poetry the idea is everything; the rest is a world of illusion, of divine illusion. Poetry attaches its emotion to the idea; the idea *is* the fact. The strongest part of our religion to-day is its unconscious poetry.'

Let me be permitted to quote these words of my own, as uttering the thought which should, in my opinion, go with us and govern us in all our study of poetry. In the present work it is the course of one great contributory stream to the world-river of poetry that we are invited to follow. We are here invited to trace the stream of English poetry. But whether we set ourselves, as here, to follow only one of the several streams that make the mighty river of poetry, or whether we seek to know them all, our governing thought should be the same. We should conceive of poetry worthily, and more highly than it has been the custom to conceive of it. We should conceive of it as capable of higher uses, and called to higher destinies, than

[1] Published in 1880 as the General Introduction to *The English Poets*, edited by T. H. Ward.

those which in general men have assigned to it hitherto.
More and more mankind will discover that we have to
turn to poetry to interpret life for us, to console us, to
sustain us. Without poetry, our science will appear incomplete; and most of what now passes with us for religion
and philosophy will be replaced by poetry. Science, I
say, will appear incomplete without it. For finely and
truly does Wordsworth call poetry 'the impassioned
expression which is in the countenance of all science';
and what is a countenance without its expression? Again,
Wordsworth finely and truly calls poetry 'the breath and
finer spirit of all knowledge': our religion, parading
evidence such as those on which the popular mind relies
now; our philosophy, pluming itself on its reasonings
about causation and finite and infinite being; what are
they but the shadows and dreams and false shows of
knowledge? The day will come when we shall wonder at
ourselves for having trusted to them, for having taken
them seriously; and the more we perceive their hollowness, the more we shall prize 'the breath and finer spirit
of knowledge' offered to us by poetry.

But if we conceive thus highly of the destinies of poetry,
we must also set our standard for poetry high, since
poetry, to be capable of fulfilling such high destinies,
must be poetry of a high order of excellence. We must
accustom ourselves to a high standard and to a strict judgment. Sainte-Beuve relates that Napoleon one day said,
when somebody was spoken of in his presence as a charlatan: 'Charlatan as much as you please; but where is
there *not* charlatanism?'—'Yes,' answers Sainte-Beuve,
'in politics, in the art of governing mankind, that is perhaps true. But in the order of thought, in art, the glory,
the eternal honour is that charlatanism shall find no
entrance; herein lies the inviolableness of that noble

portion of man's being.' It is admirably said, and let us hold fast to it. In poetry, which is thought and art in one, it is the glory, the eternal honour, that charlatanism shall find no entrance; that this noble sphere be kept inviolate and inviolable. Charlatanism is for confusing or obliterating the distinctions between excellent and inferior, sound and unsound or only half-sound, true and untrue or only half-true. It is charlatanism, conscious or unconscious, whenever we confuse or obliterate these. And in poetry, more than anywhere else, it is unpermissible to confuse or obliterate them. For in poetry the distinction between excellent and inferior, sound and unsound or only half-sound, true and untrue or only half-true, is of paramount importance. It is of paramount importance because of the high destinies of poetry. In poetry, as a criticism of life under the conditions fixed for such a criticism by the laws of poetic truth and poetic beauty, the spirit of our race will find, we have said, as time goes on and as other helps fail, its consolation and stay. But the consolation and stay will be of power in proportion to the power of the criticism of life. And the criticism of life will be of power in proportion as the poetry conveying it is excellent rather than inferior, sound rather than unsound or half-sound, true rather than untrue or half-true.

The best poetry is what we want; the best poetry will be found to have a power of forming, sustaining, and delighting us, as nothing else can. A clearer, deeper sense of the best in poetry, and of the strength and joy to be drawn from it, is the most precious benefit which we can gather from a poetical collection such as the present. And yet in the very nature and conduct of such a collection there is inevitably something which tends to obscure in us the consciousness of what our benefit should be, and to distract us from the pursuit of it. We should therefore steadily set it before our minds at the outset, and should compel ourselves to revert constantly to the thought of it as we proceed.

Yes; constantly in reading poetry, a sense for the best, the really excellent, and of the strength and joy to be drawn from it, should be present in our minds and should govern our estimate of what we read. But this real estimate, the only true one, is liable to be superseded, if we are not watchful, by two other kinds of estimate, the historic estimate and the personal estimate, both of which are fallacious. A poet of a poem may count to us historically, they may count to us on grounds personal to ourselves, and they may count to us really. They may count to us historically. The course of development of a nation's language, thought, and poetry, is profoundly interesting; and by regarding a poet's work as a stage in this course of development we may easily bring ourselves to make it of more importance as poetry than in itself it really is, we may come to use a language of quite exaggerated praise in criticising it; in short, to over-rate it. So arises in our poetic judgments the fallacy caused by the estimate which we may call historic. Then, again, a poet or a poem may count to us on grounds personal to ourselves. Our personal affinities, likings, and circumstances, have great power to sway our estimate of this or that poet's work, and to make us attach more importance to it as poetry than in itself it really possesses, because to us it is, or has been, of high importance. Here also we over-rate the object of our interest, and apply to it a language of praise which is quite exaggerated. And thus we get the source of a second fallacy in our poetic judgments—the fallacy caused by an estimate which we may call personal.

Both fallacies are natural. It is evident how naturally the study of the history and development of a poetry may incline a man to pause over reputations and works once conspicuous but now obscure, and to quarrel with a careless public for skipping, in obedience to mere tradition and habit, from one famous name or work in its national poetry to another, ignorant of what it misses, and of the reason for keeping what it keeps, and of the whole process of growth in its poetry. The French have become diligent students of their own early poetry, which they long neglected; the study makes many of them dissatisfied with their so-called classical poetry, the court-tragedy of the seventeenth century, a poetry which Pellisson long ago reproached with its want of the true poetic stamp, with its *politisse stérile et rampante*, but which nevertheless has reigned in France as absolutely as if it had been the perfection of classical poetry indeed. The dissatisfaction is natural; yet a lively and accomplished critic, M. Charles d'Héricault, the editor of Clément Marot, goes too far when he says that 'the cloud of glory playing round a classic is a mist as dangerous to the future of a literature as it is intolerable for the purposes of history.'

It hinders [he goes on], it hinders us from seeing more than one single point, the culminating and exceptional point; the summary, fictitious and arbitrary, of a thought and of a work. It substitutes a halo for a physiognomy, it puts a statue where there was once a man, and hiding from us all trace of the labour, the attempts, the weaknesses, the failures, it claims not study but veneration; it does not show us how the thing is done, it imposes upon us a model. Above all, for the historian this creation of class personages is inadmissible; for it withdraws the poet from his time, from his proper life, it breaks historical relationships, it blinds criticism by conventional admiration, and renders the investigation of literary origins unacceptable. It gives us a human personage no longer, but a God seated immovable amidst His perfect work, like Jupiter on Olympus; and hardly will it be possible for the young student, to whom such work is exhibited at such a distance from him, to believe that it did not issue ready made from that divine head.

All this is brilliantly and tellingly said, but we must plead for a distinction. Everything depends on the reality of a poet's classic character. If he is a dubious classic, let us sift him; if he is a false classic, let us explode him. But if he is a real classic, if his work belongs to the class of the very best (for this is the true and right meaning of the word *classic, classical*), then the great thing for us is to feel and enjoy his work as deeply as ever we can, and to appreciate the wide difference between it and all work which has not the same high character. This is what is salutary, this is what is formative; this is the great benefit to be got from the study of poetry. Everything which interferes with it, which hinders it, is injurious. True, we must read our classic with open eyes, and not with eyes blinded with superstition; we must perceive when his work comes short, when it drops out of the class of the very best, and we must rate it, in such cases, at its proper value. But the use of this negative criticism is not in itself, it is entirely in its enabling us to have a clearer sense and a deeper enjoyment of what is truly excellent. To trace the labour, the attempts, the weaknesses, the failures of a genuine classic, to acquaint oneself with his time and his life and his historical relationships, is mere literary dilettantism unless it has that clear sense and deeper enjoyment for its end. It may be said that the more we know about a classic the better we shall enjoy him; and, if we lived as long as Methuselah and had all of us heads of perfect clearness and wills of perfect steadfastness, this might be true in fact as it is plausible in theory. But the case here is much the same as the case with the Greek and Latin studies of our schoolboys. The elaborate philological groundwork which we require them to lay is in theory an admirable preparation for appreciating the Greek and Latin authors worthily. The more thoroughly we lay the groundwork, the better we shall be able, it may be said, to enjoy the authors. True, if time were not so short, and schoolboys' wits not so soon tired and their power of attention exhausted; only, as it is, the elaborate philological preparation goes on, but the authors are little known and less enjoyed. So with the investigator of 'historic origins' in poetry. He ought to enjoy the true classic all the better for his investigations; he often is distracted from the enjoyment of the best, and with the less good he overbusies himself, and is prone to over-rate it in proportion to the trouble which it has cost him.

The idea of tracing historic origins and historical relationships cannot be absent from a compilation like the present. And naturally the poets to be exhibited in it will be assigned to those persons for exhibition who are known to prize them highly, rather than to those who have no special inclination towards them. Moreover the very occupation with an author, and the business of exhibiting him, disposes us to affirm and amplify his importance. In the present work, therefore, we are sure of frequent temptation to adopt the historic estimate, or the personal estimate, and to forget the real estimate; which latter, nevertheless, we must employ if we are to make poetry yield us its full benefit. So high is that benefit, the benefit of clearly feeling and of deeply enjoying the really excellent, the truly classic in poetry, that we do well, I say, to set it fixedly before our minds as our object in studying poets and poetry, and to make the desire of attaining it the one principle to which, as the *Imitation* says, whatever we may read or come to know, we always return. *Cum multa legeris et cognoveris, ad unum semper oportet redire principium.*

The historic estimate is likely in especial to affect our judgment and our language when we are dealing with ancient poets; the personal estimate when we are dealing with poets our contemporaries, or at any rate modern. The exaggerations due to the historic estimate are not in themselves, perhaps, of very much gravity. Their report hardly enters the general ear; probably they do not always impose even on the literary men who adopt them. But they lead to a dangerous abuse of language. So we hear Caedmon, amongst our own poets, compared to Milton. I have already noticed the enthusiasm of one accomplished French critic for 'historic origins'. Another eminent French critic, M. Vitet, comments upon that famous document of the early poetry of his nation, the *Chanson de Roland*. It is indeed a most interesting document. The *joculator* or *jongleur* Taillefer, who was with William the Conqueror's army at Hastings, marched before the Norman troops, so said the tradition, singing 'of Charlemagne and of Roland and of Oliver, and of the vassals who died at Roncevaux'; and it is suggested that in the *Chanson de Roland* by one Turoldus or Théroulde, a poem preserved in a manuscript of the twelfth century in the Bodleian Library at Oxford, we have certainly the matter, perhaps even some of the words, of the chant which Taillefer sang. The poem has vigour and freshness; it is not without pathos. But M. Vitet is not satisfied with seeing in it a document of some poetic value, and of very high historic and linguistic value; he sees in it a grand and beautiful work, a monument of epic genius. In its general design he finds the grandiose conception, in its details he finds the constant union of simplicity with greatness, which are the marks, he truly says, of the genuine epic, and distinguish it from the artificial epic of literary ages. One thinks of Homer; this is the sort of praise which is given to Homer, and justly given. Higher praise there cannot well be, and it is the praise due to epic poetry of the highest order only, and to no other. Let us try, then, the *Chanson de Roland* at its best. Roland, mortally wounded, lays himself down under a pine-tree, with his face turned towards Spain and the enemy—

> De plusurs choses à remembrer li prist,
> De tantes teres cume li bers cunquist,
> De dulce France, des humes de sun lign,
> De Carlemagne sun seignor ki l'nurrit.[1]

That is primitive work, I repeat, with an undeniable poetic quality of its own. It deserves such praise, and such praise is sufficient for it. But now turn to Homer—

> Ὣς φάτο· τοὺς δ' ἤδη κατέχεν φυσίζοος αἶα
> ἐν Λακεδαίμονι αὖθι, φίλῃ ἐν πατρίδι γαίῃ.[2]

We are here in another world, another order of poetry altogether; here is rightly due such supreme praise as that which M. Vitet gives to the *Chanson de Roland*. If our words are to have any meaning, if our judgments are to have any solidity, we must not heap that supreme praise upon poetry of an order immeasurably inferior.

Indeed there can be no more useful help for discovering what poetry belongs to the class of the truly excellent, and can therefore do us most good, than to have always in one's mind lines and expressions of the great masters, and to apply them as a touchstone to other poetry. Of course we are not to require this other poetry

---

[1] 'Then began he to call many things to remembrance,—all the lands which his valour conquered, and pleasant France and the men of his lineage, and Charlemagne his liege lord who nourished him.'—*Chanson de Roland*, iii. 939–42.

[2] 'So said she; they long since in Earth's soft arms were reposing,
There, in their own dear land, their fatherland, Lacedæmon.'
Iliad, iii. 243, 244 (translated by Dr. Hawtrey).

to resemble them; it may be very dissimilar. But if we have any tact we shall find them, when we have lodged them well in our minds, an infallible touchstone for detecting the presence or absence of high poetic quality, and also the degree of this quality, in all other poetry which we may place beside them. Short passages, even single lines, will serve our turn quite sufficiently. Take the two lines which I have just quoted from Homer, the poet's comment on Helen's mention of brothers;—or take his

> Ἆ δειλώ, τί σφῶϊ δόμεν Πηλῆϊ ἄνακτι
> θνητῷ; ὑμεῖς δ' ἐστὸν ἀγήρω τ' ἀθανάτω τε.
> ἦ ἵνα δυστήνοισι μετ' ἀνδράσιν ἄλγε' ἔχητον;[1]

the address of Zeus to the horses of Peleus;—or take finally his

> Καὶ σέ, γέρον, τὸ πρὶν μὲν ἀκούομεν ὄλβιον εἶναι.[2]

the words of Achilles to Priam, a suppliant before him. Take that incomparable line and a half of Dante, Ugolino's tremendous words—

> Io no piangeva; sì dentro impietrai.
> Piangevan elli . . .[3]

take the lovely words of Beatrice to Virgil—

> Io son fatta da Dio, sua mercè, tale,
> Che la vostra miseria non mi tange,
> Nè fiamma d'esto incendio non m'assale . . .[4]

---

[1] 'Ah, unhappy pair, why gave we you to King Peleus, to a mortal? but ye are without old age, and immortal. Was it that with men born to misery ye might have sorrow?'—*Iliad*, xvii. 443-5.

[2] 'Nay, and thou too, old man, in former days wast, as we hear, happy.'—*Iliad*, xxiv. 543.

[3] 'I wailed not, so of stone grew I within;—*they* wailed.'—*Inferno*, xxxiii. 39, 40.

[4] 'Of such sort hath God, thanked be His mercy, made me, that your misery toucheth me not, neither doth the flame of this fire strike me.'—*Inferno*, ii. 91-93.

take the simple, but perfect, single line—

> In la sua volontade è nostra pace.[1]

Take of Shakespeare a line or two of Henry the Fourth's
expostulation with sleep—

> Wilt thou upon the high and giddy mast
> Seal up the ship-boy's eyes, and rock his brains
> In cradle of the rude imperious surge . . .

and take, as well, Hamlet's dying request to Horatio—

> If thou didst ever hold me in thy heart,
> Absent thee from felicity awhile,
> And in this harsh world draw thy breath in pain
> To tell my story . . .

Take of Milton that Miltonic passage—

> Darken'd so, yet shone
> Above them all the archangel; but his face
> Deep scars of thunder had intrench'd, and care
> Sat on his faded cheek . . .

add two such lines as—

> And courage never to submit or yield
> And what is else not to be overcome . . .

and finish with the exquisite close to the loss of Proser-
pine, the loss

> . . . which cost Ceres all that pain
> To seek her through the world.

These few lines, if we have tact and can use them, are
enough even of themselves to keep clear and sound our
judgments about poetry, to save us from fallacious estimates of it, to conduct us to a real estimate.

---

[1] 'In His will is our peace.'—*Paradiso*, iii. 85.

The specimens I have quoted differ widely from one another, but they have in common this: the possession of the very highest poetical quality. If we are thoroughly penetrated by their power, we shall find that we have acquired a sense enabling us, whatever poetry may be laid before us, to feel the degree in which a high poetical quality is present or wanting there. Critics give themselves great labour to draw out what in the abstract constitutes the characters of a high quality of poetry. It is much better simply to have recourse to concrete examples;—to take specimens of poetry of the high, the very highest quality, and to say: The characters of a high quality of poetry are what is expressed *there*. They are far better recognised by being felt in the verse of the master, than by being perused in the prose of the critic. Nevertheless if we are urgently pressed to give some critical account of them, we may safely, perhaps, venture on laying down, not indeed how and why the characters arise, but where and in what they arise. They are in the matter and substance of the poetry, and they are in its manner and style. Both of these, the substance and matter on the one hand, the style and manner on the other, have a mark, an accent, of high beauty, worth, and power. But if we are asked to define this mark and accent in the abstract, our answer must be: No, for we should thereby be darkening the question, not clearing it. The mark and accent are as given by the substance and matter of that poetry, by the style and manner of that poetry, and of all other poetry which is akin to it in quality.

Only one thing we may add as to the substance and matter of poetry, guiding ourselves by Aristotle's profound observation that the superiority of poetry over history consists in its possessing a higher truth and a higher seriousness (φιλοσοφώτερον καὶ σπουδαιότερον). Let us add, therefore, to what we have said, this: that the substance and matter of the best poetry acquire their special character from possessing, in an eminent degree, truth and seriousness. We may add yet further, what is in itself evident, that to the style and manner of the best poetry their special character, their accent, is given by their diction, and, even yet more, by their movement. And though we distinguish between the two characters, the two accents, of superiority, yet they are nevertheless vitally connected one with the other. The superior character of truth and seriousness, in the matter and substance of the best poetry, is inseparable from the superiority of diction and movement marking its style and manner. The two superiorities are closely related, and are in steadfast proportion one to the other. So far as high poetic truth and seriousness are wanting to a poet's matter and substance, so far also, we may be sure, will a high poetic stamp of diction and movement be wanting to his style and manner. In proportion as this high stamp of diction and movement, again, is absent from a poet's style and manner, we shall find, also, that high poetic truth and seriousness are absent from his substance and matter.

So stated, these are but dry generalities; their whole force lies in their application. And I could wish every student of poetry to make the application of them for himself. Made by himself, the application would impress itself upon his mind far more deeply than made by me. Neither will my limits allow me to make any full application of the generalities above propounded; but in the hope of bringing out, at any rate, some significance in them, and of establishing an important principle more firmly by their means, I will, in the space which remains to me, follow rapidly from the commencement the course of our English poetry with them in my view.

Once more I return to the early poetry of France, with which our own poetry, in its origins, is indissolubly connected. In the twelfth and thirteenth centuries, that seed-time of all modern language and literature, the poetry of France had a clear predominance in Europe. Of the two divisions of that poetry, its productions in the *langue d'oïl* and its productions in the *langue d'oc*, the poetry of the *langue d'oc*, of southern France, of the troubadours, is of importance because of its effect on Italian literature;—the first literature of modern Europe to strike the true and grand note, and to bring forth, as in Dante and Petrarch it brought forth, classics. But the predominance of French poetry in Europe, during the twelfth and thirteenth centuries, is due to its poetry of the *langue d'oïl*, the poetry of northern France and of the tongue which is now the French language. In the twelfth century the bloom of this romance-poetry was earlier and stronger in England, at the court of our Anglo-Norman kings, than in France itself. But it was a bloom of French poetry; and as our native poetry formed itself, it formed itself out of this. The romance-poems which took possession of the heart and imagination of Europe in the twelfth and thirteenth centuries are French; 'they are', as Southey justly says, 'the pride of French literature, nor have we anything which can be placed in competition with them'. Themes were supplied from all quarters; but the romance-setting which was common to them all, and which gained the ear of Europe, was French. This constituted for the French poetry, literature, and language, at the height of the Middle Age, an unchallenged predominance. The Italian Brunetto Latini, the master of Dante, wrote his *Treasure* in French because, he says, 'la parleure en est plus délitable et plus commune à toutes gens'. In the same century, the thirteenth, the French romance-writer,

Christian of Troyes, formulates the claims, in chivalry and letters, of France, his native country, as follows:

> Or vous ert par ce livre apris,
> Que Gresse ot de chevalerie
> Le premier los et de clergie;
> Puis vint chevalerie à Rome,
> Et de la clergie la some,
> Qui ore est en France venue.
> Deix doinst qu'ele i soit retenue,
> Et que li lius li abelisse
> Tant que de France n'isse
> L'onor qui s'i est arestée!

Now by this book you will learn that first Greece had the renown for chivalry and letters: then chivalry and the primacy in letters passed to Rome, and now it is come to France. God grant it may be kept there; and that the place may please it so well, that the honour which has come to make stay in France may never depart thence!

Yet it is now all gone, this French romance-poetry, of which the weight of substance and the power of style are not unfairly represented by this extract from Christian of Troyes. Only by means of the historic estimate can we persuade ourselves now to think that any of it is of poetical importance.

But in the fourteenth century there comes an Englishman nourished on this poetry, taught his trade by this poetry, getting words, rhyme, metre from this poetry; for even of that stanza which the Italians used, and which Chaucer derived immediately from the Italians, the basis and suggestion was probably given in France. Chaucer (I have already named him) fascinated his contemporaries, but so too did Christian of Troyes and Wolfram of Eschenbach. Chaucer's power of fascination, however, is enduring; his poetical importance does not need the assistance of the historic estimate; it is real. He is a genuine source of joy and strength, which is flowing still for us and will flow always. He will be read, as time goes on, far more generally than he is read now. His language is a cause of difficulty for us; but so also, and I think in quite as great a degree, is the language of Burns. In Chaucer's case, as in that of Burns, it is a difficulty to be unhesitatingly accepted and overcome.

If we ask ourselves wherein consists the immense superiority of Chaucer's poetry over the romance-poetry —why is it that in passing from this to Chaucer we suddenly feel ourselves to be in another world, we shall find that his superiority is both in the substance of his poetry and in the style of his poetry. His superiority in substance is given by his large, free, simple, clear yet kindly view of human life,—so unlike the total want, in the romance-poets, of all intelligent command of it. Chaucer has not their helplessness; he has gained the power to survey the world from a central, a truly human point of view. We have only to call to mind the Prologue to *The Canterbury Tales*. The right comment upon it is Dryden's: 'It is sufficient to say, according to the proverb, that *here is God's plenty*.' And again: 'He is a perpetual fountain of good sense.' It is by a large, free, sound representation of things, that poetry, this high criticism of life, has truth of substance; and Chaucer's poetry has truth of substance.

Of his style and manner, if we think first of the romance-poetry and then of Chaucer's divine liquidness of diction, his divine fluidity of movement, it is difficult to speak temperately. They are irresistible, and justify all the rapture with which his successors speak of his 'gold dewdrops of speech'. Johnson misses the point entirely when he finds fault with Dryden for ascribing to Chaucer the first refinement of our numbers, and says that Gower also can show smooth numbers and easy rhymes. The refinement of our numbers means something far more than this. A nation may have versifiers with smooth numbers and easy rhymes, and yet may have no real poetry at all. Chaucer is the father of our splendid English poetry; he is our 'well of English undefiled', because by the lovely charm of his diction, the lovely charm of his movement, he makes an epoch and founds a tradition. In Spenser, Shakespeare, Milton, Keats, we can follow the tradition of the liquid diction, the fluid movement, of Chaucer; at one time it is his liquid diction of which in these poets we feel the virtue, and at another time it is his fluid movement. And the virtue is irresistible.

Bounded as is my space, I must yet find room for an example of Chaucer's virtue, as I have given examples to show the virtue of the great classics. I feel disposed to say that a single line is enough to show the charm of Chaucer's verse; that merely one line like this—

O martyr souded[1] in virginitee!

has a virtue of manner and movement such as we shall not find in all the verse of romance-poetry;—but this is saying nothing. The virtue is such as we shall not find, perhaps, in all English poetry, outside the poets whom I have named as the special inheritors of Chaucer's tradition. A single line, however, is too little if we have not the strain of Chaucer's verse well in our memory; let us take a stanza. It is from *The Prioress's Tale*, the story of the Christian child murdered in a Jewry—

> My throte is cut unto my nekke-bone
> Saidè this child, and as by way of kinde
> I should have deyd, yea, longè time agone;
> But Jesu Christ, as ye in bookès finde,
> Will that his glory last and be in minde,

[1] The French *soude*; soldered, fixed fast.

> And for the worship of his mother dere
> Yet may I sing *O Alma* loud and clere.

Wordsworth has modernised this Tale, and to feel how
delicate and evanescent is the charm of verse, we have
only to read Wordsworth's first three lines of this stanza
after Chaucer's—

> My throat is cut unto the bone, I trow,
> Said this young child, and by the law of kind
> I should have died, yea, many hours ago.

The charm is departed. It is often said that the power of
liquidness and fluidity in Chaucer's verse was dependent
upon a free, a licentious dealing with language, such as
is now impossible; upon a liberty, such as Burns too
enjoyed, of making words like *neck*, *bird*, into a dissyllable
by adding to them, and words like *cause*, *rhyme*, into a dissyllable by sounding the *e* mute. It is true that Chaucer's
fluidity is conjoined with this liberty, and is admirably
served by it; but we ought not to say that it was dependent upon it. It was dependent upon his talent. Other
poets with a like liberty do not attain to the fluidity of
Chaucer; Burns himself does not attain to it. Poets, again,
who have a talent akin to Chaucer's, such as Shakespeare or Keats, have known how to attain to his fluidity
without the like liberty.

And yet Chaucer is not one of the great classics. His
poetry transcends and effaces, easily and without effort,
all the romance-poetry of Catholic Christendom; it
transcends and effaces all the English poetry contemporary with it, it transcends and effaces all the English
poetry subsequent to it down to the age of Elizabeth. Of
such avail is poetic truth of substance, in its natural and
necessary union with poetic truth of style. And yet, I say,
Chaucer is not one of the great classics. He has not their

accent. What is wanting to him is suggested by the mere
mention of the name of the first great classic of Christendom, the immortal poet who died eighty years before
Chaucer,—Dante. The accent of such a verse as

> In la sua volontade è nostra pace . . .

is altogether beyond Chaucer's reach; we praise him, but
we feel that this accent is out of the question for him. It
may be said that it was necessarily out of the reach of any
poet in the England of that stage of growth. Possibly;
but we are to adopt a real, not a historic, estimate of
poetry. However we may account for its absence, something is wanting, then, to the poetry of Chaucer, which
poetry must have before it can be placed in the glorious
class of the best. And there is no doubt what that something is. It is the σπουδαιότης, the high and excellent
seriousness, which Aristotle assigns as one of the grand
virtues of poetry. The substance of Chaucer's poetry, his
view of things and his criticism of life, has largeness,
freedom, shrewdness, benignity; but it has not this high
seriousness. Homer's criticism of life has it, Dante's has
it, Shakespeare's has it. It is this chiefly which gives to
our spirits what they can rest upon; and with the increasing demands of our modern ages upon poetry, this virtue
of giving us what we can rest upon will be more and more
highly esteemed. A voice from the slums of Paris, fifty
or sixty years after Chaucer, the voice of poor Villon out
of his life of riot and crime, has at its happy moments (as,
for instance, in the last stanza of *La Belle Heaulmière*[1]) more

---

[1] The name *Heaulmière* is said to be derived from a headdress (helm) worn
as a mark by courtesans. In Villon's ballad, a poor old creature of this class
laments her days of youth and beauty. The last stanza of the ballad runs
thus—

> 'Ainsi le bon temps regretons
> Entre nous, pauvres vieilles sottes,
> Assises bas, à croppetons,

of this important poetic virtue of seriousness than all the productions of Chaucer. But its apparition in Villon, and in men like Villon, is fitful; the greatness of the great poets, the power of their criticism of life, is that their virtue is sustained.

To our praise, therefore, of Chaucer as a poet there must be this limitation; he lacks the high seriousness of the great classics, and therewith an important part of their virtue. Still, the main fact for us to bear in mind about Chaucer is his sterling value according to that real estimate which we firmly adopt for all poets. He has poetic truth of substance, though he has not high poetic seriousness, and corresponding to his truth of substance he has an exquisite virtue of style and manner. With him is born our real poetry.

For my present purpose I need not dwell on our Elizabethan poetry, or on the continuation and close of this poetry in Milton. We all of us profess to be agreed in the estimate of this poetry; we all of us recognise it as great poetry, our greatest, and Shakespeare and Milton as our poetical classics. The real estimate, here, has universal currency. With the next age of our poetry divergency and difficulty begin. An historic estimate of that poetry has established itself; and the question is, whether it will be found to coincide with the real estimate.

The age of Dryden, together with our whole eighteenth century which followed it, sincerely believed itself to have

> Tout en ung tas comme pelottes;
> A petit feu de chenevottes
> Tost allumés, tost estainctes.
> Et jadis fusmes si mignottes!
> Ainsi en prend à maintz et maintes.'

'Thus amongst ourselves we regret the good time, poor silly old things, low-seated on our heels, all in a heap like so many balls; by a little fire of hemp-stalks, soon lighted, soon spent. And once we were such darlings! So fares it with many and many a one.'

produced poetical classics of its own, and even to have made advance, in poetry, beyond all its predecessors. Dryden regards as not seriously disputable the opinion 'that the sweetness of English verse was never understood or practised by our fathers'. Cowley could see nothing at all in Chaucer's poetry. Dryden heartily admired it, and, as we have seen, praised its matter admirably; but of its exquisite manner and movement all he can find to say is that 'there is the rude sweetness of a Scotch tune in it, which is natural and pleasing, though not perfect'. Addison, wishing to praise Chaucer's numbers, compares them with Dryden's own. And all through the eighteenth century, and down even into our own times, the stereotyped phrase of approbation for good verse found in our early poetry has been, that it even approached the verse of Dryden, Addison, Pope, and Johnson.

Are Dryden and Pope poetical classics? Is the historic estimate, which represents them as such, and which has been so long established that it cannot easily give way, the real estimate? Wordsworth and Coleridge, as is well known, denied it; but the authority of Wordsworth and Coleridge does not weigh much with the young generation, and there are many signs to show that the eighteenth century and its judgments are coming into favour again. Are the favourite poets of the eighteenth century classics?

It is impossible within my present limits to discuss the question fully. And what man of letters would not shrink from seeming to dispose dictatorially of the claims of two men who are, at any rate, such masters in letters as Dryden and Pope; two men of such admirable talent, both of them, and one of them, Dryden, a man, on all sides, of such energetic and genial power? And yet, if we are to gain the full benefit from poetry, we must have the real estimate of it. I cast about for some mode of arriving, in the present case, at such an estimate without offence. And perhaps the best way is to begin, as it is easy to begin, with cordial praise.

When we find Chapman, the Elizabethan translator of Homer, expressing himself in his preface thus: 'Though truth in her very nakedness sits in so deep a pit, that from Gades to Aurora and Ganges few eyes can sound her, I hope yet those few here will so discover and confirm that, the date being out of her darkness in this morning of our poet, he shall now gird his temples with the sun',—we pronounce that such a prose is intolerable. When we find Milton writing: 'And long it was not after, when I was confirmed in this opinion, that he, who would not be frustrate of his hope to write well hereafter in laudable things, ought himself to be a true poem',—we pronounce that such a prose has its own grandeur, but that it is obsolete and inconvenient. But when we find Dryden telling us: 'What Virgil wrote in the vigour of his age, in plenty and at ease, I have undertaken to translate in my declining years; struggling with wants, oppressed with sickness, curbed in my genius, liable to be misconstrued in all I write',—then we exclaim that here at last we have the true English prose, a prose such as we would all gladly use if we only knew how. Yet Dryden was Milton's contemporary.

But after the Restoration the time had come when our nation felt the imperious need of a fit prose. So, too, the time had likewise come when our nation felt the imperious need of freeing itself from the absorbing preoccupation which religion in the Puritan age had exercised. It was impossible that this freedom should be brought about without some negative excess, without some neglect and impairment of the religious life of the soul; and the spiritual history of the eighteenth century shows us that the freedom was not achieved without them. Still, the freedom was achieved; the preoccupation, an undoubtedly baneful and retarding one if it had continued, was got rid of. And as with religion amongst us at that period, so it was also with letters. A fit prose was a necessity; but it was impossible that a fit prose should establish itself amongst us without some touch of frost to the imaginative life of the soul. The needful qualities for a fit prose are regularity, uniformity, precision, balance. The men of letters, whose destiny it may be to bring their nation to the attainment of a fit prose, must of necessity, whether they work in prose or in verse, give a predominating, an almost exclusive attention to the qualities of regularity, uniformity, precision, balance. But an almost exclusive attention to these qualities involves some repression and silencing of poetry.

We are to regard Dryden as the puissant and glorious founder, Pope as the splendid high priest, of our age of prose and reason, of our excellent and indispensable eighteenth century. For the purposes of their mission and destiny their poetry, like their prose, is admirable. Do you ask me whether Dryden's verse, take it almost where you will, is not good?

> A milk-white Hind, immortal and unchanged,
> Fed on the lawns and in the forest ranged.

I answer: Admirable for the purposes of the inaugurator of an age of prose and reason. Do you ask me whether Pope's verse, take it almost where you will, is not good?

> To Hounslow Heath I point, and Banstead Down;
> Thence comes your mutton, and these chicks my own.

I answer: Admirable for the purposes of the high priest of an age of prose and reason. But do you ask me whether such verse proceeds from men with an adequate poetic criticism of life, from men whose criticism of life has a high seriousness, or even, without that high seriousness, has poetic largeness, freedom, insight, benignity? Do you ask me whether the application of ideas to life in the verse of these men, often a powerful application, no doubt, is a powerful *poetic* application? Do you ask me whether the poetry of these men has either the matter or the inseparable manner of such an adequate poetic criticism; whether it has the accent of

> Absent thee from felicity awhile . . .

or of

> And what is else not to be overcome . . .

or of

> O martyr souded in virginitee!

I answer: It has not and cannot have them; it is the poetry of the builders of an age of prose and reason. Though they may write in verse, though they may in a certain sense be masters of the art of versification, Dryden and Pope are not classics of our poetry, they are classics of our prose.

Gray is our poetical classic of that literature and age; the position of Gray is singular, and demands a word of notice here. He has not the volume or the power of poets who, coming in times more favourable, have attained to an independent criticism of life. But he lived with the great poets, he lived, above all with the Greeks, through perpetually studying and enjoying them; and he caught their poetic point of view for regarding life, caught their poetic manner. The point of view and the manner are not self-sprung in him, he caught them of others; and he had not the free and abundant use of them. But whereas Addison and Pope never had the use of them, Gray had the use of them at times. He is the scantiest and frailest of classics in our poetry, but he is a classic.

And now, after Gray, we are met, as we draw towards the end of the eighteenth century, we are met by the great name of Burns. We enter now on times where the personal estimate of poets begins to be rife, and where the real estimate of them is not reached without difficulty. But in spite of the disturbing pressures of personal partiality, of national partiality, let us try to reach a real estimate of the poetry of Burns.

By his English Burns in general belongs to the eighteenth century, and has little importance for us.

> Mark ruffian Violence, distain'd with crimes,
> Rousing elate in these degenerate times;
> View unsuspecting Innocence a prey,
> As guileful Fraud points out the erring way;
> While subtle Litigation's pliant tongue
> The life-blood equal sucks of Right and Wrong!

Evidently this is not the real Burns, or his name and fame would have disappeared long ago. Nor is Clarinda's love-poet, Sylvander, the real Burns either. But he tells us himself: 'These English songs gravel me to death. I have not the command of the language that I have of my native tongue. In fact, I think that my ideas are more barren in English than in Scotch. I have been at *Duncan Gray* to dress it in English, but all I can do is desperately stupid.' We English turn naturally, in Burns, to the poems in our own language, because we can read them easily; but in those poems we have not the real Burns.

The real Burns is of course in his Scotch poems. Let us boldly say that of much of this poetry, a poetry dealing perpetually with Scotch drink, Scotch religion, and Scotch manners, a Scotchman's estimate is apt to be personal. A Scotchman is used to this world of Scotch drink,

Scotch religion, and Scotch manners; he has a tenderness for it; it meets its poet half way. In this tender mood he reads tender pieces like the *Holy Fair* or *Halloween*. But this world of Scotch drink, Scotch religion, and Scotch manners is against a poet, not for him, when it is not a partial countryman who reads him; for in itself it is not a beautiful world, and no one can deny that it is of advantage to a poet to deal with a beautiful world. Burns's world of Scotch drink, Scotch religion, and Scotch manners, is often a harsh, a sordid, a repulsive world: even the world of his *Cotter's Saturday Night* is not a beautiful world. No doubt a poet's criticism of life may have such truth and power that it triumphs over its world and delights us. Burns may triumph over his world, often he does triumph over his world, but let us observe how and where. Burns is the first case we have had where the bias of the personal estimate tends to mislead; let us look at him closely, he can bear it.

Many of his admirers will tell us that we have Burns, convivial, genuine, delightful, here—

> Leeze me on drink! it gies us mair
>   Than either school or college;
> It kindles wit, it waukens lair,
>   It pangs us fou o' knowledge.
> Be't whisky gill or penny wheep
>   Or ony stronger potion,
> It never fails, on drinking deep,
>   To kittle up our notion
>   By night or day.

There is a great deal of that sort of thing in Burns, and it is unsatisfactory, not because it is bacchanalian poetry, but because it has not that accent of sincerity which bacchanalian poetry, to do it justice, very often has. There is something in it of bravado, something which makes us feel that we have not the man speaking to us with his real voice; something, therefore, poetically unsound.

With still more confidence will his admirers tell us that we have the genuine Burns, the great poet, when his strain asserts the independence, equality, dignity, of men, as in the famous song *For a' that and a' that*—

> A prince can mak' a belted knight,
>   A marquis, duke, and a' that;
> But an honest man's aboon his might,
>   Guid faith he mauna fa' that!
>   For a' that, and a' that,
>   Their dignities, and a' that,
>   The pith o' sense, and pride o' worth,
>   Are higher rank than a' that.

Here they find his grand, genuine touches; and still more, when this puissant genius, who so often set morality at defiance, falls moralising—

> The sacred lowe o' weel-placed love
>   Luxuriantly indulge it;
> But never tempt th' illicit rove,
>   Tho' naething should divulge it.
> I waive the quantum o' the sin,
>   The hazard o' concealing,
> But och! it hardens a' within,
>   And petrifies the feeling.

Or in a higher strain—

> Who made the heart, 'tis He alone
>   Decidedly can try us;
> He knows each chord, its various tone;
>   Each spring, its various bias.
> Then at the balance let's be mute,
>   We never can adjust it;
> What's *done* we partly may compute,
>   But know not what's resisted.

Or in a better strain yet, a strain, his admirers will say, unsurpassable—

> To make a happy fire-side clime
> To weans and wife,
> That's the true pathos and sublime
> Of human life.

There is criticism of life for you, the admirers of Burns will say to us; there is the application of ideas to life! There is, undoubtedly. The doctrine of the last-quoted lines coincides almost exactly with what was the aim and end, Xenophon tells us, of all the teaching of Socrates. And the application is a powerful one; made by a man of vigorous understanding, and (need I say?) a master of language.

But for supreme poetical success more is required than the powerful application of ideas to life; it must be an application under the conditions fixed by the laws of poetic truth and poetic beauty. Those laws fix as an essential condition, in the poet's treatment of such matters as are here in question, high seriousness;—the high seriousness which comes from absolute sincerity. The accent of high seriousness, born of absolute sincerity, is what gives to such verse as

> In la sua volontade è nostra pace . . .

to such criticism of life as Dante's, its power. Is this accent felt in the passages which I have been quoting from Burns? Surely not; surely, if our sense is quick, we must perceive that we have not in those passages a voice from the very inmost soul of the genuine Burns; he is not speaking to us from these depths, he is more or less preaching. And the compensation for admiring such passages less, from missing the perfect poetic accent in

them, will be that we shall admire more the poetry where
that accent is found.

No; Burns, like Chaucer, comes short of the high seriousness of the great classics, and the virtue of matter and
manner which goes with that high seriousness is wanting
to his work. At moments he touches it in a profound and
passionate melancholy, as in those four immortal lines
taken by Byron as a motto for *The Bride of Abydos*, but
which have in them a depth of poetic quality such as
resides in no verse of Byron's own—

> Had we never loved sae kindly,
> Had we never loved sae blindly,
> Never met, or never parted,
> We had ne'er been broken-hearted.

But a whole poem of that quality Burns cannot make;
the rest, in the *Farewell to Nancy*, is verbiage.

We arrive best at the real estimate of Burns, I think,
by conceiving his work as having truth of matter and
truth of manner, but not the accent or the poetic virtue
of the highest masters. His genuine criticism of life, when
the sheer poet in him speaks, is ironic; it is not—

> Thou Power Supreme, whose mighty scheme
>   These woes of mine fulfil,
> Here firm I rest, they must be best
>   Because they are Thy will!

It is far rather: *Whistle owre the lave o't!* Yet we may say
of him as of Chaucer, that of life and the world, as they
come before him, his view is large, free, shrewd, benig-
nant,—truly poetic, therefore; and his manner of rendering what he sees is to match. But we must note, at the
same time, his great difference from Chaucer. The
freedom of Chaucer is heightened, in Burns, by a fiery,

reckless energy; the benignity of Chaucer deepens, in
Burns, into an overwhelming sense of the pathos of
things;—of the pathos of human nature, the pathos, also,
of non-human nature. Instead of the fluidity of Chaucer's
manner, the manner of Burns has spring, bounding swift-
ness. Burns is by far the greater force, though he has perhaps less charm. The world of Chaucer is fairer, richer,
more significant than that of Burns; but when the largeness
and freedom of Burns get full sweep, as in *Tam o' Shanter*,
or still more in that puissant and splendid production,
The Jolly Beggars, his world may be what it will, his
poetic genius triumphs over it. In the world of *The Jolly
Beggars* there is more than hideousness and squalor, there
is bestiality; yet the piece is a superb poetic success. It
has a breadth, truth, and power which make the famous
scene in Auerbach's Cellar, of Goethe's *Faust*, seem artificial and tame beside it, and which are only matched by
Shakspeare and Aristophanes.

Here, where his largeness and freedom serve him so
admirably, and also in those poems and songs where to
shrewdness he adds infinite archness and wit, and to
benignity infinite pathos, where his manner is flawless,
and a perfect poetic whole is the result,—in things like
the address to the mouse whose home he had ruined, in
things like *Duncan Gray, Tam Glen, Whistle and I'll come to
you my Lad, Auld Lang Syne* (this list might be made much
longer),—here we have the genuine Burns, of whom the
real estimate must be high indeed. Not a classic, nor
with the excellent σπουδαιότης of the great classics, nor
with a verse rising to a criticism of life and a virtue like
theirs; but a poet with a thorough truth of substance and
an answering truth of style, giving us a poetry sound to
the core. We all of us have a leaning towards the
pathetic, and may be inclined perhaps to prize Burns

most for his touches of piercing, sometimes almost intolerable, pathos; for verse like—

> We twa hae paidl't i' the burn
> From morning' sun till dine;
> But seas between us braid hae roar'd
> Sin auld lang syne . . .

where he is as lovely as he is sound. But perhaps it is by the perfection of soundness of his lighter and archer masterpieces that he is poetically most wholesome for us. For the votary misled by a personal estimate of Shelley, as so many of us have been, are, and will be,—of that beautiful spirit building his many-coloured haze of words and images

> Pinnacled dim in the intense inane

—no contact can be wholesomer than the contact with Burns at his archest and soundest. Side by side with the

> On the brink of the night and the morning
> My coursers are wont to respire,
> But the Earth has just whispered a warning
> That their flight must be swifter than fire . . .

of *Prometheus Unbound*, how salutary, how very salutary, to place this from *Tam Glen*—

> My minnie does constantly deave me
> And bids me beware o' young men;
> They flatter, she says, to deceive me;
> But wha can think sae o' Tam Glen?

But we enter on burning ground as we approach the poetry of times so near to us—poetry like that of Byron, Shelley, and Wordsworth—of which the estimates are so often not only personal, but personal with passion. For my purpose, it is enough to have taken the single case of Burns, the first poet we come to of whose work the estimate formed is evidently apt to be personal, and to have suggested how we may proceed, using the poetry of the great classics as a sort of touchstone, to correct this estimate, as we had previously corrected by the same means the historic estimate where we met with it. A collection like the present, with its succession of celebrated names and celebrated poems, offers a good opportunity to us for resolutely endeavouring to make our estimates of poetry real. I have sought to point out a method which will help us in making them so, and to exhibit it in use so far as to put any one who likes in a way of applying it for himself.

At any rate the end to which the method and the estimate are designed to lead, and from leading to which, if they do lead to it, they get their whole value,—the benefit of being able clearly to feel and deeply to enjoy the best, the truly classic in poetry,—is an end, let me say it once more at parting, of supreme importance. We are often told that an era is opening in which we are to see multitudes of a common sort of readers, and masses of a common sort of literature; that such readers do not want and could not relish anything better than such literature, and that to provide it is becoming a vast and profitable industry. Even if good literature entirely lost currency with the world, it would still be abundantly worth while to continue to enjoy it by oneself. But it never will lose currency with the world, in spite of momentary appearances: it never will lose supremacy. Currency and supremacy are insured to it, not indeed by the world's deliberate and conscious choice, but by something far deeper,—by the instinct of self-preservation in humanity.

ON TRANSLATING HOMER

(*Abridged*)

(1861)

... Nunquamne reponam?

IT has more than once been suggested to me that I should translate Homer. That is a task for which I have neither the time nor the courage; but the suggestion led me to regard yet more closely a poet whom I had already long studied, and for one or two years the works of Homer were seldom out of my hands. The study of classical literature is probably on the decline; but, whatever may be the fate of this study in general, it is certain that, as instruction spreads and the number of readers increases, attention will be more and more directed to the poetry of Homer, not indeed as part of a classical course, but as the most important poetical monument existing. Even within the last ten years two fresh translations of the *Iliad* have appeared in England: one by a man of great ability and genuine learning, Professor Newman; the other by Mr. Wright, the conscientious and painstaking translator of Dante. It may safely be asserted that neither of these works will take rank as the standard translation of Homer; that the task of rendering him will still be attempted by other translators. It may perhaps be possible to render to these some service, to save them some loss of labour, by pointing out rocks on which their predecessors have split, and the right objects on which a translator of Homer should fix his attention.

It is disputed what aim a translator should propose to himself in dealing with his original. Even this preliminary is not yet settled. On one side it is said that the translation ought to be such 'that the reader should, if possible, forget that it is a translation at all, and be lulled into the illusion that he is reading an original work—something original' (if the translation be English), 'from an English hand'. The real original is in this case, it is said, 'taken as a basis on which to rear a poem that shall affect our countrymen as the original may be conceived to have affected its natural hearers'. On the other hand, Mr. Newman, who states the foregoing doctrine only to condemn it, declares that he 'aims at precisely the opposite: to retain every peculiarity of the original, so far as he is able, *with the greater care the more foreign it may happen to be*'; so that it may 'never be forgotten that he is imitating, and imitating in a different material'. The translator's 'first duty', says Mr. Newman 'is a historical one, to be *faithful*'. Probably both sides would agree that the translator's 'first duty is to be faithful'; but the question at issue between them is, in what faithfulness consists.

My one object is to give practical advice to a translator; and I shall not the least concern myself with theories of translation as such. But I advise the translator not to try 'to rear on the basis of the *Iliad*, a poem that shall affect our countrymen as the original may be conceived to have affected its natural hearers'; and for this simple reason, that we cannot possibly tell *how* the *Iliad* 'affected its natural hearers'. It is probably meant merely that he should try to affect Englishmen powerfully, as Homer affected Greeks powerfully; but this direction is not enough, and can give no real guidance. For all great poets affect their hearers powerfully, but the effect of one poet is one thing, that of another poet another thing: it is our translator's business to reproduce the effect of Homer, and the most powerful emotion of the unlearned English reader can never assure him whether he has *re*produced this, or whether he has produced something else. So, again, he may follow Mr. Newman's directions, he may try to be 'faithful', he may 'retain every peculiarity of his original'; but who is to assure him, who is to assure Mr. Newman himself, that, when he has done this, he has done that for which Mr. Newman enjoins this to be done, 'adhered closely to Homer's manner and habit of thought'? Evidently the translator needs some more practical directions than these. No one can tell him how Homer affected the Greeks; but there are those who can tell him how Homer affects *them*. These are scholars; who possess, at the same time with knowledge of Greek, adequate poetical taste and feeling. No translation will seem to them of much worth compared with the original; but they alone can say whether the translation produces more or less the same effect upon them as the original. They are the only competent tribunal in this matter: the Greeks are dead; the unlearned Englishman has not the data for judging; and no man can safely confide in his own single judgment of his own work. Let not the translator, then, trust to his notions of what the ancient Greeks would have thought of him; he will lose himself in the vague. Let him not trust to what the ordinary English reader thinks of him; he will be taking the blind for his guide. Let him not trust to his own judgment of his own work; he may be misled by individual caprices. Let him ask how his work affects those who both know Greek and can appreciate poetry; whether to read it gives the Provost of Eton, or Professor Thompson at Cambridge, or Professor Jowett here in Oxford, at all the same feeling which to read the original gives them. I consider that when Bentley said of Pope's translation, 'It was a pretty poem, but must not be called Homer', the work, in spite of all its power and attractiveness, was judged.

'Ὡς ἂν ὁ φρόνιμος ὁρίσειεν, 'as the judicious would determine', that is a test to which everyone professes himself willing to submit his works. Unhappily, in most cases, no two persons agree as to who 'the judicious' are. In the present case, the ambiguity is removed: I suppose the translator at one with me as to the tribunal to which alone he should look for judgment; and he has thus obtained a practical test by which to estimate the real success of his work. How is he to proceed, in order that his work, tried by this test, may be found most successful?

First of all, there are certain negative counsels which I will give him. Homer has occupied men's minds so much, such a literature has arisen about him, that every one who approaches him should resolve strictly to limit himself to that which may directly serve the object for which he approaches him. I advise the translator to have nothing to do with the questions, whether Homer ever existed; whether the poet of the *Iliad* be one or many; whether the *Iliad* be one poem or an *Achilleis* and an *Iliad* stuck together; whether the Christian doctrine of the Atonement is shadowed forth in the Homeric mythology; whether the Goddess Latona in any way prefigures the Virgin Mary, and so on. These are questions which have been discussed with learning, with ingenuity, nay, with genius; but they have two inconveniences,—one general for all who approach them, one particular for the translator. The general inconvenience is that there really exist no data for determining them. The particular inconvenience is that their solution by the translator, even were it possible, could be of no benefit to his translation.

I advise him, again, not to trouble himself with constructing a special vocabulary for his use in translation; with excluding a certain class of English words, and with confining himself to another class, in obedience to any theory about the peculiar qualities of Homer's style. Mr. Newman says that 'the entire dialect of Homer being essentially archaic, that of a translator ought to be as much Saxo-Norman as possible, and owe as little as possible to the elements thrown into our language by classical learning'. Mr. Newman is unfortunate in the observance of his own theory; for I continually find in his translation words of Latin origin, which seem to me quite alien to the simplicity of Homer,—'responsive', for instance, which is a favourite word of Mr. Newman, to represent the Homeric ἀμειβόμενος:

> Great Hector of the motley helm thus spake to her *responsive*.
> But thus *responsively* to him spake godlike Alexander.

And the word 'celestial', again, in the grand address of Zeus to the horses of Achilles,

> You, who are born *celestial*, from Eld and Death exempted!

seems to me in that place exactly to jar upon the feeling as too bookish. But, apart from the question of Mr. Newman's fidelity to his own theory, such a theory seems to me both dangerous for a translator and false in itself. Dangerous for a translator; because, wherever one finds such a theory announced (and one finds it pretty often), it is generally followed by an explosion of pedantry; and pedantry is of all things in the world the most un-Homeric. False in itself; because, in fact, we owe to the Latin element in our language most of that very rapidity and clear decisiveness by which it is contradistinguished from the German, and in sympathy with the languages of Greece and Rome: so that to limit an English translator of Homer to words of Saxon origin is to deprive him of one of his special advantages for translating Homer. In Voss's well-known translation of Homer, it is precisely the qualities of his German language itself, something heavy and trailing both in the structure of its sentences and in the words of which it is composed, which prevent his translation, in spite of the hexameters, in spite of the fidelity, from creating in us the impression created by the Greek. Mr. Newman's prescription, if followed, would just strip the English translator of the advantage which he has over Voss. . . .

These are negative counsels; I come to the positive. When I say the translator of Homer should above all be penetrated by a sense of four qualities of his author;— that he is eminently rapid; that he is eminently plain and direct, both in the evolution of his thought and in the expression of it, that is, both in his syntax and in his words; that he is eminently plain and direct in the substance of his thought, that is, in his matter and ideas; and, finally that he is eminently noble;—I probably seem to be saying what is too general to be of much service to anybody. Yet it is strictly true that, for want of duly penetrating themselves with the first-named quality of Homer, his rapidity, Cowper and Mr. Wright have failed in rendering him; that, for want of duly appreciating the second-named quality, his plainness and directness of style and diction, Pope and Mr. Sotheby have failed in rendering him; that for want of appreciating the third, his plainness and directness of ideas, Chapman has failed in rendering him; while for want of appreciating the fourth, his nobleness, Mr. Newman, who has clearly seen some of the faults of his predecessors, has yet failed more conspicuously than any of them.

Coleridge says, in his strange language, speaking of the union of the human soul with the divine essence, that this takes place

> Whene'er the mist, which stands 'twixt God and thee,
> Defecates to a pure transparency;

and so, too, it may be said of that union of the translator with his original, which alone can produce a good translation, that it takes place when the mist which stands between them—the mist of alien modes of thinking, speaking, and feeling on the translator's part—'defecates to a pure transparency', and disappears. But between Cowper and Homer—(Mr. Wright repeats in the main Cowper's manner, as Mr. Sotheby repeats Pope's manner, and neither Mr. Wright's translation nor Mr. Sotheby's has, I must be forgiven for saying, any proper reason for existing)—between Cowper and Homer there is interposed the mist of Cowper's elaborate Miltonic manner, entirely alien to the flowing rapidity of Homer; between Pope and Homer there is interposed the mist of Pope's literary artificial manner, entirely alien to the plain naturalness of Homer's manner; between Chapman and Homer there is interposed the mist of the fancifulness of the Elizabethan age, entirely alien to the plain directness of Homer's thought and feeling; while between Mr. Newman and Homer is interposed a cloud of more than Egyptian thickness,—namely, a manner, in Mr. Newman's version, eminently ignoble, while Homer's manner is eminently noble.

I do not despair of making all these propositions clear to a student who approaches Homer with a free mind. First, Homer is eminently rapid, and to this rapidity the elaborate movement of Miltonic blank verse is alien. The reputation of Cowper, that most interesting man and excellent poet, does not depend on his translation of Homer; and in his preface to the second edition, he himself tells us that he felt,—he had too much poetical taste not to feel,—on returning to his own version after six or seven years, 'more dissatisfied with it himself than the most difficult to be pleased of all his judges'. And he was dissatisfied with it for the right reason,—that 'it seemed to him deficient *in the grace of ease*'. Yet he seems to have originally misconceived the manner of Homer so much, that it is no wonder he rendered him amiss. 'The similitude of Milton's manner to that of Homer is such', he says, 'that no person familiar with both can read either without being reminded of the other; and it is in those breaks and pauses to which the numbers of the English poet are so much indebted, both for their dignity and variety, that he chiefly copies the Grecian.' It would be more true to say: 'The unlikeness of Milton's manner to that of Homer is such, that no person familiar with both can read either without being struck with his difference from the other; and it is in his breaks and pauses that the English poet is most unlike the Grecian.'

The inversion and pregnant conciseness of Milton or Dante are, doubtless, most impressive qualities of style; but they are the very opposites of the directness and flowingness of Homer, which he keeps alike in passages of the simplest narrative, and in those of the deepest emotion. Not only, for example, are these lines of Cowper un-Homeric:

So numerous seemed those fires the banks between
Of Xanthus, blazing, and the fleet of Greece
In prospect all of Troy;

where the position of the word 'blazing' gives an entirely un-Homeric movement to this simple passage, describing the fires of the Trojan camp outside of Troy; but the following lines, in that very highly-wrought passage where the horse of Achilles answers his master's reproaches for having left Patroclus on the field of battle, are equally un-Homeric:

> For not through sloth or tardiness on us
> Aught chargeable, have Ilium's sons thine arms
> Stript from Patroclus' shoulders; but a God
> Matchless in battle, offspring of bright-haired
> Latona, him contending in the van
> Slew, for the glory of the chief of Troy.

Here even the first inversion, 'have Ilium's sons thine arms Stript from Patroclus' shoulders', gives the reader a sense of a movement not Homeric; and the second inversion, 'a God him contending in the van Slew', gives this sense ten times stronger. Instead of moving on without check, as in reading the original, the reader twice finds himself, in reading the translation, brought up and checked. Homer moves with the same simplicity and rapidity in the highly-wrought as in the simple passage.

It is in vain that Cowper insists on his fidelity: 'my chief boast is that I have adhered closely to my original': —'the matter found in me, whether the reader like it or not, is found also in Homer; and the matter not found in me, how much soever the reader may admire it, is found only in Mr. Pope'. To suppose that it is *fidelity* to an original to give its matter, unless you at the same time give its manner; or, rather, to suppose that you can really give its matter at all, unless you can give its manner, is just the mistake of our pre-Raphaelite school of painters, who do not understand that the peculiar effect of nature resides in the whole and not in the parts. So the peculiar effect of a poet resides in his manner and movement, not in his words taken separately. It is well known how conscientiously literal is Cowper in his translation of Homer. It is well known how extravagantly free is Pope.

> So let it be!
> Portents and prodigies are lost on me;

that is Pope's rendering of the words,

> Ξάνθε, τί μοι θάνατον μαντεύεαι; οὐδέ τί σε χρή·[1]

> Xanthus, why prophesiest thou my death to me? thou
> needest not at all:

yet, on the whole, Pope's translation of the *Iliad* is more Homeric than Cowper's, for it is more rapid.

Pope's movement, however, though rapid, is not of the same kind as Homer's; and here I come to the real objection to rhyme in a translation of Homer. It is commonly said that rhyme is to be abandoned in a translation of Homer, because 'the exigencies of rhyme', to quote Mr. Newman, 'positively forbid faithfulness'; because 'a just translation of any ancient poet in rhyme', to quote Cowper, 'is impossible'. This, however, is merely an accidental objection to rhyme. If this were all, it might be supposed, that if rhymes were more abundant Homer could be adequately translated in rhyme. But this is not so; there is a deeper, a substantial objection to rhyme in a translation of Homer. It is, that rhyme inevitably tends to pair lines which in the original are independent, and thus the movement of the poem is changed. In these

---

[1] *Iliad*, xix. 420.

lines of Chapman, for instance, from Sarpedon's speech to Glaucus, in the twelfth book of the *Iliad*:

> O friend, if keeping back
> Would keep back age from us, and death, and that we might not wrack
> In this life's human sea at all, but that deferring now
> We shunned death ever,—nor would I half this vain valor show,
> Nor glorify a folly so, to wish thee to advance;
> But since we *must* go, though not here, and that besides the chance
> Proposed now, there are infinite fates, etc.

Here the necessity of making the line,

> Nor glorify a folly so, to wish thee to advance,

rhyme with the line which follows it, entirely changes and spoils the movement of the passage.

> οὔτε κεν αὐτὸς ἐνὶ πρώτοισι μαχοίμην,
> οὔτε κε σὲ στέλλοιμι μάχην ἐς κυδιάνειραν.[1]

Neither would I myself go forth to fight with the foremost,
Nor would I urge thee on to enter the glorious battle,

says Homer; there he stops, and begins an opposed movement:

> νῦν δ'—ἔμπης γὰρ Κῆρες ἐφεστᾶσιν θανάτοιο—

But—for a thousand fates of death stand close to us always—

This line, in which Homer wishes to go away with the most marked rapidity from the line before, Chapman is forced, by the necessity of rhyming, intimately to connect with the line before.

> But since we *must* go, though not here, and that besides the chance.

[1] *Iliad*, xii. 324.

The moment the word *chance* strikes our ear, we are irresistibly carried back to *advance* and to the whole previous line, which, according to Homer's own feeling, we ought to have left behind us entirely, and to be moving farther and farther away from.

Rhyme certainly, by intensifying antithesis, can intensify separation, and this is precisely what Pope does; but this balanced rhetorical antithesis, though very effective, is entirely un-Homeric. And this is what I mean by saying that Pope fails to render Homer, because he does not render his plainness and directness of style and diction. Where Homer marks separation by moving away, Pope marks it by antithesis. No passage could show this better than the passage I have just quoted, on which I will pause for a moment.

Robert Wood, whose *Essay on the Genius of Homer* is mentioned by Goethe as one of the books which fell into his hands when his powers were first developing themselves, and strongly interested him, relates of this passage a striking story. He says that in 1762, at the end of the Seven Years' War, being then Under-Secretary of State, he was directed to wait upon the President of the Council, Lord Granville, a few days before he died, with the preliminary articles of the Treaty of Paris. 'I found him', he continues, 'so languid, that I proposed postponing my business for another time; but he insisted that I should stay, saying, it could not prolong his life to neglect his duty; and repeating the following passage out of Sarpedon's speech, he dwelt with particular emphasis on the third line, which recalled to his mind the distinguishing part he had taken in public affairs:

ὦ πέπον, εἰ μὲν γάρ, πόλεμον περὶ τόνδε φυγόντε,
αἰεὶ δὴ μέλλοιμεν ἀγήρω τ' ἀθανάτω τε

ἔσσεθ᾽, οὔτε κεν αὐτὸς ἐνὶ πρώτοισι μαχοίμην,[1]
οὔτε κε σὲ στέλλοιμι μάχην ἐς κυδιάνειραν·
νῦν δ᾽—ἔμπης γὰρ Κῆρες ἐφεστᾶσιν θανάτοιο
μυρίαι, ἃς οὐκ ἔστι φυγεῖν βρότον, οὐδ᾽ ὑπαλύξαι—
ἴομεν.

His Lordship repeated the last word several times with a calm and determinate resignation; and, after a serious pause of some minutes, he desired to hear the Treaty read, to which he listened with great attention, and recovered spirits enough to declare the approbation of a dying statesman (I use his own words) "on the most glorious war, and most honourable peace, this nation ever saw".[2]

I quote this story, first, because it is interesting as exhibiting the English aristocracy at its very height of culture, lofty spirit, and greatness, towards the middle of the 18th century. I quote, secondly, because it seems to me to illustrate Goethe's saying which I mentioned, that our life, in Homer's view of it, represents a conflict and a hell; and it brings out, too, what there is tonic and fortifying in this doctrine. I quote it, lastly, because it shows that the passage is just one of those in translating which Pope will be at his best, a passage of strong emotion and oratorical movement, not of simple narrative or description.

Pope translates the passage thus:

> Could all our care elude the gloomy grave
> Which claims no less the fearful than the brave,
> For lust of fame I should not vainly dare
> In fighting fields, nor urge thy soul to war:
> But since, alas! ignoble age must come,
> Disease, and death's inexorable doom;

---

[1] These are the words on which Lord Granville 'dwelled with particular emphasis'.

[2] Robert Wood, *Essay on the Original Genius and Writings of Homer*, London, 1775, p. vii.

The life which others pay, let us bestow,
And give to fame what we to nature owe.

Nothing could better exhibit Pope's prodigious talent; and nothing, too, could be better in its own way. But, as Bentley said, 'You must not call it Homer'. One feels that Homer's thought has passed through a literary and rhetorical crucible, and come out highly intellectualised; come out in a form which strongly impresses us, indeed, but which no longer impresses us in the same way as when it was uttered by Homer. The antithesis of the last two lines—

The life which others pay, let us bestow,
And give to fame what we to nature owe

is excellent, and is just suited to Pope's heroic couplet; but neither the antithesis itself, nor the couplet which conveys it is suited to the feeling or to the movement of the Homeric ἴομεν.

A literary and intellectualised language is, however, in its own way well suited to grand matters; and Pope, with a language of this kind and his own admirable talent, comes off well enough as long as he has passion, or oratory, or a great crisis to deal with. Even here, as I have been pointing out, he does not render Homer: but but he and his style are in themselves strong. It is when he comes to level passages, passages of narrative or description, that he and his style are sorely tried, and prove themselves weak. A perfectly plain direct style can of course convey the simplest matter as naturally as the grandest; indeed, it must be harder for it, one would say, to convey a grand matter worthily and nobly, than to convey a common matter, as alone such a matter should be conveyed, plainly and simply. But the style of Rasselas is

incomparably better fitted to describe a sage philosophis-
ing than a soldier lighting his camp-fire. The style of
Pope is not the style of *Rasselas*; but it is equally a literary
style, equally unfitted to describe a simple matter with
the plain naturalness of Homer.

Everyone knows the passage at the end of the eighth
book of the *Iliad*, where the fires of the Trojan encamp-
ment are likened to the stars. It is very far from my wish
to hold Pope up to ridicule, so I shall not quote the commencement of the passage, which in the original is of
great and celebrated beauty, and in translating which
Pope has been singularly and notoriously fortunate. But
the latter part of the passage, where Homer leaves the
stars, and comes to the Trojan fires, treats of the plainest,
most matter-of-fact subject possible, and deals with this,
as Homer always deals with every subject, in the plainest
and most straightforward style.

So many in number, between the ships and the streams of
Xanthus, shone forth in front of Troy the fires kindled by the
Trojans. There were kindled a thousand fires in the plain; and
by each one there sat fifty men in the light of the blazing
fire. And the horses, munching white barley and rye, and
standing by the chariots, waited for the bright-throned
Morning.[1]

In Pope's translation, this plain story becomes the
following:

> So many flames before proud Ilion blaze,
> And brighten glimmering Xanthus with their rays;
> The long reflections of the distant fires
> Gleam on the walls, and tremble on the spires.
> A thousand piles the dusky horrors gild,
> And shoot a shady lustre o'er the field.

[1] *Iliad*, viii. 560.

> Full fifty guards each flaming pile attend,
> Whose umbered arms, by fits, thick flashes send;
> Loud neigh the coursers o'er their heaps of corn,
> And ardent warriors wait the rising morn.

It is for passages of this sort, which, after all, form the bulk of a narrative poem, that Pope's style is so bad. In elevated passages he is powerful, as Homer is powerful, though not in the same way; but in plain narrative, where Homer is still powerful and delightful, Pope, by the inherent fault of his style, is ineffective and out of taste. Wordsworth says somewhere, that wherever Virgil seems to have composed 'with his eye on the object', Dryden fails to render him. Homer invariably composes 'with his eye on the object', whether the object be a moral or a material one: Pope composes with his eye on his style, into which he translates his object, whatever it is. That, therefore, which Homer conveys to us immediately, Pope conveys to us through a medium. He aims at turning Homer's sentiments pointedly and rhetorically; at investing Homer's description with ornament and dignity. A sentiment may be changed by being put into a pointed and oratorical form, yet may still be very effective in that form; but a description, the moment it takes its eyes off that which it is to describe, and begins to think of ornamenting itself, is worthless.

Therefore, I say, the translator of Homer should penetrate himself with a sense of the plainness and directness of Homer's style; of the simplicity with which Homer's thought is evolved and expressed. He has Pope's fate before his eyes, to show him what a divorce may be created even between the most gifted translator and Homer by an artificial evolution of thought and a literary cast of style. . . .

Mr. Newman does not leave us in doubt as to the

general effect which Homer makes upon him. As I have told you what is the general effect which Homer makes upon me,—that of a most rapidly moving poet, that of a poet most plain and direct in his style, that of a poet most plain and direct in his ideas, that of a poet eminently noble,—so Mr. Newman tells us his general impression of Homer. 'Homer's style', he says, 'is direct, popular, forcible, quaint, flowing, garrulous.' Again: 'Homer rises and sinks with his subject, is prosaic when it is tame, is low when it is mean.'

I lay my finger on four words in these two sentences of Mr. Newman, and I say that the man who could apply those words to Homer can never render Homer truly. The four words are these: *quaint, garrulous, prosaic, low.* Search the English language for a word, which does not apply to Homer, and you could not fix on a better than *quaint*, unless perhaps you fixed on one of the other three.

Again; 'to translate Homer suitably', says Mr. Newman, 'we need a diction sufficiently antiquated to obtain pardon of the reader for its frequent homeliness'. 'I am concerned', he says again, 'with the artistic problem of attaining a plausible aspect of moderate antiquity, while remaining easily intelligible.' And again, he speaks of 'the more antiquated style suited to this subject'. Quaint! antiquated!—but to whom? Sir Thomas Browne is quaint, and the diction of Chaucer is antiquated: does Mr. Newman suppose that Homer seemed quaint to Sophocles, when he read him, as Sir Thomas Browne seems quaint to us, when we read him? or that Homer's diction seemed antiquated to Sophocles, as Chaucer's diction seems antiquated to us? But we cannot really know, I confess, how Homer seemed to Sophocles: well then, to those who can tell us how he seems to them, to the living scholar, to our only present witness on this matter,—does Homer make on the Provost of Eton, when he reads him, the impression of a poet quaint and anti- quated? does he make this impression on Professor Thompson or Professor Jowett. When Shakespeare says, 'The princes *orgulous*', meaning, 'the proud princes', we say, 'This is antiquated'; when he says of the Trojan gates, that they

> With massy staples
> And corresponsive and fulfilling bolts
> *Sperr* up the sons of Troy,

we say, 'This is both quaint and antiquated'. But does Homer ever compose in a language which produces on the scholar at all the same impression as this language which I have quoted from Shakespeare? Never once. Shakespeare is quaint and antiquated in the lines which I have just quoted; but Shakespeare—need I say it?— can compose, when he likes, when he is at his best, in a language perfectly simple, perfectly intelligible; in a lan- guage which, in spite of the two centuries and a half which part its author from us, stops us or surprises us as little as the language of a contemporary. And Homer has not Shakespeare's variations: Homer always com- poses as Shakespeare composes at his best: Homer is always simple and intelligible, as Shakespeare is often; Homer is never quaint and antiquated, as Shakespeare is sometimes.

When Mr. Newman says that Homer is garrulous, he seems perhaps to depart less widely from the common opinion than when he calls him quaint; for is there not Horace's authority for asserting that 'the good Homer sometimes nods', *bonus dormitat Homerus*? and a great many people have come, from the currency of this well-known criticism, to represent Homer to themselves as a diffuse old man, with the full-stocked mind, but also with the occasional slips and weakness of old age. Horace has said better things than his 'bonus dormitat Homerus'; but he never meant by this, as I need not remind anyone who knows the passage, that Homer was garrulous, or anything of the kind. Instead, however, of either discussing what Horace meant, or discussing Homer's garrulity as a general question, I prefer to bring to my mind some style which *is* garrulous, and to ask myself, to ask you, whether anything at all of the impression made by that style is ever made by the style of Homer. The medieval romancers, for instance, are garrulous; the following, to take out of a thousand instances the first which comes to hand, is in a garrulous manner. It is from the romance of Richard Cœur de Lion.

> Of my tale be not a-wondered!
> The French says he slew an hundred
> [Whereof is made this English saw)
> Or he rested him any thraw.
> Him followed many an English knight
> That eagerly holp him for to fight

and so on. Now the manner of that composition I call garrulous; everyone will feel it to be garrulous; everyone will understand what is meant when it is called garrulous. Then I ask the scholar,—does Homer's manner ever make upon you, I do not say, the same impression of its garrulity as that passage, but does it make, ever for one moment, an impression in the slightest way resembling, in the remotest degree akin to, the impression made by that passage of the mediæval poet? I have no fear of the answer.

I follow the same method with Mr. Newman's two

other epithets, *prosaic* and *low*. 'Homer rises and sinks with his subject', says Mr. Newman; 'is prosaic when it is tame, is low when it is mean.' First I say, Homer is never, in any sense, to be with truth called prosaic; he is never to be called low. He does not rise and sink with his subject; on the contrary, his manner invests his subject, whatever his subject be, with nobleness. Then I look for an author of whom it may with truth be said that he 'rises and sinks with his subject, is prosaic when it is tame, is low when it is mean'. Defoe is eminently such an author; of Defoe's manner it may with perfect precision be said, that it follows his matter; his lifelike composition takes its character from the facts which it conveys, not from the nobleness of the composer. In *Moll Flanders* and *Colonel Jack*, Defoe is undoubtedly prosaic when his subject is tame, low when his subject is mean. Does Homer's manner in the *Iliad*, I ask the scholar, ever make upon him an impression at all like the impression made by Defoe's manner in *Moll Flanders* and *Colonel Jack*? Does it not, on the contrary, leave him with an impression of nobleness, even when it deals with Thersites or with Irus?

Well then, Homer is neither quaint, nor garrulous, nor prosaic, nor mean: and Mr. Newman, in seeing him so, sees him differently from those who are to judge Mr. Newman's rendering of him. By pointing out how a wrong conception of Homer affects Mr. Newman's translation, I hope to place in still clearer light those four cardinal truths which I pronounce essential for him who would have a right conception of Homer: that Homer is rapid, that he is plain and direct in word and style, that he is plain and direct in his ideas, and that he is noble.

Mr. Newman says that in fixing on a style for suitably rendering Homer, as he conceives him, he 'alights on the delicate line which separates the *quaint* from the *grotesque*'.

'I ought to be quaint,' he says, 'I ought not to be grotesque.' This is a most unfortunate sentence. Mr. Newman is grotesque, which he himself says he ought not to
be; and he ought not to be quaint, which he himself says
he ought to be.

'No two persons will agree', says Mr. Newman, 'as to
where the quaint ends and the grotesque begins'; and
perhaps this is true. But, in order to avoid all ambiguity
in the use of the two words, it is enough to say, that most
persons would call an expression which produced on
them a very strong sense of its incongruity, and which
violently surprised them, *grotesque*; and an expression,
which produced on them a slighter sense of its incongruity,
and which more gently surprised them, *quaint*. Using
the two words in this manner, I say, that when Mr.
Newman translates Helen's words to Hector in the sixth
book,

$$Δᾶερ ἐμεῖο, κυνὸς κακομηχάνου, ὀκρυοέσσης,^1$$

O, brother thou of me, who am a mischief-working vixen,
A numbing horror,

he is grotesque; that is, he expresses himself in a manner
which produces on us a very strong sense of its incongruity, and which violently surprises us. I say, again,
that when Mr. Newman translates the common line,

$$Τὴν δ' ἠμείβετ' ἔπειτα μέγας κορυθαίολος Ἕκτωρ,$$

Great Hector of the motley helm then spake to her responsive,

or the common expression, εὔκνήμιδες Ἀχαιοί, 'dapper-
greaved Achaians', he is quaint; that is, he expresses
himself in a manner which produces on us a slighter sense

<hr>

¹ *Iliad*, vi. 344.

of incongruity, and which more gently surprises us. But
violent and gentle surprise are alike far from the scholar's
spirit when he reads in Homer κυνὸς κακομηχάνου, or
κορυθαίολος Ἕκτωρ, or, ἐϋκνήμιδες Ἀχαιοί. These expressions no more seem odd to him than the simplest expressions in English. He is not more checked by any feeling
of strangeness, strong or weak, when he reads them, than
when he reads in an English book 'the painted savage',
or, 'the phlegmatic Dutchman'. Mr. Newman's rendering
of them must, therefore, be wrong expressions in a
translation of Homer, because they excite in the scholar,
their only competent judge, a feeling quite alien to that
excited in him by what they profess to render.

Mr. Newman, by expressions of this kind, is false to his
original in two ways. He is false to him inasmuch as he is
ignoble; for a noble air, and a grotesque air, the air of
the address,

Δᾶερ ἐμεῖο, κυνὸς κακομηχάνου, ὀκρυοέσσης,

and the air of the address,

O, brother thou of me, who am a mischief-working vixen,
A numbing horror,

are just contrary the one to the other: and he is false to
him inasmuch as he is odd; for an odd diction like Mr.
Newman's, and a perfectly plain natural diction like
Homer's,—'dapper-greaved Achaians' and ἐϋκνήμιδες
Ἀχαιοί,—are also just contrary the one to the other.
Where, indeed, Mr. Newman got his diction, with whom
he can have lived, what can be his test of antiquity and
rarity for words, are questions which I ask myself with
bewilderment. He has prefixed to his translation a list of
what he calls 'the more antiquated or rarer words' which
he has used. In this list appear, on the one hand, such

words as *doughty*, *grisly*, *lusty*, *noisome*, *ravin*, which are
familiar, one would think, to all the world; on the other
hand such words as *bragly*, meaning, Mr. Newman tells
us, 'proudly fine'; *bulkin*, 'a calf'; *plump*, a 'mass'; and
so on. 'I am concerned', says Mr. Newman, 'with the
artistic problem of attaining a plausible aspect of moderate
antiquity, while remaining easily intelligible.' But it seems
to me that *lusty* is not antiquated: and that *bragly* is not
a word readily understood. That this word, indeed, and
bulkin, may have 'a plausible aspect of moderate antiquity', I admit; but that they are 'easily intelligible', I
deny.

Mr. Newman's syntax has, I say it with pleasure, a
much more Homeric cast than his vocabulary; his syntax, the mode in which his thought is evolved, although
not the actual words in which it is expressed, seems to
me right in its general character, and the best feature of
his version. It is not artificial or rhetorical like Cowper's
syntax or Pope's: it is simple, direct, and natural, and
so far it is like Homer's. It fails, however, just where, from
the inherent fault of Mr. Newman's conception of Homer,
one might expect it to fail,—it fails in nobleness. It presents the thought in a way which is something more than
unconstrained,—over-familiar; something more than
easy,—free and easy. In this respect it is like the movement of Mr. Newman's version, like his rhythm, for this,
too, fails, in spite of some qualities, by not being noble
enough; this, while it avoids the faults of being slow and
elaborate, falls into a fault in the opposite direction, and
is slip-shod. Homer presents his thought naturally; but
when Mr. Newman has,

A thousand fires along the plain, *I say*, that night were
burning,

he presents his thought familiarly; in a style which may be the genuine style of ballad-poetry, but which is not the style of Homer. Homer moves freely; but when Mr. Newman has,

> Infatuate! O that thou wert lord to some other army,[1]

he gives himself too much freedom; he leaves us too much to do for his rhythm ourselves, instead of giving to us a rhythm like Homer's, easy indeed, but mastering our ear with a fulness of power which is irresistible.

I said that a certain style might be the genuine style of ballad-poetry, but yet not the style of Homer. The analogy of the ballad is ever present to Mr. Newman's thoughts in considering Homer; and perhaps nothing has more caused his faults than this analogy,—this popular, but, it is time to say, this erroneous analogy. 'The moral qualities of Homer's style', says Mr. Newman, 'being like to those of the English ballad, we need a metre of the same genius. Only those metres, which by the very possession of these qualities are liable to degenerate into *doggerel*, are suitable to reproduce the ancient epic.' 'The style of Homer', he says, in a passage which I have before quoted, 'is direct, popular, forcible, quaint, flowing, garrulous: in all these respects it is similar to the old English ballad.' Mr. Newman, I need not say, is by no means alone in this opinion. 'The most really and truly Homeric of all the creations of the English muse is', says

---

[1] From the reproachful answer of Ulysses to Agamemnon, who had proposed an abandonment of their expedition. This is one of the 'tonic' passages of the *Iliad*, so I quote it:

Ah, unworthy king, some other inglorious army
Should'st thou command, not rule over *us*, whose portion for ever
Zeus hath made it, from youth right up to age, to be winding
Skeins of grievous wars, till every soul of us perish.

Iliad, xiv. 84.

Mr. Newman's critic in the *National Review*, 'the ballad-poetry of ancient times; and the association between metre and subject is one that it would be true wisdom to preserve.' 'It is confessed', says Chapman's last editor, Mr. Hooper, 'that the fourteen-syllable verse' (that is, a ballad-verse) 'is peculiarly fitting for Homeric translation.' And the editor of Dr. Maginn's clever and popular *Homeric Ballads* assumes it as one of his author's greatest and most undisputable merits, that he was 'the first who consciously realised to himself the truth that Greek ballads can be really represented in English only by a similar measure'.

This proposition that Homer's poetry is *ballad-poetry*, analogous to the well-known ballad-poetry of the English and other nations, has a certain small portion of truth in it, and at one time probably served a useful purpose, when it was employed to discredit the artificial and literary manner in which Pope and his school rendered Homer. But it has been so extravagantly over-used, the mistake which it was useful in combating has so entirely lost the public favour, that it is now much more important to insist on the large part of error contained in it, than to extol its small part of truth. It is time to say plainly that, whatever the admirers of our old ballads may think, the supreme form of epic poetry, the genuine Homeric mould, is not the form of the Ballad of Lord Bateman. I have myself shown the broad difference between Milton's manner and Homer's; but, after a course of Mr. Newman and Dr. Maginn, I turn round in desperation upon them and upon the balladists who have misled them, and I exclaim: 'Compared with you, Milton is Homer's double; there is, whatever you may think, ten thousand times more of the real strain of Homer in

> Blind Thamyris, and blind Mæonides,
> And Tiresias, and Phineus, prophets old,

than in

> Now Christ thee save, thou proud portèr,
> Now Christ thee save and see,[1]

or in

> While the tinker did dine, he had plenty of wine.'[2]

For Homer is not only rapid in movement, simple in style, plain in language, natural in thought; he is also, and above all, *noble*. I have advised the translator not to go into the vexed question of Homer's identity. Yet I will just remind him that the grand argument—or rather, not argument, for the matter affords no data for arguing, but the grand source from which conviction, as we read the *Iliad*, keeps pressing in upon us, that there is one poet of the *Iliad*, one Homer—is precisely this nobleness of the poet, this grand manner; we feel that the analogy drawn from other joint compositions does not hold good here, because those works do not bear, like the *Iliad*, the magic stamp of a master; and the moment you have *anything* less than a masterwork, the co-operation or consolidation of several poets becomes possible, for talent is not uncommon; the moment you have *much* less than a masterwork, they become easy, for mediocrity is everywhere, I can imagine fifty Bradies joined with as many Tates to make the New Version of the Psalms. I can imagine several poets having contributed to any one of the old English ballads in Percy's collection. I can imagine several poets, possessing, like Chapman, the Elizabethan vigour and the Elizabethan mannerism, united with

---

[1] From the ballad of *King Estmere*, in Percy's *Reliques of Ancient English Poetry*, i. 69 (edit. of 1767).
[2] *Reliques*, i. 241.

Chapman to produce his version of the *Iliad*. I can imagine several poets, with the literary knack of the twelfth century, united to produce the *Nibelungen Lay* in the form in which we have it,—a work which the Germans, in their joy at discovering a national epic of their own, have rated vastly higher than it deserves. And lastly, though Mr. Newman's translation of Homer bears the strong mark of his own idiosyncrasy, yet I can imagine Mr. Newman and a school of adepts trained by him in his art of poetry, jointly producing that work, so that Aristarchus himself should have difficulty in pronouncing which line was the master's, and which a pupil's. But I cannot imagine several poets, or one poet, joined with Dante in the composition of his *Inferno*, though many poets have taken for their subject a descent into Hell. Many artists, again, have represented Moses; but there is only one Moses of Michael Angelo. So the insurmountable obstacle to believing the *Iliad* a consolidated work of several poets is this: that the work of great masters is unique; and the *Iliad* has a great master's genuine stamp, and that stamp is *the grand style*.

Poets who cannot work in the grand style instinctively seek a style in which their comparative inferiority may feel itself at ease, a manner which may be, so to speak, indulgent to their inequalities. The ballad-style offers to an epic poet, quite unable to fill the canvas of Homer, or Dante, or Milton, a canvas which he is capable of filling. The ballad-measure is quite able to give due effect to the vigour and spirit which its employer, when at his very best, may be able to exhibit; and, when he is not at his best, when he is a little trivial, or a little dull, it will not betray him, it will not bring out his weakness into broad relief. This is a convenience; but it is a convenience which the ballad-style purchases by resigning all pretensions to the highest, to the grand manner. It is true of its movement, as it is *not* true of Homer's, that it is 'liable to degenerate into doggerel'. It is true of its 'moral qualities', as it is *not* true of Homer's, that 'quaintness' and 'garrulity' are among them. It is true of its employers, as it is *not* true of Homer that they 'rise and sink with their subject, are prosaic when it is tame, and low when it is mean'. For this reason the ballad-style and the ballad-measure are eminently *in*appropriate to render Homer. Homer's manner and movement are always both noble and powerful: the ballad-manner and movement are often either jaunty and smart, so not noble; or jog-trot and hum-drum, so not powerful. . . .

LAST WORDS ON TRANSLATING HOMER

A Reply to Francis W. Newman

'Multi, qui persequuntur me, et tribulant me: a testimoniis non declinavi.'

BUFFON, the great French naturalist, imposed on himself the rule of steadily abstaining from all answers to attacks made upon him. 'Je n'ai jamais répondu à aucune critique', he said to one of his friends who, on the occasion of a certain criticism, was eager to take up arms in his behalf; 'je n'ai jamais répondu à aucune critique, et je garderai le même silence sur celle-ci.' On another occasion, when accused of plagiarism, and pressed by his friends to answer, 'Il vaut mieux', he said, 'laisser ces mauvaises gens dans l'incertitude.' Even when reply to an attack was made successfully, he disapproved of it, he

regretted that those he esteemed should make it. Montesquieu, more sensitive to criticism than Buffon, had
answered, and successfully answered, an attack made
upon his great work, the *Esprit des Lois*, by the *Gazetier
Janséniste*. This Jansenist Gazetteer was a periodical of
those times, a periodical such as other times, also, have
occasionally seen, very pretentious, very aggressive, and,
when the point to be seized was at all a delicate one, very
apt to miss it. 'Notwithstanding this example', said
Buffon, who, as well as Montesquieu, had been attacked
by the Jansenist Gazetteer, 'notwithstanding this example,
I think I may promise my course will be different. I shall
not answer a single word.'

And to anyone who has noticed the baneful effects of
the controversy, with all its train of personal rivalries
and hatreds, on men of letters or men of science; to anyone who has observed how it tends to impair, not only
their dignity and repose, but their productive force, their
genuine activity; how it always checks the free play of the
spirit, and often ends by stopping it altogether; it can
hardly seem doubtful that the rule thus imposed on himself by Buffon was a wise one. His own career, indeed,
admirably shows the wisdom of it. That career was as
glorious as it was serene; but it owed to its serenity no
small part of its glory. The regularity and completeness
with which he gradually built up the great work which
he had designed, the air of equable majesty which he
shed over it, struck powerfully the imagination of his
contemporaries, and surrounded Buffon's fame with a
peculiar respect and dignity. 'He is', said Frederick the
Great of him, 'the man who has best deserved the great
celebrity which he has acquired.' And this celebrity of
production, this equableness of temper, he maintained
by his resolute disdain of personal controversy.

Buffon's example seems to be worthy of all imitation, and in my humble way I mean always to follow it. I never have replied, I never will reply, to any literary assailant; in such encounters tempers are lost, the world laughs, and truth is not served. Least of all should I think of using this Chair as a place from which to carry on such a conflict. But when a learned and estimable man thinks he has reason to complain of language used by me in this Chair, when he attributes to me intentions and feelings towards him which are far from my heart, I owe him some explanation, and I am bound, too, to make the explanation as public as the words which gave offence. This is the reason why I revert once more to the subject of translating Homer. But being thus brought back to that subject, and not wishing to occupy you solely with an explanation which, after all, is Mr. Newman's affair and mine, not the public's, I shall take the opportunity, not certainly to enter into any conflict with anyone, but to try to establish our old friend, the coming translator of Homer, yet a little firmer in the positions which I hope we have now secured for him; to protect him against the danger of relaxing, in the confusion of dispute, his attention to those matters which alone I consider important for him; to save him from losing sight, in the dust of the attacks delivered over it, of the real body of Patroclus. He will, probably, when he arrives, requite my solicitude very ill, and be in haste to disown his benefactor: but my interest in him is so sincere that I can disregard his probable ingratitude.

First, however, for the explanation. Mr. Newman has published a reply to the remarks which I made on his translation of the *Iliad*. He seems to think that the respect which at the outset of those remarks I professed for him must have been professed ironically; he says that I use 'forms of attack against him which he does not know how to characterize'; that I 'speak scornfully' of him, treat him with 'gratuitous insult, gratuitous rancour'; that I 'propagate slanders' against him, that I wish to 'damage him with my readers', to 'stimulate my readers to despise' him. He is entirely mistaken. I respect Mr. Newman sincerely; I respect him as one of the few learned men we have, one of the few who love learning for its own sake; this respect for him I had before I read his translation of the *Iliad*, I retained it while I was commenting on that translation, I have not lost it after reading his reply. Any vivacities of expression which may have given him pain I sincerely regret, and can only assure him that I used them without a thought of insult or rancour. When I took the liberty of creating the verb *to Newmanize*, my intentions were no more rancorous than if I had said to *Miltonize*; when I exclaimed, in my astonishment at his vocabulary, 'With whom can Mr. Newman have lived?' I meant merely to convey, in a familiar form of speech, the sense of bewilderment one has at finding a person to whom words one thought all the world knew seem strange, and words one thought entirely strange, intelligible. Yet this simple expression of my bewilderment Mr. Newman construes into an accusation that he is 'often guilty of keeping low company', and says that I shall 'never want a stone to throw at him'. And what is stranger still, one of his friends gravely tells me that Mr. Newman 'lived with the fellows of Balliol'. As if that made Mr. Newman's glossary less inexplicable to me! As if he could have got his glossary from the fellows of Balliol! As if I could believe that the members of that distinguished society, of whose discourse, not so many years afterwards, I myself was an unworthy hearer, were in Mr. Newman's time so far removed from the Attic purity of speech which we all of us admired, that when one of them called a calf a *bulkin*, the rest 'easily understood' him; or, when he wanted to say that a newspaper-article was 'proudly fine', it mattered little whether he said it was that or *bragly*! No; his having lived with the fellows of Balliol does not explain Mr. Newman's glossary to me. I will no longer ask 'with whom he can have lived', since that gives him offence; but I must still declare that where he got his test of rarity or intelligibility for words is a mystery to me. . . .

But Mr. Newman does not confine himself to complaints on his own behalf, he complains on Homer's behalf too. He says that my 'statements about Greek literature are against the most notorious and elementary fact'; that I 'do a public wrong to literature by publishing them'; and that the Professors to whom I appealed in my three Lectures, 'would only lose credit if they sanctioned the use I make of their names'. He does these eminent men the kindness of adding, however, that 'whether they are pleased with this parading of their names in behalf of paradoxical error, he may well doubt', and that 'until they endorse it themselves, he shall treat my process as a piece of forgery'. He proceeds to discuss my statements at great length, and with an erudition and ingenuity which nobody can admire more than I do. And he ends by saying that my ignorance is great.

Alas! that is very true. Much as Mr. Newman was mistaken when he talked of my rancour, he is entirely right when he talks of my ignorance. And yet, perverse as it seems to say so, I sometimes find myself wishing, when dealing with these matters of poetical criticism, that my ignorance were even greater than it is. To handle these matters properly there is needed a poise so perfect that the least overweight in any direction tends to destroy the balance. Temper destroys it, a crotchet destroys it, even erudition may destroy it. To press to the sense of the thing itself with which one is dealing, not to go off on some collateral issue about the thing, is the hardest matter in the world. The 'thing itself' with which one is here dealing, the critical perception of poetic truth, is of all things the most volatile, elusive, and evanescent; by even pressing too impetuously after it, one runs the risk of losing it. The critic of poetry should have the finest tact, the nicest moderation, the most free, flexible, and elastic spirit imaginable; he should be indeed the 'ondoyant et divers', the *undulating and diverse* being of Montaigne. The less he can deal with his object simply and freely the more things he has to take into account in dealing with it, the more, in short, he has to encumber himself, so much the greater force of spirit he needs to retain his elasticity. But one cannot exactly have this greater force by wishing for it; so, for the force of spirit one has, the load put upon it is often heavier than it will well bear. The late Duke of Wellington said of a certain peer that 'it was a great pity his education had been so far too much for his abilities'. In like manner, one often sees erudition out of all proportion to its owner's critical faculty. Little as I know, therefore, I am always apprehensive, in dealing with poetry, lest even that little should prove 'too much for my abilities'.

With this consciousness of my own lack of learning, nay, with this sort of acquiescence in it, with this belief that for the labourer in the field of poetical criticism learning has its disadvantages, I am not likely to dispute with Mr. Newman about matters of erudition. All that he says on these matters in his Reply I read with great interest; in general I agree with him; but only, I am sorry to say, up to a certain point. Like all learned men, accustomed to desire definite rules, he draws his conclusions too absolutely; he wants to include too much under his rules; he does not quite perceive that in poetical criticism the shade, the fine distinction, is everything; and that, when he has once missed this, in all he says he is in truth but beating the air. For instance: because I think Homer noble, he imagines I must think him elegant; and in fact he says in plain words that I do think him so, that to me Homer seems 'pervadingly elegant'. But he does not. Virgil is elegant, 'pervadingly elegant', even in passages of the highest emotion:

> O, ubi campi,
> Spercheosque, et virginibus bacchata Lacænis
> Taygeta![1]

Even there Virgil, though of a divine elegance, is still elegant, but Homer is not elegant; the word is quite a wrong one to apply to him, and Mr. Newman is quite right in blaming anyone he finds so applying it. Again; arguing against my assertion that Homer is not quaint, he says: 'It is quaint to call waves *wet*, milk *white*, blood *dusky*, horses *single-hoofed*, words *winged*, Vulcan *Lobfoot* (Κυλλοποδίων), spear *longshadowy*', and so on. I find I know not how many distinctions to draw here. I do not think it quaint to call waves *wet*, or milk *white*, or words *winged*; but I do think it quaint to call horses *single-hoofed*, or Vulcan *Lobfoot*, or a spear *long-shadowy*. As to calling blood *dusky*, I do not feel quite sure; I will tell Mr. Newman my opinion when I see the passage in which he calls it so. But then, again, because it is quaint to call

---

[1] 'O for the fields of Thessaly and the streams of Spercheios! O for the hills alive with the dances of the Laconian maidens, the hills of Taygetus'!— *Georgics*, ii. 486.

Vulcan *Lobfoot*, I cannot admit that it was quaint to call him Κυλλοποδίων; nor that, because it is quaint to call a spear *longshadowy*, it was quaint to call it δολιχόσκιον. Here Mr. Newman's erudition misleads him: he knows the literal value of the Greek so well, that he thinks his literal rendering identical with the Greek, and that the Greek must stand or fall along with his rendering. But the real question is, not whether he has given us, so to speak, full change for the Greek, but *how* he gives us our change: we want it in gold, and he gives it us in copper. Again: 'It is quaint', says Mr. Newman, 'to address a young friend as "O Pippin"! it is quaint to compare Ajax to an ass whom boys are belabouring.' Here, too, Mr. Newman goes much too fast, and his category of quaintness is too comprehensive. To address a young friend as 'O Pippin'! is, I cordially agree with him, very quaint; although I do not think it was quaint in Sarpedon to address Glaucus as ὦ πέπον: but in comparing, whether in Greek or in English, Ajax to an ass whom boys are belabouring, I do not see that there is of necessity anything quaint at all. Again; because I said that *eld*, *lief*, *in sooth*, and other words, are, as Mr. Newman uses them in certain places, bad words, he imagines that I must mean to stamp these words with an absolute reprobation; and because I said that 'my Bibliolatry is excessive', he imagines that I brand all words as ignoble which are not in the Bible. Nothing of the kind: there are no such absolute rules to be laid down in these matters. The Bible vocabulary is to be used as an assistance, not as an authority. Of the words which, placed where Mr. Newman places them, I have called bad words, everyone may be excellent in some other place. Take *eld*, for instance: when Shakespeare, reproaching man with the dependence in which his youth is passed, says:

                    all thy blessed youth
              Becomes as aged, and doth beg the alms
              Of palsied *eld*, . . .

it seems to me that *eld* comes in excellently there, in
a passage of curious meditation; but when Mr. Newman
renders ἀγήρω τ' ἀθανάτω τε by 'from *Eld* and Death
exempted', it seems to me he infuses a tinge of quaintness
into the transparent simplicity of Homer's expression,
and so I call *eld* a bad word in that place. . . .

Perplexed by his knowledge of the philological aspect
of Homer's language, encumbered by his own learning,
Mr. Newman, I say, misses the poetical aspect, misses that
which alone we are here concerned. 'Homer *is* odd', he
persists, fixing his eyes on his own philological analysis of
μῶνυξ, and μέροψ, and Κυλλοποδίων, and not on these
words in their synthetic character;—just as Professor
Max Müller, going a little farther back, and fixing his
attention on the elementary value of the word θυγάτηρ,
might say Homer was 'odd' for using *that* word;—'if the
whole Greek nation, by long familiarity, had become
inobservant of Homer's oddities', of the oddities of this
'noble barbarian', as Mr. Newman elsewhere calls him,
this 'noble barbarian' with the 'lively eye of the savage',
'that would be no fault of mine. That would not justify
Mr. Arnold's blame of me for rendering the words correctly'. *Correctly*,—ah, but what *is* correctness in this
case? This correctness of his is the very rock on which Mr.
Newman has split. He is so correct that at last he finds
peculiarity everywhere. The true knowledge of Homer
becomes at last, in his eyes, a knowledge of Homer's
'peculiarities, pleasant and unpleasant'. Learned men
know these peculiarities', and Homer is to be translated
because the unlearned are impatient to know them too.
'That', he exclaims, 'is just why people want to read an

English Homer, to *know all his oddities, just as learned men do*'. Here I am obliged to shake my head, and to declare that, in spite of all my respect for Mr Newman, I cannot go these lengths with him. He talks of my 'monomaniac fancy that there is nothing quaint or antique in Homer'. Terrible learning, I cannot help in my turn exclaiming, terrible learning, which discovers so much!

. . . But, after all, Homer is not a better poet than the balladists, because he has taken in the hexameter a better instrument; he took this instrument because he was a *different* poet from them; so different, not only so much better, but so essentially different, that he has not to be classed with them at all. Poets receive their distinctive character, not from their subject, but from their application to that subject of the ideas (to quote the *Excursion*)

On God, on Nature, and on human life,

which they have acquired for themselves. In the ballad-poets in general, as in men of a rude and early stage of the world, in whom their humanity is not yet variously and fully developed, the stock of these ideas is scanty, and the ideas themselves not very effective or profound. From them the narrative itself is the great matter, not the spirit and significance which underlies the narrative. Even in later times of richly developed life and thought, poets appear who have what may be called a *balladist's mind*; in whom a fresh and lively curiosity for the outward spectacle of the world is much more strong than their sense of the inward significance of that spectacle. When they apply ideas to their narrative of human events, you feel that they are, so to speak, travelling out of their own province: in the best of them you feel this perceptibly, but in those of a lower order you feel it very strongly. Even Sir Walter Scott's efforts of this kind, even, for instance, the

> Breathes there the man with soul so dead,

or the

> O woman! in our hours of ease,

even these leave, I think, as high poetry, much to be desired; far more than the same poet's description of a hunt or a battle. But Lord Macaulay's

> Then out spake brave Horatius,
> The captain of the gate:
> 'To all the men upon this earth
> Death cometh soon or late'.

(and here, since I have been reproached with undervaluing Lord Macaulay's *Lays of Ancient Rome*, let me frankly say that, to my mind, a man's power to detect the ring of false metal in those Lays is a good measure of his fitness to give an opinion about poetical matters at all), I say, Lord Macaulay's

> To all the men upon this earth
> Death cometh soon or late,

it is hard to read without a cry of pain. But with Homer it is very different. This 'noble barbarian', this 'savage with the lively eye', whose verse, Mr. Newman thinks, would affect us, if we could hear the living Homer, 'like an elegant and simple melody from an African of the Gold Coast', is never more at home, never more nobly himself, than in applying profound ideas to his narrative. As a poet he belongs, narrative as is his poetry, and early as is his date, to an incomparably more developed spiritual and intellectual order than the balladists, or than Scott and Macaulay; he is here as much to be distinguished from them, and in the same way, as Milton is to be distinguished from them. He is, indeed, rather to be classed with Milton than with the balladists and Scott; for what he has in common with Milton, the noble and

profound application of ideas to life is the most essential
part of poetic greatness. . . .

The general public carries away little from discussions
of this kind, except some vague notion that one advocates
English hexameters, or that one has attacked Mr. Newman. On the mind of an adversary one never makes the
faintest impression. Mr. Newman reads all one can say
about diction, and his last word on the subject is, that he
'regards it as a question about to open hereafter, whether
a translator of Homer ought not to adopt the old dis-
syllabic *landis, houndis, hartis*' (for lands, hounds, harts),
and also 'the final *en* of the plural of verbs (we *dancen*,
they *singen*, etc.), which still subsists in Lancashire'. A
certain critic reads all one can say about style, and at the
end of it arrives at the inference that, 'after all, there is
some style grander than the grand style itself, since
Shakspeare has not the grand manner, and yet has the
supremacy over Milton'; another critic reads all one can
say about rhythm, and the result is, that he thinks Scott's
rhythm, in the description of the death of Marmion, all
the better for being *saccadé*, because the dying ejaculations
of Marmion were likely to be 'jerky'. How vain to rise up
early, and to take rest late, from any zeal for proving to
Mr. Newman that he must not, in translating Homer,
say *houndis* and *dancen*; or to the first of the two critics
above quoted, that one poet may be a greater poetical
force than another, and yet have a more unequal style;
or to the second, that the best art, having to represent
the death of a hero, does not set about imitating his
dying noises! Such critics, however, provide for an
opponent's vivacity the charming excuse offered by Rivarol
for his, when he was reproached with giving offence by it:
'Ah'! he exclaimed, 'no one considers how much pain every
man of taste has had to *suffer*, before he ever inflicts any.'

WORDSWORTH[1]
(1879)

I REMEMBER hearing Lord Macaulay say, after Wordsworth's death, when subscriptions were being collected to found a memorial of him, that ten years earlier more money could have been raised in Cambridge alone, to do honour to Wordsworth, than was now raised all through the country. Lord Macaulay had, as we know, his own heightened and telling way of putting things, and we must always make allowance for it. But probably it is true that Wordsworth has never, either before or since, been so accepted and popular, so established in possession of the minds of all who profess to care for poetry, as he was between the years 1830 and 1840, and at Cambridge. From the very first, no doubt, he had his believers and witnesses. But I have myself heard him declare that, for he knew not how many years, his poetry had never brought him in enough to buy his shoe-strings. The poetry-reading public was very slow to recognise him, and was very easily drawn away from him. Scott effaced him with this public, Byron effaced him.

The death of Byron, seemed, however, to make an opening for Wordsworth. Scott, who had for some time ceased to produce poetry himself, and stood before the public as a great novelist; Scott, too genuine himself not to feel the profound genuineness of Wordsworth, and with an instinctive recognition of his firm hold on nature and of his local truth, always admired him sincerely, and

[1] The preface to *The Poems of Wordsworth*, chosen and edited by Matthew Arnold.

praised him generously. The influence of Coleridge upon young men of ability was then powerful, and was still gathering strength; this influence told entirely in favour of Wordsworth's poetry. Cambridge was a place where Coleridge's influence had great action, and where Wordsworth's poetry, therefore, flourished especially. But even amongst the general public its sale grew large, the eminence of its author was widely recognised, and Rydal Mount became an object of pilgrimage. I remember Wordsworth relating how one of the pilgrims, a clergyman, asked him if he had ever written anything besides the *Guide to the Lakes*. Yes, he answered modestly, he had written verses. Not every pilgrim was a reader, but the vogue was established, and the stream of pilgrims came.

Mr. Tennyson's decisive appearance dates from 1842. One cannot say that he effaced Wordsworth as Scott and Byron had effaced him. The poetry of Wordsworth had been so long before the public, the suffrage of good judges was so steady and so strong in its favour, that by 1842 the verdict of posterity, one may almost say, had been already pronounced, and Wordsworth's English fame was secure. But the vogue, the ear and applause of the great body of poetry-readers, never quite thoroughly perhaps his, he gradually lost more and more, and Mr. Tennyson gained them. Mr. Tennyson drew to himself, and away from Wordsworth, the poetry-reading public, and the new generations. Even in 1850, when Wordsworth died, this diminution of popularity was visible, and occasioned the remark of Lord Macaulay which I quoted at starting.

The diminution has continued. The influence of Coleridge has waned, and Wordsworth's poetry can no longer draw succour from this ally. The poetry has not, however, wanted eulogists; and it may be said to have brought its eulogists luck, for almost every one who has praised Wordsworth's poetry has praised it well. But the public has remained cold, or, at least, undetermined. Even the abundance of Mr. Palgrave's fine and skilfully chosen specimens of Wordsworth, in the *Golden Treasury*, surprised many readers, and gave offence to not a few. To tenth-rate critics and compilers, for whom any violent shock to the public taste would be a temerity not to be risked, it is still quite permissible to speak of Wordsworth's poetry, not only with ignorance, but with impertinence. On the Continent he is almost unknown.

I cannot think, then, that Wordsworth has, up to this time, at all obtained his deserts. 'Glory,' said M. Renan the other day, 'glory after all is the thing which has the best chance of not being altogether vanity'. Wordsworth was a homely man, and himself would certainly never have thought of talking of glory as that which, after all, has the best chance of not being altogether vanity. Yet we may well allow that few things are less vain than *real* glory. Let us conceive of the whole group of civilised nations as being, for intellectual and spiritual purposes, one great confederation, bound to a joint action and working towards a common result; a confederation whose members have a due knowledge both of the past, out of which they all proceed, and of one another. This was the ideal of Goethe, and it is an ideal which will impose itself upon the thoughts of our modern societies more and more. Then to be recognised by the verdict of such a confederation as a master, or even as a seriously and eminently worthy workman, in one's own line of intellectual or spiritual activity, is indeed glory; a glory which it would be difficult to rate too highly. For what could be more beneficent, more salutary? The world is forwarded by having its attention fixed on the best things;

and here is a tribunal, free from all suspicion of national
and provincial partiality, putting a stamp on the best
things, and recommending them for general honour and
acceptance. A nation, again, is furthered by recognition of
its real gifts and successes; it is encouraged to develop
them further. And here is an honest verdict, telling us
which of our supposed successes are really, in the judgment of the great impartial world, and not in our own
private judgment only, successes, and which are not.

It is so easy to feel pride and satisfaction in one's own
things, so hard to make sure that one is right in feeling it!
We have a great empire. But so had Nebuchadnezzar.
We extol the 'unrivalled happiness' of our national
civilisation. But then comes a candid friend, and remarks
that our upper class is materialised, our middle class
vulgarised, and our lower class brutalised. We are proud
of our painting, our music. But we find that in the judgment of other people our painting is questionable, and our
music non-existent. We are proud of our men of science.
And here it turns out that the world is with us; we find
that in the judgment of other people, too, Newton among
the dead, and Mr Darwin among the living, hold as high
a place as they hold in our national opinion.

Finally, we are proud of our poets and poetry. Now
poetry is nothing less than the most perfect speech of
man, that in which he comes nearest to being able to
utter the truth. It is no small thing, therefore, to succeed
eminently in poetry. And so much is required for duly
estimating success here, that about poetry it is perhaps
hardest to arrive at a sure general verdict, and takes
longest. Meanwhile, our own conviction of the superiority
of our national poets is not decisive, is almost certain to
be mingled, as we see constantly in English eulogy of
Shakespeare, with much of provincial infatuation. And

we know what was the opinion current amongst our neighbours the French—people of taste, acuteness, and quick literary tact—not a hundred years ago, about our great poets. The old *Biographie Universelle* notices the pretension of the English to a place for their poets among the chief poets of the world, and says that this is a pretension which to no one but an Englishman can ever seem admissible. And the scornful, disparaging things said by foreigners about Shakespeare and Milton, and about our national over-estimate of them, have been often quoted, and will be in every one's remembrance.

A great change has taken place, and Shakespeare is now generally recognised, even in France, as one of the greatest of poets. Yes, some anti-Gallican cynic will say, the French rank him with Corneille and with Victor Hugo! But let me have the pleasure of quoting a sentence about Shakespeare, which I met with by accident not long ago in the *Correspondent*, a French review which not a dozen English people, I suppose, look at. The writer is praising Shakespeare's prose. With Shakespeare, he says, 'prose comes in whenever the subject, being more familiar, is unsuited to the majestic English iambic'. And he goes on: 'Shakespeare is the king of poetic rhythm and style, as well as the king of the realm of thought; along with his dazzling prose, Shakespeare has succeeded in giving us the most varied, the most harmonious verse which has ever sounded upon the human ear since the verse of the Greeks.' M. Henry Cochin, the writer of this sentence, deserves our gratitude for it; it would not be easy to praise Shakespeare, in a single sentence, more justly. And when a foreigner and a Frenchman writes thus of Shakespeare, and when Goethe says of Milton, in whom there was so much to repel Goethe rather than to attract him, that 'nothing has been ever done so entirely in the sense of the Greeks as *Samson Agonistes*', and that 'Milton is in very truth a poet whom we must treat with all reverence', then we understand what constitutes a European recognition of poets and poetry as contra-distinguished from a merely national recognition, and that in favour both of Milton and of Shakespeare the judgment of the high court of appeal has finally gone.

I come back to M. Renan's praise of glory, from which I started. Yes, real glory is a most serious thing, glory authenticated by the Amphictyonic Court of final appeal, definitive glory. And even for poets and poetry, long and difficult as may be the process of arriving at the right award, the right award comes at last, the definitive glory rests where it is deserved. Every establishment of such a real glory is good and wholesome for mankind at large, good and wholesome for the nation which produced the poet crowned with it. To the poet himself it can seldom do harm; for he, poor man, is in his grave, probably, long before his glory crowns him.

Wordsworth has been in his grave for some thirty years, and certainly his lovers and admirers cannot flatter themselves that this great and steady light of glory as yet shines over him. He is not fully recognised at home; he is not recognised at all abroad. Yet I firmly believe that the poetical performance of Wordsworth is, after that of Shakespeare and Milton, of which all the world now recognises the worth, undoubtedly the most considerable in our language from the Elizabethan age to the present time. Chaucer is anterior; and on other grounds, too, he cannot well be brought into the comparison. But taking the roll of our chief poetical names, besides Shakespeare and Milton, from the age of Elizabeth downwards, and going through it,—Spenser, Dryden, Pope, Gray, Goldsmith, Cowper, Burns, Coleridge, Scott, Campbell,

Moore, Byron, Shelley, Keats (I mention those only who are dead),—I think it certain that Wordsworth's name deserves to stand, and will finally stand, above them all. Several of the poets named have gifts and excellences which Wordsworth has not. But taking the performance of each as a whole, I say that Wordsworth seems to me to have left a body of poetical work superior in power, in interest, in the qualities which give enduring freshness, to that which any one of the others has left.

But this is not enough to say. I think it certain, further, that if we take the chief poetical names of the Continent since the death of Molière, and, omitting Goethe, confront the remaining names with that of Wordsworth, the result is the same. Let us take Klopstock, Lessing, Schiller, Uhland, Rückert, and Heine for Germany; Filicaia, Alfieri, Manzoni, and Leopardi for Italy; Racine, Boileau, Voltaire, André Chenier, Béranger, Lamartine, Musset, M. Victor Hugo (he has been so long celebrated that although he still lives I may be permitted to name him) for France. Several of these, again, have evidently gifts and excellences to which Wordsworth can make no pretension. But in real poetical achievement it seems to me indubitable that to Wordsworth, here again, belongs the palm. It seems to me that Wordsworth has left behind him a body of poetical work which wears, and will wear, better on the whole than the performance of any one of these personages, so far more brilliant and celebrated, most of them, than the homely poet of Rydal. Wordsworth's performance in poetry is on the whole, in power, in interest, in the qualities which give enduring freshness, superior to theirs.

This is a high claim to make for Wordsworth. But if it is a just claim, if Wordsworth's place among the poets who have appeared in the last two or three centuries is

after Shakespeare, Molière, Milton, Goethe, indeed, but
before all the rest, then in time Wordsworth will have his
due. We shall recognise him in his place, as we recognise
Shakespeare and Milton; and not only we ourselves shall
recognise him, but he will be recognised by Europe also.
Meanwhile, those who recognise him already may do
well, perhaps, to ask themselves whether there are not in
the case of Wordsworth certain special obstacles which
hinder or delay his due recognition by others, and whether
these obstacles are not in some measure removable.

The *Excursion* and the *Prelude*, his poems of greatest
bulk, are by no means Wordsworth's best work. His best
work is in his shorter pieces, and many indeed are there
of these which are of first-rate excellence. But in his seven
volumes the pieces of high merit are mingled with a mass
of pieces very inferior to them; so inferior to them that it
seems wonderful how the same poet should have produced
both. Shakespeare frequently has lines and passages in
a strain quite false, and which are entirely unworthy of
him. But one can imagine his smiling if one could meet
him in the Elysian Fields and tell him so; smiling and
replying that he knew it perfectly well himself, and what
did it matter? But with Wordsworth the case is different.
Work altogether inferior, work quite uninspired, flat and
dull, is produced by him with evident unconsciousness of
its defects, and he presents it to us with the same faith and
seriousness as his best work. Now a drama or an epic fill
the mind, and one does not look beyond them; but in
a collection of short pieces the impression made by one
piece requires to be continued and sustained by the piece
following. In reading Wordsworth the impression made
by one of his fine pieces is too often dulled and spoiled by
a very inferior piece coming after it.

Wordsworth composed verses during a space of some

sixty years; and it is no exaggeration to say that within one single decade of those years, between 1798 and 1808, almost all his really first-rate work was produced. A mass of inferior work remains, work done before and after this golden prime, imbedding the first-rate work and clogging it, obstructing our approach to it, chilling, not unfrequently, the high-wrought mood with which we leave it. To be recognised far and wide as a great poet, to be possible and receivable as a classic, Wordsworth needs to be relieved of a great deal of the poetical baggage which now encumbers him. To administer this relief is indispensable, unless he is to continue to be a poet for the few only,—a poet valued far below his real worth by the world.

There is another thing. Wordsworth classified his poems not according to any commonly received plan of arrangement, but according to a scheme of mental physiology. He has poems of the fancy, poems of the imagination, poems of sentiment and reflection, and so on. His categories are ingenious but far-fetched, and the result of his employment of them is unsatisfactory. Poems are separated one from another which possess a kinship of subject or of treatment far more vital and deep than the supposed unity of mental origin, which was Wordsworth's reason for joining them with others.

The tact of the Greeks in matters of this kind was infallible. We may rely upon it that we shall not improve upon the classification adopted by the Greeks for kinds of poetry; that their categories of epic, dramatic, lyric, and so forth, have a natural propriety, and should be adhered to. It may sometimes seem doubtful to which of two categories a poem belongs; whether this or that poem is to be called, for instance, narrative or lyric, lyric or elegiac. But there is to be found in every good poem a strain, a predominant note, which determines the poem as belonging to one of these kinds rather than the other; and here is the best proof of the value of the classification, and of the advantage of adhering to it. Wordsworth's poems will never produce their due effect until they are freed from their present artificial arrangement, and grouped more naturally.

Disengaged from the quantity of inferior work which now obscures them, the best poems of Wordsworth, I hear many people say, would indeed stand out in great beauty, but they would prove to be very few in number, scarcely more than half a dozen. I maintain, on the other hand, that what strikes me with admiration, what establishes in my opinion Wordsworth's superiority, is the great and ample body of powerful work which remains to him, even after all his inferior work has been cleared away. He gives us so much to rest upon, so much which communicates his spirit and engages ours!

This is of very great importance. If it were a comparison of single pieces, or of three or four pieces, by each poet, I do not say that Wordsworth would stand decisively above Gray, or Burns, or Coleridge, or Keats, or Manzoni, or Heine. It is in his ampler body of powerful work that I find his superiority. His good work itself, his work which counts, is not all of it, of course, of equal value. Some kinds of poetry are in themselves lower kinds than others. The ballad kind is a lower kind; the didactic kind, still more, is a lower kind. Poetry of this latter sort counts, too, sometimes, by its biographical interest partly, not by its poetical interest pure and simple; but then this can only be when the poet producing it has the power and importance of Wordsworth, a power and importance which he assuredly did not establish by such didactic poetry alone. Altogether, it is, I say, by the great body of powerful and significant work which remains to him, after every reduction and deduction has been made, that Wordsworth's superiority is proved.

To exhibit this body of Wordsworth's best work, to clear away obstructions from around it, and to let it speak for itself, is what every lover of Wordsworth should desire. Until this has been done, Wordsworth, whom we, to whom he is dear, all of us know and feel to be so great a poet, has not had a fair chance before the world. When once it has been done, he will make his way best, not by our advocacy of him, but by his own worth and power. We may safely leave him to make his way thus, we who believe that a superior worth and power in poetry finds in mankind a sense responsive to it and disposed at last to recognise it. Yet at the outset, before he has been duly known and recognised, we may do Wordsworth a service, perhaps, by indicating in what his superior power and worth will be found to consist, and in what it will not.

Long ago, in speaking of Homer, I said that the noble and profound application of ideas to life is the most essential part of poetic greatness. I said that a great poet receives his distinctive character of superiority from his application, under the conditions immutably fixed by the laws of poetic beauty and poetic truth, from his application, I say, to his subject, whatever it may be, of the ideas

On man, on nature, and on human life,

which he has acquired for himself. The line quoted is Wordsworth's own; and his superiority arises from his powerful use, in his best pieces, his powerful application to his subject, of ideas 'on man, on nature, and on human life'.

Voltaire, with his signal acuteness, most truly remarked that 'no nation has treated in poetry moral ideas with more energy and depth than the English nation.' And he adds: 'There, it seems to me, is the great merit of the English poets.' Voltaire does not mean, by 'treating in poetry moral ideas,' the composing moral and didactic poems;—that brings us but a very little way in poetry. He means just the same thing as was meant when I spoke above 'of the noble and profound application of ideas to life'; and he means the application of these ideas under the conditions fixed for us by the laws of poetic beauty and poetic truth. If it is said that to call these ideas *moral* ideas is to introduce a strong and injurious limitation, I answer that it is to do nothing of the kind, because moral ideas are really so main a part of human life. The question, *how to live*, is itself a moral idea; and it is the question which most interests every man, and with which, in some way or other, he is perpetually occupied. A large sense is of course to be given to the term *moral*. Whatever bears upon the question, 'how to live', comes under it.

> Nor love thy life, nor hate; but, what thou liv'st,
> Live well; how long or short, permit to heaven.

In those fine lines Milton utters, as every one at once perceives, a moral idea. Yes, but so too, when Keats consoles the forward-bending lover on the Grecian Urn, the lover arrested and presented in immortal relief by the sculptor's hand before he can kiss, with the line,

> For ever wilt thou love, and she be fair

—he utters a moral idea. When Shakespeare says, that

> We are such stuff
> As dreams are made of, and our little life
> Is rounded with a sleep,

he utters a moral idea.

Voltaire was right in thinking that the energetic and profound treatment of moral ideas, in this large sense, is what distinguishes the English poetry. He sincerely meant praise, not dispraise or hint of limitation; and they err who suppose that poetic limitation is a necessary consequence of the fact, the fact being granted as Voltaire states it. If what distinguishes the greatest poets is their powerful and profound application of ideas to life, which surely no good critic will deny, then to prefix to the term ideas here the term moral makes hardly any difference, because human life itself is in so preponderating a degree moral.

It is important, therefore, to hold fast to this: that poetry is at bottom a criticism of life; that the greatness of a poet lies in his powerful and beautiful application of ideas to life,—to the question: How to live. Morals are often treated in a narrow and false fashion; they are bound up with systems of thought and belief which have had their day; they are fallen into the hands of pedants and professional dealers; they grow tiresome to some of us. We find attraction, at times, even in a poetry of revolt against them; in a poetry which might take for its motto Omar Kheyam's words: 'Let us make up in the tavern for the time we have wasted in the mosque.' Or we find attractions in a poetry indifferent to them; in a poetry where the contents may be what they will, but where the form is studied and exquisite. We delude ourselves in either case; and the best cure for our delusion is to let our minds rest upon that great and inexhaustible word *life*, until we learn to enter into its meaning. A poetry of revolt against moral ideas is a poetry of revolt against *life*; a poetry of indifference towards moral ideas is a poetry of indifference towards *life*.

Epictetus had a happy figure for things like the play of the senses, or literary form and finish, or argumentative ingenuity, in comparison with 'the best and master thing' for us, as he called it, the concern, how to live. Some people were afraid of them, he said, or they disliked and undervalued them. Such people were wrong; they were unthankful or cowardly. But the things might also be over-prized, and treated as final when they are not. They bear to life the relation which inns bear to home. 'As if a man, journeying home, and finding a nice inn on the road, and liking it, were to stay for ever at the inn! Man, thou hast forgotten thine object; thy journey was not *to* this, but *through* this. 'But this inn is taking.' And how many other inns, too, are taking, and how many fields and meadows! but as places of passage merely. You have an object, which is this: to get home, to do your duty to your family, friends, and fellow-countrymen, to attain inward freedom, serenity, happiness, contentment. Style takes your fancy, arguing takes your fancy, and you forget your home and want to make your abode with them and to stay with them, on the plea that they are taking. Who denies that they are taking? but as places of passage, as inns. And when I say this, you suppose me to be attacking the care for style, the care for argument. I am not; I attack the resting in them, the not looking to the end which is beyond them.'

Now, when we come across a poet like Théophile Gautier, we have a poet who has taken up his abode at an inn, and never got farther. There may be inducements to this or that one of us, at this or that moment, to find delight in him, to cleave to him; but after all, we do not change the truth about him,—we only stay ourselves in his inn along with him. And when we come across a poet like Wordsworth, who sings

Of truth, of grandeur, beauty, love and hope.
And melancholy fear subdued by faith,

> Of blessed consolations in distress,
> Of moral strength and intellectual power,
> Of joy in widest commonalty spread

—then we have a poet intent on 'the best and master thing', and who prosecutes his journey home. We say, for brevity's sake, that he deals with *life*, because he deals with that in which life really consists. This is what Voltaire means to praise in the English poets,—this dealing with what is really life. But always it is the mark of the greatest poets that they deal with it; and to say that the English poets are remarkable for dealing with it, is only another way of saying, what is true, that in poetry the English genius has especially shown its power.

Wordsworth deals with it, and his greatness lies in his dealing with it so powerfully. I have named a number of celebrated poets above all of whom he, in my opinion, deserves to be placed. He is to be placed above poets like Voltaire, Dryden, Pope, Lessing, Schiller, because these famous personages, with a thousand gifts and merits, never, or scarcely ever, attain the distinctive accent and utterance of the high and genuine poets—

> Quique pii vates et Phœbo digna locuti,

at all. Burns, Keats, Heine, not to speak of others in our list, have this accent;—who can doubt it? And at the same time they have treasures of humour, felicity, passion, for which in Wordsworth we shall look in vain. Where, then, is Wordsworth's superiority? It is here; he deals with more of *life* than they do; he deals with *life*, as a whole, more powerfully.

No Wordsworthian will doubt this. Nay, the fervent Wordsworthian will add, as Mr. Leslie Stephen does, that Wordsworth's poetry is precious because his philosophy is sound; that his 'ethical system is as distinctive

and capable of exposition as Bishop Butler's'; that his
poetry is informed by ideas which 'fall spontaneously
into a scientific system of thought'. But we must be on our
guard against the Wordsworthians, if we want to secure
for Wordsworth his due rank as a poet. The Wordsworthians are apt to praise him for the wrong things, and
to lay far too much stress upon what they call his philosophy. His poetry is the reality, his philosophy,—so far,
at least, as it may put on the form and habit of 'a scientific
system of thought', and the more that it puts them on,—
is the illusion. Perhaps we shall one day learn to make
this proposition general, and to say: Poetry is the reality,
philosophy the illusion. But in Wordsworth's case, at any
rate, we cannot do him justice until we dismiss his formal
philosophy.

The *Excursion* abounds with philosophy, and therefore
the *Excursion* is to the Wordsworthian what it never can
be to the disinterested lover of poetry,—a satisfactory
work. 'Duty exists', says Wordsworth, in the *Excursion*;
and then he proceeds thus—

> . . . Immutably survive,
> For our support, the measures and the forms,
> Which an abstract Intelligence supplies,
> Whose kingdom is, where time and space are not.

And the Wordsworthian is delighted, and thinks that here
is a sweet union of philosophy and poetry. But the disinterested lover of poetry will feel that the lines carry
us really not a step farther than the proposition which
they would interpret; that they are a tissue of elevated
but abstract verbiage, alien to the very nature of poetry.

Or let us come direct to the centre of Wordsworth's
philosophy, as 'an ethical system, as distinctive and capable of systematical exposition as Bishop Butler's'—

> . . . One adequate support
> For the calamities of mortal life
> Exists, one only;—an assured belief
> That the procession of our fate, howe'er
> Sad or disturbed, is ordered by a Being
> Of infinite benevolence and power;
> Whose everlasting purposes embrace
> All accidents, converting them to good.

That is doctrine such as we hear in church too, religious and philosophic doctrine; and the attached Wordsworthian loves passages of such doctrine, and brings them forward in proof of his poet's excellence. But however true the doctrine may be, it has, as here presented, none of the characters of *poetic* truth, the kind of truth which we require from a poet, and in which Wordsworth is really strong.

Even the 'intimations' of the famous Ode, those cornerstones of the supposed philosophic system of Wordsworth,—the idea of the high instincts and affections coming out in childhood, testifying of a divine home recently left, and fading away as our life proceeds,—this idea, of undeniable beauty as a play of fancy, has itself not the character of poetic truth of the best kind; it has no real solidity. The instinct of delight in Nature and her beauty had no doubt extraordinary strength in Wordsworth himself as a child. But to say that universally this instinct is mighty in childhood, and tends to die away afterwards, is to say what is extremely doubtful. In many people, perhaps with the majority of educated persons the love of nature is nearly imperceptible at ten years old, but strong and operative at thirty. In general we may say of these high instincts of early childhood, the base of the alleged systematic philosophy of Wordsworth, what Thucydides says of the early achievements of the Greek race: 'It is impossible to speak with certainty of what is so remote; but from all that we can really investigate, I should say that they were no very great things.'

Finally, the 'scientific system of thought' in Wordsworth gives us at last such poetry as this, which the devout Wordsworthian accepts—

> O for the coming of that glorious time
> When, prizing knowledge as her noblest wealth
> And best protection, this Imperial Realm,
> While she exacts allegiance, shall admit
> An obligation, on her part, to *teach*
> Them who are born to serve her and obey;
> Binding herself by statute to secure,
> For all the children whom her soil maintains,
> The rudiments of letters, and inform
> The mind with moral and religious truth.

Wordsworth calls Voltaire dull, and surely the production of these un-Voltairian lines must have been imposed on him as a judgment! One can hear them being quoted at a Social Science Congress; one can call up the whole scene. A great room in one of our dismal provincial towns; dusty air and jaded afternoon daylight; benches full of men with bald heads and women in spectacles; an orator lifting up his face from a manuscript written within and without to declaim these lines of Wordsworth; and in the soul of any poor child of nature who may have wandered in thither, an unutterable sense of lamentation, and mourning, and woe!

'But turn we', as Wordsworth says, 'from these bold, bad men,' the haunters of Social Science Congresses. And let us be on our guard, too, against the exhibitors and extollers of a 'scientific system of thought' in Wordsworth's poetry. The poetry will never be seen aright while they thus exhibit it. The cause of its greatness is simple, and may be told quite simply. Wordsworth's poetry is great because of the extraordinary power with which Wordsworth feels the joy offered to us in nature, the joy offered to us in the simple primary affections and duties; and because of the extraordinary power with which, in case after case, he shows us this joy, and renders it so as to make us share it.

The source of joy from which he thus draws is the truest and most unfailing source of joy accessible to man. It is also accessible universally. Wordsworth brings us word, therefore, according to his own strong and characteristic line, he brings us word

Of joy in widest commonalty spread.

Here is an immense advantage for a poet. Wordsworth tells of what all seek, and tells of it at its truest and best source, and yet a source where all may go and draw for it.

Nevertheless, we are not to suppose that everything is precious which Wordsworth, standing even at this perennial and beautiful source, may give us. Wordsworthians are apt to talk as if it must be. They will speak with the same reverence of *The Sailor's Mother*, for example, as of *Lucy Gray*. They do their master harm by such lack of discrimination. *Lucy Gray* is a beautiful success; *The Sailor's Mother* is a failure. To give aright what he wishes to give, to interpret and render successfully, is not always within Wordsworth's own command. It is within no poet's command; here is the part of the Muse, the inspiration, the God, the 'not ourselves'. In Wordsworth's case, the accident, for so it may almost be called, of inspiration, is of peculiar importance. No poet, perhaps, is so evidently filled with a new and sacred energy when the inspiration is upon him; no poet, when it fails him, is so left 'weak as is a breaking wave.' I remember hearing him say that 'Goethe's poetry was not inevitable enough'. The remark is striking and true; no line in Goethe, as Goethe said himself, but its maker knew well how it came there. Wordsworth is right, Goethe's poetry is not inevitable; not inevitable enough. But Wordsworth's poetry, when he is at his best, is inevitable, as inevitable as Nature herself. It might seem that Nature not only gave him the matter for his poem, but wrote his poem for him. He has no style. He was too conversant with Milton not to catch at times his master's manner, and he has fine Miltonic lines; but he has no assured poetic style of his own, like Milton. When he seeks to have a style he falls into ponderosity and pomposity. In the *Excursion* we have his style, as an artistic product of his own creation; and although Jeffrey completely failed to recognise Wordsworth's real greatness, he was yet not wrong in saying of the *Excursion*, as a work of poetic style: 'This will never do.' And yet magical as is that power, which Wordsworth has not, of assured and possessed poetic style, he has something which is an equivalent for it.

Every one who has any sense for these things feels the subtle turn, the heightening, which is given to a poet's verse by his genius for style. We can feel it in the

> After life's fitful fever, he sleeps well

—of Shakespeare; in the

> . . . though fall'n on evil days,
> On evil days though fall'n, and evil tongues

—of Milton. It is the incomparable charm of Milton's power of poetic style which gives such worth to *Paradise Regained*, and makes a great poem of a work in which Milton's imagination does not soar high. Wordsworth has in constant possession, and at command, no style of

this kind; but he had too poetic a nature, and had read
the great poets too well, not to catch, as I have already
remarked, something of it occasionally. We find it not
only in his Miltonic lines; we find it in such a phrase as
this, where the manner is his own, not Milton's—

> . . . the fierce confederate storm
> Of sorrow barricadoed evermore
> Within the walls of cities;

although even here, perhaps, the power of style which is
undeniable, is more properly that of eloquent prose than
the subtle heightening and change wrought by genuine
poetic style. It is style, again, and the elevation given by
style, which chiefly makes the effectiveness of *Laodameia*.
Still the right sort of verse to choose from Wordsworth, if
we are to seize his true and most characteristic form of
expression, is a line like this from *Michael*—

> And never lifted up a single stone.

There is nothing subtle in it, no heightening, no study of
poetic style, strictly so called, at all; yet it is expression
of the highest and most truly expressive kind.

Wordsworth owed much to Burns, and a style of perfect plainness, relying for effect solely on the weight and
force of that which with entire fidelity it utters, Burns
could show him.

> The poor inhabitant below
> Was quick to learn and wise to know,
> And keenly felt the friendly glow
> And softer flame;
> But thoughtless follies laid him low
> And stain'd his name.

Every one will be conscious of a likeness here to Wordsworth; and if Wordsworth did great things with this

nobly plain manner, we must remember, what indeed he himself would always have been forward to acknowledge, that Burns used it before him.

Still Wordsworth's use of it has something unique and unmatchable. Nature herself seems, I say, to take the pen out of his hand, and to write for him with her own bare, sheer, penetrating power. This arises from two causes; from the profound sincereness with which Wordsworth feels his subject, and also from the profoundly sincere and natural character of his subject itself. He can and will treat such a subject with nothing but the most plain, first-hand, almost austere naturalness. His expression may often be called bald, as, for instance, in the poem of *Resolution and Independence*; but it is bald as the bare mountain tops are bald, with a baldness which is full of grandeur.

Wherever we meet with the successful balance, in Wordsworth, of profound truth of subject with profound truth of execution, he is unique. His best poems are those which most perfectly exhibit this balance. I have a warm admiration for *Laodameia* and for the great *Ode*; but if I am to tell the very truth, I find *Laodameia* not wholly free from something artificial, and the great *Ode* not wholly free from something declamatory. If I had to pick out poems of a kind most perfectly to show Wordsworth's unique power, I should rather choose poems such as *Michael*, *The Fountain*, *The Highland Reaper*. And poems with the peculiar and unique beauty which distinguishes these, Wordsworth produced in considerable number; besides very many other poems of which the worth, although not so rare as the worth of these, is still exceedingly high.

On the whole, then, as I said at the beginning, not only is Wordsworth eminent by reason of the goodness of his best work, but he is eminent also by reason of the great body of good work which he has left to us. With the ancients I will not compare him. In many respects the ancients are far above us, and yet there is something that we demand which they can never give. Leaving the ancients, let us come to the poets and poetry of Christendom. Dante, Shakespeare, Molière, Milton, Goethe, are altogether larger and more splendid luminaries in the poetical heaven than Wordsworth. But I know not where else, among the moderns, we are to find his superiors.

To disengage the poems which show his power, and to present them to the English-speaking public and to the world, is the object of this volume. I by no means say that it contains all which in Wordsworth's poems is interesting. Except in the case of *Margaret*, a story composed separately from the rest of the *Excursion*, and which belongs to a different part of England, I have not ventured on detaching portions of poems, or on giving any piece otherwise than as Wordsworth himself gave it. But under the conditions imposed by this reserve, the volume contains, I think, everything, or nearly everything, which may best serve him with the majority of lovers of poetry, nothing which may disserve him.

I have spoken lightly of Wordsworthians; and if we are to get Wordsworth recognised by the public and by the world, we must recommend him not in the spirit of a clique, but in the spirit of disinterested lovers of poetry. But I am a Wordsworthian myself. I can read with pleasure and edification *Peter Bell*, and the whole series of *Ecclesiastical Sonnets*, and the address to Mr. Wilkinson's spade, and even the *Thanksgiving Ode*;—everything of Wordsworth, I think, except *Vaudracour and Julia*. It is not for nothing that one has been brought up in the veneration of a man so truly worthy of homage; that one has seen him and heard him, lived in his neighbourhood, and been familiar with his country. No Wordsworthian has a tenderer affection for this pure and sage master than I, or is less really offended by his defects. But Wordsworth is something more than the pure and sage master of a small band of devoted followers, and we ought not to rest satisfied until he is seen to be what he is. He is one of the very chief glories of English Poetry; and by nothing is England so glorious as by her poetry. Let us lay aside every weight which hinders our getting him recognised as this, and let our one study be to bring to pass, as widely as possible and as truly as possible, his own word concerning his poems: 'They will co-operate with the benign tendencies in human nature and society, and will, in their degree, be efficacious in making men wiser, better, and happier.'

COUNT LEO TOLSTOI[1]

(1887)

IN reviewing at the time of its first publication, thirty years ago, Flaubert's remarkable novel of *Madame Bovary*, Sainte-Beuve observed that in Flaubert we come to another manner, another kind of inspiration, from those which had prevailed hitherto; we find ourselves dealing, he said, with a man of a new and different generation from novelists like George Sand. The ideal has ceased, the lyric vein is dried up; the new men are cured of lyricism and the ideal; 'a severe and pitiless truth has made its entry, as the last word of experience, even into art itself'. The characters of the new literature of fiction are 'science, a spirit of observation, maturity, force, a touch of hardness'. *L'idéal a cessé, le lyrique a tari.*

The spirit of observation and the touch of hardness (let us retain these mild and inoffensive terms) have since been carried in the French novel very far. So far have they been carried, indeed, that in spite of the advantage which the French language, familiar to the cultivated classes everywhere, confers on the French novel, this novel has lost much of its attraction for those classes; it no longer commands their attention as it did formerly. The famous English novelists have passed away, and have left no successor of like fame. It is not the English novel, therefore, which has inherited the vogue lost by the French novel. It is the novel of a country new to literature, or at any rate unregarded, till lately, by the general

[1] Published in the *Fortnightly Review*, December 1887.

public of readers: it is the novel of Russia. The Russian novel has now the vogue, and deserves to have it. If fresh literary productions maintain this vogue and enhance it, we shall all be learning Russian.

The Slav nature, or at any rate the Russian nature, the Russian nature as it shows itself in the Russian novels, seems marked by an extreme sensitiveness, a consciousness most quick and acute both for what the man's self is experiencing, and also for what others in contact with him are thinking and feeling. In a nation full of life, but young, and newly in contact with an old and powerful civilisation, this sensitiveness and self-consciousness are prompt to appear. In the Americans, as well as in the Russians, we see them active in a high degree. They are somewhat agitating and disquieting agents to their possessor, but they have, if they get fair play, great powers for evoking and enriching a literature. But the Americans, as we know, are apt to set them at rest in the manner of my friend Colonel Higginson of Boston.

As I take it, Nature said, some years since: 'Thus far the English is my best race; but we have had Englishmen enough; we need something with a little more buoyancy than the Englishman; let us lighten the structure, even at some peril in the process. Put in one drop more of nervous fluid, and make the American.' With that drop, a new range of promise opened on the human race, and a lighter, finer, more highly organised type of mankind was born.

People who by this sort of thing give rest to their sensitive and busy self-consciousness may very well, perhaps, be on their way to great material prosperity, to great political power; but they are scarcely on the right way to a great literature, a serious art.

The Russian does not assuage his sensitiveness in this fashion. The Russian man of letters does not make Nature

say: 'The Russian is my best race.' He finds relief to his
sensitiveness in letting his perceptions have perfectly
free play, and in recording their reports with perfect
fidelity. The sincereness with which the reports are given
has even something childlike and touching. In the novel
of which I am going to speak there is not a line, not a
trait, brought in for the glorification of Russia, or to feed
vanity; things and characters go as nature takes them, and
the author is absorbed in seeing how nature takes them
and in relating it. But we have here a condition of things
which is highly favourable to the production of good
literature, of good art. We have great sensitiveness,
subtlety, and finesse, addressing themselves with entire
disinterestedness and simplicity to the representation of
human life. The Russian novelist is thus master of a spell
to which the secrets of human nature—both what is
external and what is internal, gesture and manner no
less than thought and feeling—willingly make themselves
known. The crown of literature is poetry, and the Russians have not yet had a great poet. But in that form of
imaginative literature which in our day is the most popular and most possible, the Russians at the present moment
seem to me to hold, as Mr. Gladstone would say, the field.
They have great novelists, and of one of their great
novelists I wish now to speak.

Count Leo Tolstoi is about sixty years old, and tells us
that he shall write novels no more. He is now occupied
with religion and with the Christian life. His writings
concerning these great matters are not allowed, I believe,
to obtain publication in Russia, but instalments of them
in French and English reach us from time to time. I find
them very interesting, but I find his novel of *Anna
Karénine* more interesting still. I believe that many readers
prefer to *Anna Karénine* Count Tolstoi's other great novel,

La Guerre et la Paix. But in the novel one prefers, I think, to have the novelist dealing with the life which he knows from having lived it, rather than with the life which he knows from books or hearsay. If one has to choose a representative work of Thackeray, it is *Vanity Fair* which one would take rather than *The Virginians.* In like manner I take *Anna Karénine* as the novel best representing Count Tolstoi. I use the French translation; in general, as I long ago said, work of this kind is better done in France than in England, and *Anna Karénine* is perhaps also a novel which goes better into French than into English just as Frederika Bremer's *Home* goes into English better than into French. After I have done with *Anna Karénine* I must say something of Count Tolstoi's religious writings. Of these too I use the French translation, so far as it is available. The English translation, however, which came into my hands late, seems to be in general clear and good. Let me say in passing that it has neither the same arrangement, nor the same titles, nor altogether the same contents, with the French translation.

There are too many characters in *Anna Karénine*—too many if we look in it for a work of art in which the action shall be vigorously one, and to that one action everything shall converge. There are even two main actions extending throughout the book, and we keep passing from one of them to the other—from the affairs of Anna and Wronsky to the affairs of Kitty and Levine. People appear in connection with these two main actions whose appearance and proceedings do not in the least contribute to develop them; incidents are multiplied which we expect are to lead to something important, but which do not. What, for instance does the episode of Kitty's friend Warinka and Levine's brother Serge Ivanitch, their inclination for one another and its failure to come to anything, contribute to the development of either the character or the fortunes of Kitty and Levine? What does the incident of Levine's long delay in getting to church to be married, a delay which as we read of it seem to have significance, really import? It turns out to import absolutely nothing, and to be introduced solely to give the author the pleasure of telling us that all Levine's shirts had been packed up.

But the truth is we are not to take *Anna Karénine* as a work of art; we are to take it as a piece of life. A piece of life it is. The author has not invented and combined it, he has seen it; it has all happened before his inward eye, and it was in this wise that it happened. Levine's shirts were packed up, and he was late for his wedding in consequence; Warinka and Serge Ivanitch met at Levine's country-house and went out walking together; Serge was very near proposing, but did not. The author saw it all happening so—saw it, and therefore relates it; and what his novel in this way loses in art it gains in reality.

For this is the result which, by his extraordinary fineness of perception, and by his sincere fidelity to it, the author achieves; he works in us a sense of the absolute reality of his personages and their doings. Anna's shoulders, and masses of hair, and half-shut eyes; Alexis Karénine's updrawn eyebrows, and tired smile, and cracking finger-joints; Stiva's eyes suffused with facile moisture—these are as real to us as any of those outward peculiarities which in our own circle of acquaintance we are noticing daily, while the inner man of our own circle of acquaintance, happily or unhappily, lies a great deal less clearly revealed to us than that of Count Tolstoi's creation.

I must speak of only a few of these creations, the chief personages and no more. The book opens with 'Stiva', and who that has once made Stiva's acquaintance will ever forget him? We are living, in Count Tolstoi's novel, among the great people of Moscow and St. Petersburg, the nobles and the high functionaries, the governing class of Russia. Stépane Arcadiévitch—'Stiva'—is Prince Oblonsky, and descended from Rurik, although to think of him as anything except 'Stiva' is difficult. His *air souriant*, his good looks, his satisfaction; his 'ray', which made the Tartar waiter at the club joyful in contemplating it; his pleasure in oysters and champagne, his pleasure in making people happy and in rendering services; his need of money, his attachment to the French governess, his distress at his wife's distress, his affection for her and the children; his emotion and suffused eyes, while he quite dismisses the care of providing funds for household expenses and education; and the French attachment, contritely given up to-day only to be succeeded by some other attachment to-morrow—no never, certainly, shall we come to forget Stiva. Anna, the heroine, is Stiva's sister. His wife Dolly (these English diminutives are common among Count Tolstoi's ladies) is daughter oɪ the Prince and Princess Cherbatzky, grandees who show us Russian high life by its most respectable side; the Prince, in particular, is excellent—simple, sensible, right-feeling; a man of dignity and honour. His daughters, Dolly and Kitty, are charming. Dolly, Stiva's wife, is sorely tried by her husband, full of anxieties for the children, with no money to spend on them or herself, poorly dressed, worn and aged before her time. She has moments of despairing doubt whether the gay people may not be after all in the right, whether virtue and principle answer; whether happiness does not dwell with adventuresses and profligates, brilliant and perfectly dressed adventuresses and profligates, in a land flowing with roubles and champagne. But in a quarter of an hour she comes right again and is herself—a nature straight, honest, faithful, loving, sound to the core; such she is and such she remains; she can be no other. Her sister Kitty is at bottom of the same temper, but she has her experience to get, while Dolly, when the book begins, has already acquired hers. Kitty is adored by Levine, in whom we are told that many traits are to be found of the character and history of Count Tolstoi himself. Levine belongs to the world of great people by his birth and property, but he is not at all a man of the world. He has been a reader and thinker, he has a conscience, he has public spirit and would ameliorate the condition of the people, he lives on his estate in the country, and occupies himself zealously with local business, schools, and agriculture. But he is shy, apt to suspect and to take offence, somewhat impracticable, out of his element in the gay world of Moscow. Kitty likes him, but her fancy has been taken by a brilliant guardsman, Count Wronsky, who has paid her attentions. Wronsky is described to us by Stiva; he is 'one of the first specimens of the *jeunesse dorée* of St. Petersburg; immensely rich, handsome, aide-de-camp to the emperor, great interest at his back, and a good fellow notwithstanding; more than a good fellow, intelligent besides and well read—a man who has a splendid career before him'. Let us complete the picture by adding that Wronsky is a powerful man, over thirty, bald at the top of his head, with irreproachable manners, cool and calm, but a little haughty. A hero, one murmurs to oneself, too much of the Guy Livingstone type, though without the bravado and exaggeration. And such is, justly enough perhaps, the first impression, an impression which continues all through the first volume; but Wronsky, as we shall see, improves towards the end.

Kitty discourages Levine, who retires in misery and confusion. But Wronsky is attracted by Anna Karénine, and ceases his attentions to Kitty. The impression made on her heart by Wronsky was not deep; but she is so keenly mortified with herself, so ashamed, and so upset, that she falls ill, and is sent with her family to winter abroad. There she regains health and mental composure, and discovers at the same time that her liking for Levine was deeper than she knew, that it was a genuine feeling, a strong and lasting one. On her return they meet, their hearts come together, they are married; and in spite of Levine's waywardness, irritability, and unsettlement of mind, of which I shall have more to say presently, they are profoundly happy. Well, and who could help being happy with Kitty? So I find myself adding impatiently. Count Tolstoi's heroines are really so living and charming that one takes them, fiction though they are, too seriously.

But the interest of the book centres in Anna Karénine. She is Stiva's sister, married to a high official at St. Petersburg, Alexis Karénine. She has been married to him nine years, and has one child, a boy named Serge. The marriage had not brought happiness to her, she had found in it no satisfaction to her heart and soul, she had a sense of want and isolation; but she is devoted to her boy, occupied, calm. The charm of her personality is felt even before she appears, from the moment when we hear of her being sent for as the good angel to reconcile Dolly with Stiva. Then she arrives at the Moscow station from St. Petersburg, and we see the gray eyes with their long eyelashes, the graceful carriage, the gentle and caressing smile on the fresh lips, the vivacity restrained but waiting to break through, the fulness of life, the softness and strength joined, the harmony, the bloom, the charm. She goes to Dolly, and achieves, with infinite tact and tenderness, the task of reconciliation. At a ball a few days later, we add to our first impression of Anna's beauty, dark hair, a quantity of little curls over her temples and at the back of her neck, sculptural shoulders, firm throat, and beautiful arms. She is in a plain dress of black velvet with a pearl necklace, a bunch of forget-me-nots in the front of her dress, another in her hair. This is Anne Karénine.

She had travelled from St. Petersburg with Wronsky's mother; had seen him at the Moscow station, where he came to meet his mother, had been struck with his looks and manner, and touched by his behaviour in an accident which happened while they were in the station to a poor workman crushed by a train. At the ball she meets him again; she is fascinated by him and he by her. She had been told of Kitty's fancy, and had gone to the ball meaning to help Kitty; but Kitty is forgotten, or at any rate neglected; the spell which draws Wronsky and Anna is irresistible. Kitty finds herself opposite to them in a quadrille together:

She seemed to remark in Anna the symptoms of an over-excitement which she herself knew from experience—that of success. Anna appeared to her as if intoxicated with it. Kitty knew to what to attribute that brilliant and animated look, that happy and triumphant smile, those half-parted lips, those movements full of grace and harmony.

Anna returns to St. Petersburg, and Wronsky returns there at the same time; they meet on the journey, they keep meeting in society, and Anna begins to find her husband, who before had not been sympathetic, intolerable. Alexis Karénine is much older than herself, a bureaucrat, a formalist, a poor creature; he has conscience, there is a root of goodness in him, but on the surface and until deeply stirred he is tiresome, pedantic, vain, exasperating. The change in Anna is not in the slightest degree comprehended by him; he sees nothing which an intelligent man might in such a case see, and does nothing which an intelligent man would do. Anna abandons herself to her passion for Wronsky.

I remember M. Nisard saying to me many years ago at the École Normale in Paris, that he respected the English because they are *une nation qui sait se gêner*—people who can put constraint on themselves and go through what is disagreeable. Perhaps in the Slav nature this valuable faculty is somewhat wanting; a very strong impulse is too much regarded as irresistible, too little as what can be resisted and ought to be resisted, however difficult and disagreeable the resistance may be. In our high society with its pleasure and dissipation, laxer notions may to some extent prevail; but in general an English mind will be startled by Anna's suffering herself to be so overwhelmed and irretrievably carried away by her passion, by her almost at once regarding it, apparently, as something which it was hopeless to fight against. And this I say irrespectively of the worth of her lover. Wronsky's gifts and graces hardly qualify him, one might think to be the object of so instantaneous and mighty a passion on the part of a woman like Anna. But that is not the question. Let us allow that these passions are incalculable; let us allow that one of the male sex scarcely does justice, perhaps, to the powerful and handsome guardsman and his attractions. But if Wronsky had been even such a lover as Alcibiades or the Master of Ravenswood, still that Anna, being what she is and her circumstances being what they are, should show not a hope, hardly a thought, of conquering her passion, of escaping from its fatal power, is to our notions strange and a little bewildering.

I state the objection; let me add that it is the triumph of Anna's charm that it remains paramount for us nevertheless; that throughout her course, with its failures, errors, and miseries, still the impression of her large, fresh, rich, generous, delightful nature, never leaves us—keeps our sympathy, keeps even, I had almost said, our respect.

To return to the story. Soon enough poor Anna begins to experience the truth of what the Wise Man told us long ago, that 'the way of transgressors is hard'. Her agitation at a steeplechase where Wronsky is in danger attracts her husband's notice and provokes his remonstrance. He is bitter and contemptuous. In a transport of passion Anna declares to him that she is his wife no longer; that she loves Wronsky, belongs to Wronsky. Hard at first, formal, cruel, thinking only of himself, Karénine, who, as I have said, has a conscience, is touched by grace at the moment when Anna's troubles reach their height. He returns to her to find her with a child just born to her and Wronsky, the lover in the house and Anna apparently dying. Karénine has words of kindness and forgiveness only. The noble and victorious effort transfigures him, and all that her husband gains in the eyes of Anna, her lover Wronsky loses. Wronsky comes to Anna's bedside, and standing there by Karénine, buries his face in his hands. Anna says to him, in the hurried voice of fever:

'Uncover your face; look at that man; he is a saint. Yes, uncover your face; uncover it,' she repeated with an angry air. 'Alexis, uncover his face; I want to see him.'

Alexis took the hands of Wronsky and uncovered his face, disfigured by suffering and humiliation.

'Give him your hand; pardon him.'

Alexis stretched out his hand without even seeking to restrain his tears.

'Thank God, thank God!' she said; 'all is ready now. How ugly those flowers are,' she went on, pointing to the wall-paper; 'they are not a bit like violets. My God, my God! when will all this end? Give me morphine, doctor—I want morphine. Oh, my God, my God!'

She seems dying, and Wronsky rushes out and shoots himself. And so, in a common novel, the story would end. Anna would die, Wronsky would commit suicide, Karénine would survive, in possession of our admiration and sympathy. But the story does not always end so in life: neither does it end so in Count Tolstoi's novel. Anna recovers from her fever, Wronsky from his wound. Anna's passion for Wronsky reawakens, her estrangement from Karénine returns. Nor does Karénine remain at the height at which in the forgiveness scene we saw him. He is formal, pedantic, irritating. Alas! even if he were not all these, perhaps even his *pince-nez*, and his rising eye-brows, and his cracking finger-joints, would have been provocation enough. Anna and Wronsky depart together. They stay for a time in Italy, then return to Russia. But her position is false, her disquietude incessant, and happi-ness is impossible for her. She takes opium every night, only to find that 'not poppy nor mandragora shall ever medicine her to that sweet sleep which she owed yester-day'. Jealousy and irritability grow upon her; she tor-tures Wronsky, she tortures herself. Under these trials Wronsky, it must be said, comes out well, and rises in our esteem. His love for Anna endures; he behaves, as our English phrase is, 'like a gentleman'; his patience is in general exemplary. But then Anna, let us remember, is to the last, through all the fret and misery, still Anna; always with something which charms; nay, with some-thing, even, something in her nature, which consoles and does good. Her life, however, was becoming impossible under its existing conditions. A trifling misunderstanding brought the inevitable end. After a quarrel with Anna, Wronsky had gone one morning into the country to see his mother; Anna summons him by telegraph to return at once, and receives an answer from him that he cannot return before ten at night. She follows him to his mother's place in the country, and at the station hears what leads her to believe that he is not coming back. Maddened with jealousy and misery, she descends the platform and throws herself under the wheels of a goods train passing through the station. It is over—the graceful head is untouched, but all the rest is a crushed formless heap. Poor Anna!

We have been in a world which misconducts itself nearly as much as the world of a French novel all palpitating with 'modernity'. But there are two things in which the Russian novel—Count Tolstoi's novel at any rate—is very advantageously distinguished from the type of novel now so much in request in France. In the first place, there is no fine sentiment, at once tiresome and false. We are not told to believe, for example, that Anna is wonderfully exalted and ennobled by her passion for Wronsky. The English reader is thus saved from many a groan of impatience. The other thing is yet more important. Our Russian novelist deals abundantly with criminal passion and with adultery, but he does not seem to feel himself owing service to the goddess Lubricity, or bound to put in touches at this goddess's dictation. Much in *Anna Karénine* is painful, much is unpleasant, but nothing is of a nature to trouble the senses, or to please those who wish their senses troubled. This taint is wholly absent. In the French novels where it is so abundantly present its baneful effects do not end with itself. Burns long ago remarked with deep truth that it *petrifies feeling*. Let us revert for a moment to the powerful novel of which I spoke at the outset, *Madame Bovary*. Undoubtedly the taint in question is present in *Madame Bovary*, although to a much less degree than in more recent French novels, which will be in every one's mind. But *Madame Bovary*, with this taint, is a work of *petrified feeling*; over it hangs an atmosphere of bitterness, irony, impotence; not a personage in the book to rejoice or console us; the springs of freshness and feeling are not there to create such personages. Emma Bovary follows a course in some respects like that of Anna, but where, in Emma Bovary, is Anna's charm? The treasures of compassion, tenderness, insight, which alone, amid such guilt and misery, can enable charm to subsist and to emerge are wanting to Flaubert. He is cruel, with the cruelty of petrified feeling, to his poor heroine; he pursues her without pity or pause, as with malignity; he is harder upon her himself than any reader even, I think, will be inclined to be.

But where the springs of feeling have carried Count Tolstoi, since he created Anna ten or twelve years ago, we have now to see.

We must return to Constantine Dmitrich Levine. Levine, as I have already said, thinks. Between the age of twenty and that of thirty-five he had lost, he tells us, the Christian belief in which he had been brought up, a loss of which examples nowadays abound certainly everywhere, but which in Russia, as in France, is among all young men of the upper and cultivated classes more a matter of course, perhaps, more universal, more avowed, than it is with us. Levine had adopted the scientific notions current all round him; talked of cells, organisms, the indestructibility of matter, the conservation of force, and was of opinion, with his comrades of the university, that religion no longer existed. But he was of a serious nature, and the question what his life meant, whence it came, whither it tended, presented themselves to him in moments of crisis and affliction with irresistible importunity, and getting no answer, haunted him, tortured him, made him think of suicide.

Two things, meanwhile, he noticed. One was, that he and his university friends had been mistaken in supposing that Christian belief no longer existed; they had lost it, but they were not all the world. Levine observed that the persons to whom he was most attached, his own wife Kitty amongst the number, retained it and drew comfort from it; that the women generally, and almost the whole of the Russian common people, retained it and drew comfort from it. The other was, that his scientific friends, though not troubled like himself by questionings about the meaning of human life, were untroubled by such questionings, not because they had got an answer to them, but because, entertaining themselves intellectually with the consideration of the cell theory, and evolution, and the indestructibility of matter, and the conservation of force, and the like, they were satisfied with this entertainment, and did not perplex themselves with investigating the meaning and object of their own life at all.

But Levine noticed further that he himself did not actually proceed to commit suicide; on the contrary, he lived on his lands as his father had done before him, busied himself with all the duties of his station, married Kitty, was delighted when a son was born to him. Nevertheless he was indubitably not happy at bottom, restless and disquieted, his disquietude sometimes amounting to agony.

Now on one of his bad days he was in the field with his peasants, and one of them happened to say to him, in answer to a question from Levine why one farmer should in a certain case act more humanely than another: 'Men are not all alike; one man lives for his belly, like Mitio-vuck, another for his soul, for God, like old Plato.'[1] 'What do you call,' cried Levine, 'living for his soul, for God?' The peasant answered: 'It's quite simple—living by the rule of God, of the truth. All men are not the same, that's certain. You yourself, for instance, Constantine Dmitrich, you wouldn't do wrong by a poor man.' Levine gave no answer, but turned away with the phrase, *living by the rule of God, of the truth,* sounding in his ears.

Then he reflected that he had been born of parents professing this rule, as their parents again had professed it before them; that he had sucked it in with his mother's milk; that some sense of it, some strength and nourishment from it, had been ever with him although he knew it not; that if he had tried to do the duties of his station it was by help of the secret support ministered by this rule; that if in his moments of despairing restlessness and agony, when he was driven to think of suicide, he had yet not committed suicide it was because this rule had silently enabled him to do his duty in some degree, and had given him some hold upon life and happiness in consequence.

The words came to him as a clue of which he could never again lose sight, and which with full consciousness and strenuous endeavour he must henceforth follow. He sees his nephews and nieces throwing their milk at one another and scolded by Dolly for it. He says to himself that these children are wasting their subsistence because they have not to earn it for themselves and do not know its value, and he explains inwardly: 'I, a Christian, brought up in the faith, my life filled with the benefits of Christianity, living on these benefits without being conscious of it, I, like these children, I have been trying to

---

[1] A common name among Russian peasants.

destroy what makes and builds up my life.' But now the feeling has been borne in upon him, clear and precious, that what he has to do is to *be good*; he has 'cried to *Him*'. What will come of it?

I shall probably continue to get out of temper with my coachman, to go into useless arguments, to air my ideas unseasonably; I shall always feel a barrier between the sanctuary of my soul and the soul of other people, even that of my wife; I shall always be holding her responsible for my annoyances and feeling sorry for it directly afterwards. I shall continue to pray without being able to explain to myself why I pray; but my inner life has won its liberty; it will no longer be at the mercy of events, and every minute of my existence will have a meaning sure and profound which it will be in my power to impress on every single one of my actions, that of *being good*.

With these words the novel of *Anna Karénine* ends. But in Levine's religious experiences Count Tolstoi was relating his own, and the history is continued in three autobiographical works translated from him, which have within the last two or three years been published in Paris: *Ma Confession*, *Ma Religion*, and *Que Faire*. Our author announces further, 'two great works', on which he has spent six years: one a criticism of dogmatic theology, the other a new translation of the four Gospels, with a concordance of his own arranging. The results which he claims to have established in these two works are, however, indicated sufficiently in the three published volumes which I have named above.

These autobiographical volumes show the same extraordinary penetration, the same perfect sincerity, which are exhibited in the author's novel. As autobiography they are of profound interest, and they are full, moreover, of acute and fruitful remarks. I have spoken of the advantages which the Russian genius possesses for imaginative literature. Perhaps for Biblical exegesis, for the criticism of religion and its documents, the advantage lies more with the older nations of the West. They will have more of the experience, width of knowledge, patience, sobriety, requisite for these studies; they may probably be less impulsive, less heady.

Count Tolstoi regards the change accomplished in himself during the last half-dozen years, he regards his recent studies and the ideas which he has acquired through them, as epoch-making in his life and of capital importance:

Five years ago faith came to me; I believed in the doctrine of Jesus, and all my life suddenly changed. I ceased to desire that which previously I desired, and, on the other hand, I took to desiring what I had never desired before. That which formerly used to appear good in my eyes appeared evil, that which used to appear evil appeared good.

The novel of *Anna Karénine* belongs to that past which Count Tolstoi has left behind him; his new studies and the works founded on them are what is important; light and salvation are there. Yet I will venture to express my doubt whether these works contain, as their contribution to the cause of religion and to the establishment of the true mind and message of Jesus, much that had not already been given or indicated by Count Tolstoi in relating, in *Anna Karénine*, Levine's mental history. Points raised in that history are developed and enforced; there is an abundant and admirable exhibition of knowledge of human nature, penetrating insight, fearless sincerity, wit, sarcasm, eloquence, style. And we have too the direct autobiography of a man not only interesting to us from his soul and talent, but highly interesting also from his nationality, position, and course of proceeding. But to light and salvation in the Christian religion we are not, I think, brought very much nearer than in Levine's history. I ought to add that what was already present in that history seems to me of high importance and value. Let us see what it amounts to.

I must be general and I must be brief; neither my limits nor my purpose permit the introduction of what is abstract. But in Count Tolstoi's religious philosophy there is very little which is abstract, arid. The idea of *life* is his master idea in studying and establishing religion. He speaks impatiently of St. Paul as a source, in common with the Fathers and the Reformers, of that ecclesiastical theology which misses the essential and fails to present Christ's Gospel aright. Yet Paul's 'law of the spirit of life in Christ Jesus freeing me from the law of sin and death' is the pith and ground of all Count Tolstoi's theology. Moral life is the gift of God, is God, and this true life, this union with God to which we aspire, we reach through union with Jesus. We reach it through union with Jesus and by adopting his life. This doctrine is proved true for us by the life in God, to be acquired through Jesus, being what our nature feels after and moves to, by the warning of misery if we are severed from it, the sanction of happiness if we find it. Of the access for *us* at any rate, to the spirit of life, us who are born in Christendom, are in touch, conscious or unconscious, with Christianity, this is the true account. Questions over which the churches spend so much labour and time— questions about the Trinity, about the godhead of Christ, about the procession of the Holy Ghost, are not vital: what is vital is the doctrine of access to the spirit of life through Jesus.

Sound and saving doctrine, in my opinion, this is. It may be gathered in a great degree from what Count

Tolstoi had already given us in the novel of *Anna Karénine*. But of course it is greatly developed in the special works which have followed. Many of these developments are, I will repeat, of striking force, interest, and value. In *Anna Karénine* we had been told of the scepticism of the upper and educated classes in Russia. But what reality is added by such an anecdote as the following from *Ma Confession*:

I remember that when I was about eleven years old we had a visit one Sunday from a boy, since dead, who announced to my brother and me, as great news, a discovery just made at his public school. This discovery was to the effect that God had no existence, and that everything which we were taught about Him was pure invention.

Count Tolstoi touched, in *Anna Karénine*, on the failure of science to tell a man what his life means. Many a sharp stroke does he add in his latter writings:

Development is going on, and there are laws which guide it. You yourself are a part of the whole. Having come to understand the whole so far as is possible, and having comprehended the law of development, you will comprehend also your place in that whole, you will understand yourself.

In spite of all the shame the confession costs me, there was a time, I declare, when I tried to look as if I was satisfied with this sort of thing!

But the men of science may take comfort from hearing that Count Tolstoi treats the men of letters no better than them, although he is a man of letters himself:

The judgment which my literary companions passed on life was to the effect that life in general is in a state of progress, and that in this development we, the men of letters, take the principal part. The vocation of us artists and poets is to instruct the world; and to prevent my coming out with the natural question, 'What am I, and what am I to teach?' it was explained to me that it was useless to know that, and that the artist and the poet taught without perceiving how. I passed for a superb artist, a great poet, and consequently it was but natural I should appropriate this theory. I, the artist, the poet —I wrote, I taught, without myself knowing what. I was paid for what I did. I had everything: splendid fare and lodging, women, society; I had *la gloire*. Consequently, what I taught was very good. This faith in the importance of poetry and of the development of life was a religion, and I was one of its priests—a very agreeable and advantageous office.

And I lived ever so long in this belief, never doubting but that it was true!

The adepts of this literary and scientific religion are not numerous, to be sure, in comparison with the mass of the people, and the mass of the people, as Levine had remarked, find comfort still in the old religion of Christendom; but of the mass of the people our literary and scientific instructors make no account. Like Solomon and Schopenhauer, these gentlemen, and 'society' along with them, are, moreover, apt to say that life is, after all, vanity: but then they all know of no life except their own.

It used to appear to me that the small number of cultivated, rich, and idle men, of whom I was one, composed the whole of humanity, and that the millions and millions of other men who had lived and are still living were not in reality men at all. Incomprehensible as it now seems to me, that I should have gone on considering life without seeing the life which was surrounding me on all sides, the life of humanity; strange as it is to think that I should have been so mistaken, and have fancied my life, the life of the Solomons and the Schopenhauers, to be the veritable and normal life, while the life of the masses was but a matter of no importance—strangely odd as this seems to me now, so it was, notwithstanding.

And this pretentious minority, who call themselves 'society', 'the world', and to whom their own life, the life of 'the world', seems the only life worth naming, are all the while miserable! Our author found it so in his own experience:

In my life, an exceptionally happy one from a worldly point of view, I can number such a quantity of sufferings endured for the sake of 'the world', that they would be enough to furnish a martyr for Jesus. All the most painful passages in my life, beginning with the orgies and duels of my student days, the wars I have been in, the illnesses, and the abnormal and unbearable conditions in which I am living now—all this is but one martyrdom endured in the name of the doctrine of the world. Yes, and I speak of my own life, exceptionally happy from the world's point of view.

Let any sincere man pass his life in review, and he will perceive that never, not once, has he suffered through practising the doctrine of Jesus; the chief part of the miseries of his life have proceeded solely from his following, contrary to his inclination, the spell of the doctrine of the world.

On the other hand, the simple, the multitudes, outside of this spell, are comparatively contented:

In opposition to what I saw in our circle, where life without faith is possible, and where I doubt whether one in a thousand would confess himself a believer, I conceive that among the people (in Russia) there is not one sceptic to many thousands of believers. Just contrary to what I saw in our circle, where life passes in idleness, amusements, and discontent with life, I saw that of these men of the people the whole life was passed in severe labour, and yet they were contented with life. Instead of complaining like the persons in our world of the hardship of their lot, these poor people received sickness and disappointments without any revolt, without opposition, but with a firm and tranquil confidence that so it was to be, that it could not be otherwise, and that it was all right.

All this is but development, sometimes rather surprising, but always powerful and interesting, of what we have

already had in the pages of *Anna Karénine*. And like
Levine in that novel, Count Tolstoi was driven by his
inward struggle and misery very near to suicide. What is
new in the recent books is the solution and cure announced. Levine had accepted a provisional solution of
the difficulties oppressing him; he had lived right on, so
to speak, obeying his conscience, but not asking how far
all his actions hung together and were consistent:

He advanced money to a peasant to get him out of the
clutches of a money-lender, but did not give up the arrears
due to himself; he punished thefts of wood strictly, but would
have scrupled to impound a peasant's cattle trespassing on his
fields; he did not pay the wages of a labourer whose father's
death caused him to leave work in the middle of harvest, but
he pensioned and maintained his old servants; he let his
peasants wait while he went to give his wife a kiss after he
came home, but would not have made them wait while he
went to visit his bees.

Count Tolstoi has since advanced to a far more definite
and stringent rule of life—the positive doctrine, he
thinks, of Jesus. It is the determination and promulgation
of this rule which is the novelty in our author's recent
works. He extracts this essential doctrine, or rule of
Jesus, from the Sermon on the Mount, and presents it in
a body of commandments—Christ's commandments; the
pith, he says, of the New Testament, as the Decalogue is
the pith of the Old. These all-important commandments
of Christ are 'commandments of peace', and five in number. The first commandment is: 'Live in peace with all
men; treat no one as contemptible and beneath you. Not
only allow yourself no anger, but do not rest until you
have dissipated even unreasonable anger in others
against yourself.' The second is: 'No libertinage and no
divorce; let every man have one wife and every woman

one husband.' The third: 'Never on any pretext take an oath of service of any kind; all such oaths are imposed for a bad purpose.' The fourth: 'Never employ force against the evil-doer; bear whatever wrong is done to you without opposing the wrong-doer or seeking to have him punished.' The fifth and last: 'Renounce all distinction of nationality; do not admit that men of another nation may ever be treated by you as enemies; love all men alike as alike near to you; do good to all alike.'

If these five commandments were generally observed, says Count Tolstoi, all men would become brothers. Certainly the actual society in which we live would be changed and dissolved. Armies and wars would be renounced; courts of justice, police, property, would be renounced also. And whatever the rest of us may do, Count Tolstoi at least will do his duty and follow Christ's commandments sincerely. He has given up rank, office, and property, and earns his bread by the labour of his own hands. 'I believe in Christ's commandments,' he says, 'and this faith changes my whole former estimate of what is good and great, bad and low, in human life.' At present—

Everything which I used to think bad and low—the rusticity of the peasant, the plainness of lodging, food, clothing, manners—all this has become good and great in my eyes. At present I can no longer contribute to anything which raises me externally above others, which separates me from them. I cannot, as formerly, recognise either in my own case or in that of others any title, rank, or quality beyond the title and quality of man. I cannot seek fame and praise; I cannot seek a culture which separates me from men. I cannot refrain from seeking in my whole existence—in my lodging, my food, my clothing, and my ways of going on with people—whatever, far from separating me from the mass of mankind, draws me nearer to them.

Whatever else we have or have not in Count Tolstoi, we have at least a great soul and a great writer. In his Biblical exegesis, in the criticism by which he extracts and constructs his Five Commandments of Christ which are to be the rule of our lives, I find much which is questionable along with much which is ingenious and powerful. But I have neither space, nor, indeed, inclination, to criticise his exegesis here. The right moment, besides, for criticising this will come when the 'two great works', which are in preparation, shall have appeared.

For the present I limit myself to a single criticism only —a general one. Christianity cannot be packed into any set of commandments. As I have somewhere or other said, 'Christianity is a *source*; no one supply of water and refreshment that comes from it can be called the sum of Christianity. It is a mistake, and may lead to much error, to exhibit any series of maxims, even those of the Sermon on the Mount, as the ultimate sum and formula into which Christianity may be run up.'

And the reason mainly lies in the character of the Founder of Christianity and in the nature of his utterances. Not less important than the teachings given by Jesus is the *temper* of their giver, his temper of sweetness and reasonableness, of *epieikeia*. Goethe calls him a *Schwärmer*, a fanatic; he may much more rightly be called an opportunist. But he is an opportunist of an opposite kind from those who in politics, that 'wild and dreamlike trade' of insincerity, give themselves this name. They push or slacken, press their points hard or let them be, as may best suit the interests of their self-aggrandisement and of their party. Jesus has in view simply 'the rule of God, of the truth'. But this is served by waiting as well as by hasting forward, and sometimes served better.

Count Tolstoi sees rightly that whatever the propertied

and satisfied classes may think, the world, ever since Jesus Christ came, is judged; 'a new earth' is in prospect. It was ever in prospect with Jesus, and should be ever in prospect with his followers. And the ideal in prospect has to be realised. 'If ye know these things, happy are ye if you do them.' But they are to be done through a great and widespread and long-continued change, and a change of the inner man to begin with. The most important and fruitful utterances of Jesus, therefore, are not things which can be drawn up as a table of stiff and stark external commands, but the things which have most soul in them; because these can best sink down into our soul, work there, set up an influence, form habits of conduct, and prepare the future. The Beatitudes are on this account more helpful than the utterances from which Count Tolstoi builds up his Five Commandments. The very *secret* of Jesus, 'He that loveth his life shall lose it, he that will lose his life shall save it', does not give us a command to be taken and followed in the letter, but an idea to work in our mind and soul, and of inexhaustible value there.

Jesus paid tribute to the government and dined with the publicans, although neither the empire of Rome nor the high finance of Judea were compatible with his ideal and with the 'new earth' which that ideal must in the end create. Perhaps Levine's provisional solution, in a society like ours, was nearer to 'the rule of God, of the truth', than the more trenchant solution which Count Tolstoi has adopted for himself since. It seems calculated to be of more use. I do not know how it is in Russia, but in an English village the determination of 'our circle' to earn their bread by the work of their hands would produce only dismay, not fraternal joy, amongst that 'majority' who are so earning it already. 'There are plenty of us to compete as things stand', the gardeners, carpenters, and smiths would say; 'pray stick to your articles, your poetry and nonsense; in manual labour you will interfere with us, and be taking the bread out of our mouths'.

So I arrive at the conclusion that Count Tolstoi has perhaps not done well in abandoning the work of the poet and artist, and that he might with advantage return to it. But whatever he may do in the future, the work which he has already done, and his work in religion as well as his work in imaginative literature, is more than sufficient to signalise him as one of the most marking, interesting, and sympathy-inspiring men of our time— an honour, I must add, to Russia, although he forbids us to heed nationality.

HAMLET ONCE MORE

BY AN OLD PLAYGOER

(1884)

At the very moment when Mr. Wilson Barrett is bringing out *Hamlet* at the Princess's, there comes into my hands *Shakespeare and Montaigne, an Endeavour to explain the Tendency of 'Hamlet' from Allusions in Contemporary Works,* by Mr. Jacob Feis, an author not known to me. Mr. Feis seeks to establish that Shakespeare in *Hamlet* identifies Montaigne's philosophy with madness, branding it as a pernicious one, as contrary to the intellectual conquests his own English nation has made when breaking with the Romanist dogma. 'Shakespeare', says Mr. Feis, 'wished to warn his contemporaries that the attempt of reconciling two opposite circles of ideas—namely, on the one hand the doctrine that we are to be guided by the laws of nature, and on the other the yielding ourselves up to superstitious dogmas which declare human nature to be sinful, must inevitably produce deeds of madness.'

Mr. Feis's name has a German look, and the first instinct of the 'genuine British narrowness' will be to say that here is another German critic who has discovered a mare's nest. 'Hamlet dies wounded and poisoned, as if Shakespeare had intended expressing his abhorrence of so vacillating a character, who places the treacherous excesses of passion above the power of that human reason in whose free service alone Greeks and Romans did their most exalted deeds of virtue.'

Shakespeare is 'the great humanist', in sympathy with

the clear unwarped reason of 'a living Horace or Horatio', an Horatio intrepid as the author of 'non vultus instantis tyranni'. This is fantastic. Far from abhorring Hamlet, Shakespeare was probably in considerable sympathy with him: nor is he likely to have thought either that salvation for mankind was to be had from the Odes of Horace.

Mr. Feis is too entire, too absolute. Nevertheless his book is of real interest and value. He has proved the pre-occupation of Shakespeare's mind when he made *Hamlet* with Montaigne's *Essays*. John Sterling had inferred it, but Mr. Feis has established it. He shows how passage after passage in the second quarto of *Hamlet*, published in 1604, has been altered and expanded in correspondence with things in the first English translation of Montaigne's *Essays*, Florio's, published in 1603.

The *Essays* had already passed through many editions in French, and were known to Shakespeare in that language. Their publication in English was an event in the brilliant and intellectual London world, then keenly interested in the playhouses; and Shakespeare, in revising his *Hamlet* in 1604, gives proof of the actual occupation of his patrons with the Englished Montaigne, and confirms, too, the fact of his own occupation with the *Essays* previously.

For me the interest of this discovery does not lie in its showing that Shakespeare thought Montaigne a dangerous author, and meant to give in *Hamlet* a shocking example of what Montaigne's teaching led to. It lies in its explaining how it comes about that *Hamlet*, in spite of the prodigious mental and poetic power shown in it, is really so tantalising and ineffective a play. To the common public *Hamlet* is a famous piece by a famous poet, with crime, a ghost, battle, and carnage; and that is sufficient. To the youthful enthusiast *Hamlet* is a piece handling the mystery of the universe, and having throughout cadences, phrases, and words full of divinest Shakespearian magic; and that, too, is sufficient. To the pedant, finally, *Hamlet* is an occasion for airing his psychology; and what does pedant require more? But to the spectator who loves true and powerful drama, and can judge whether he gets it or not, *Hamlet* is a piece which opens, indeed, simply and admirably, and then: 'The rest is puzzle'!

The reason is, apparently, that Shakespeare conceived this play with his mind running on Montaigne, and placed its action and its hero in Montaigne's atmosphere and world. What is that world? It is the world of man viewed as a being *ondoyant et divers*, balancing and indeterminate, the plaything of cross motives and shifting impulses, swayed by a thousand subtle influences, physiological and pathological. Certainly the action and hero of the original Hamlet story are not such as to compel the poet to place them in this world and no other, but they admit of being placed there, Shakespeare resolved to place them there, and they lent themselves to his resolve. The resolve once taken to place the action in this world of problem, the problem became brightened by all the force of Shakespeare's faculties, of Shakespeare's subtlety. *Hamlet* thus comes at last to be not a drama followed with perfect comprehension and profoundest emotion, which is the ideal for tragedy, but a problem soliciting interpretation and solution.

It will never, therefore, be a piece to be seen with pure satisfaction by those who will not deceive themselves. But such is its power and such is its fame that it will always continue to be acted, and we shall all of us continue to go and see it. Mr. Wilson Barrett has put it effectively and finely on the stage. In general the critics have marked his merits, with perfect justice. He is successful with his

King and Queen. The King in *Hamlet* is too often a blatant horror, and his Queen is to match. Mr. Willard and Miss Leighton are a King and Queen whom one sees and hears with pleasure. Ophelia, too—what suffering have Ophelias caused us! And nothing can make this part advantageous to an actress or enjoyable for the spectator. I confess, therefore, that I trembled at each of Miss Easterlake's entrances; but the impression finally left, by the madness scene more especially, was one of approval and respect. Mr. Wilson Barrett himself, as Hamlet, is fresh, natural, young, prepossessing, animated, coherent; the piece moves. All Hamlets whom I have seen dissatisfy us in something. Macready wanted person, Charles Kean mind, Fechter English; Mr. Wilson Barrett wants elocution. No ingenuity will ever enable us to follow the drama of *Hamlet* as we follow the first part of *Faust*, but we may be made to feel the noble poetry.

Perhaps John Kemble, in spite of his limitations, was the best Hamlet after all. But John Kemble is beyond reach of the memory of even

AN OLD PLAYGOER

EQUALITY[1]

(1878)

THERE is a maxim which we all know, which occurs in our copy-books, which occurs in that solemn and beautiful formulary against which the Nonconformist genius is just now so angrily chafing,—the Burial Service. The maxim is this: 'Evil communications corrupt good manners.' It is taken from a chapter of the First Epistle to the Corinthians; but originally it is a line of poetry, of Greek poetry. *Quid Athenis et Hierosolymis?* asks a Father; what have Athens and Jerusalem to do with one another? Well, at any rate, the Jerusalemite Paul, exhorting his converts, enforces what he is saying by a verse of Athenian comedy, —a verse, probably, from the great master of that comedy, a man unsurpassed for fine and just observation of human life, Menander. Φθείρουσιν ἤθη χρήσθ' ὁμιλίαι κακαί 'Evil communications corrupt good manners.'

In that collection of single, sententious lines, printed at the end of Menander's fragments, where we now find the maxim quoted by St. Paul, there is another striking maxim, not alien certainly to the language of the Christian religion, but which has not passed into our copybooks: 'Choose equality and flee greed.' The same profound observer, who laid down the maxim so universally accepted by us that it has become commonplace, the maxim that evil communications corrupt good manners, laid down also, as a no less sure result of the accurate study of human life, this other maxim as well: 'Choose

[1] Address delivered at the Royal Institution.

equality and flee greed'—'Ἰσότητα δ' αἱροῦ καὶ πλεονεξίαν
φύγε.

Pleonexia, or greed, the wishing and trying for the
bigger share, we know under the name of covetousness.
We understand by covetousness something different
from what *pleonexia* really means: we understand by
it the longing for other people's goods: and covetousness, so understood, it is a commonplace of morals and
of religion with us that we should shun. As to the duty
of pursuing equality, there is no such consent amongst
us. Indeed, the consent is the other way, the consent is
against equality. Equality before the law we all take as a
matter of course; that is not the equality which we mean
when we talk of equality. When we talk of equality, we
understand social equality; and for equality in this
Frenchified sense of the term almost everybody in England
has a hard word. About four years ago Lord Beaconsfield
held it up to reprobation in a speech to the students at
Glasgow;—a speech so interesting, that being asked soon
afterwards to hold a discourse at Glasgow, I said that if
one spoke there at all at that time it would be impossible
to speak on any other subject but equality. However, it is
a great way to Glasgow, and I never yet have been able
to go and speak there.

But the testimonies against equality have been steadily
accumulating from the date of Lord Beaconsfield's Glasgow speech down to the present hour. Sir Erskine May
winds up his new and important *History of Democracy* by
saying: 'France has aimed at social equality. The fearful troubles through which she has passed have checked
her prosperity, demoralised her society, and arrested the
intellectual growth of her people.' Mr. Froude, again,
who is more his own master than I am, has been able to
go to Edinburgh and to speak there upon equality. Mr.

Froude told his hearers that equality splits a nation into a 'multitude of disconnected units', that 'the masses require leaders whom they can trust', and that 'the natural leaders in a healthy country are the gentry'. And only just before the *History of Democracy* came out, we had that exciting passage of arms between Mr. Lowe and Mr. Gladstone, where equality, poor thing, received blows from them both. Mr. Lowe declared that 'no concession should be made to the cry for equality, unless it appears that the State is menaced with more danger by its refusal than by its admission. No such case exists now or ever has existed in this country.' And Mr. Gladstone replied that equality was so utterly unattractive to the people of this country, inequality was so dear to their hearts, that to talk of concessions being made to the cry for equality was absurd. 'There is no broad political idea', says Mr. Gladstone quite truly, 'which has entered less into the formation of the political system of this country than the love of equality.' And he adds: 'It is not the love of equality which has carried into every corner of the country the distinct undeniable popular preference, wherever other things are equal, for a man who is a lord over a man who is not. The love of freedom itself is hardly stronger in England than the love of aristocracy.' Mr. Gladstone goes on to quote a saying of Sir William Molesworth, that with our people the love of aristocracy 'is a religion'. And he concludes in his copious and eloquent way: 'Call this love of inequality by what name you please, —the complement of the love of freedom, or its negative pole, or the shadow which the love of freedom casts, or the reverberation of its voice in the halls of the constitution,— it is an active, living, and life-giving power, which forms an inseparable essential element in our political habits of mind, and asserts itself at every step in the processes of our system.'

And yet, on the other side, we have a consummate critic of life like Menander, delivering, as if there were no doubt at all about the matter, the maxim: 'Choose equality!' An Englishman with any curiosity must surely be inclined to ask himself how such a maxim can ever have got established, and taken rank along with 'Evil communications corrupt good manners'. Moreover, we see that among the French, who have suffered so grievously, as we hear, from choosing equality, the most gifted spirits continue to believe passionately in it nevertheless. 'The human ideal, as well as the social ideal, is', says George Sand, 'to achieve equality.' She calls equality 'the goal of man and the law of the future'. She asserts that France is the most civilised of nations, and that its pre-eminence in civilisation it owes to equality.

But Menander lived a long while ago, and George Sand was an enthusiast. Perhaps their differing from us about equality need not trouble us much. France, too, counts for but one nation, as England counts for one also. Equality may be a religion with the people of France, as inequality, we are told, is a religion with the people of England. But what do other nations seem to think about the matter?

Now, my discourse to-night is most certainly not meant to be a disquisition on law, and on the rules of bequest. But it is evident that in the societies of Europe, with a constitution of property such as that which the feudal Midde Age left them with,—a constitution of property full of inequality,—the state of the law of bequest shows us how far each society wishes the inequality to continue. The families in possession of great estates will not break them up if they can help it. Such owners will do all they can, by entail and settlement, to prevent their successors from breaking them up. They will preserve inequality.

Freedom of bequest, then, the power of making entails and settlements, is sure, in an old European country like ours, to maintain inequality. And with us, who have the religion of inequality, the power of entailing and settling, and of willing property as one likes, exists, as is well known, in singular fulness,—greater fulness than in any country of the Continent. The proposal of a measure such as the Real Estates Intestacy Bill is, in a country like ours, perfectly puerile. A European country like ours, wishing not to preserve inequality but to abate it, can only do so by interfering with the freedom of bequest. This is what Turgot, the wisest of French statesmen, pronounced before the Revolution to be necessary, and what was done in France at the great Revolution. The *Code Napoléon*, the actual law of France, forbids entails altogether, and leaves a man free to dispose of but one-fourth of his property, of whatever kind, if he have three children or more, of one-third if he have two children, of one-half if he have but one child. Only in the rare case, therefore, of a man's having but one child, can that child take the whole of his father's property. If there are two children, two-thirds of the property must be equally divided between them; if there are more than two, three-fourths. In this way has France, desiring equality, sought to bring equality about.

Now the interesting point for us is, I say, to know how far other European communities, left in the same situation with us and with France, having immense inequalities of class and property created for them by the Middle Age, have dealt with these inequalities by means of the law of bequest. Do they leave bequest free, as we do? then, like us, they are for inequality. Do they interfere with the freedom of bequest, as France does? then, like France, they are for equality. And we shall be most interested, surely, by what the most civilised European communities do in this matter,—communities such as those of Germany, Italy, Belgium, Holland, Switzerland. And among those communities we are most concerned, I think, with such as, in the conditions of freedom and of self-government which they demand for their life, are most like ourselves. Germany, for instance, we shall less regard, because the conditions which the Germans seem to accept for their life are so unlike what we demand for ours; there is so much personal government there, so much *junkerism*, militarism, officialism; the community is so much more trained to submission than we could bear, so much more used to be, as the popular phrase is, sat upon. Countries where the community has more a will of its own, or can more show it, are the most important for our present purpose,—such countries as Belgium, Holland, Italy, Switzerland. Well, Belgium adopts purely and simply, as to bequest and inheritance, the provisions of the *Code Napoléon*. Holland adopts them purely and simply. Italy has adopted them substantially. Switzerland is a republic, where the general feeling against inequality is strong, and where it might seem less necessary, therefore, to guard against inequality by interfering with the power of bequest. Each Swiss canton has its own law of bequest. In Geneva, Vaud, and Zurich,— perhaps the three most distinguished cantons,—the law is identical with that of France. In Berne, one-third is the fixed proportion which a man is free to dispose of by will; the rest of his property must go among his children equally. In all the other cantons there are regulations of a like kind. Germany, I was saying, will interest us less then these freer countries. In Germany,—though there is not the English freedom of bequest, but the rule of the Roman law prevails, the rule obliging the parent to assign a certain portion to each child,—in Germany entails and settlements in favour of an eldest son are generally permitted. But there is a remarkable exception. The Rhine countries, which in the early part of this century were under French rule, and which then received the *Code Napoléon*, these countries refused to part with it when they were restored to Germany; and to this day Rhenish Prussia, Rhenish Hesse, and Baden, have the French law of bequest, forbidding entails, and dividing property in the way we have seen.

The United States of America have the English liberty of bequest. But the United States are, like Switzerland, a republic, with the republican sentiment for equality. Theirs is, besides, a new society; it did not inherit the system of classes and of property which feudalism established in Europe. The class by which the United States were settled was not a class with feudal habits and ideas. It is notorious that to acquire great landed estates and to entail them upon an eldest son, is neither the practice nor the desire of any class in America. I remember hearing it said to an American in England: 'But, after all, you have the same freedom of bequest and inheritance as we have, and if a man to-morrow chose in your country to entail a great landed estate rigorously, what could you do?' The American answered: 'Set aside the will on the ground of insanity.'

You see we are in a manner taking the votes for and against equality. We ought not to leave out our own colonies. In general they are, of course, like the United States of America, new societies. They have the English liberty of bequest. But they have no feudal past, and were not settled by a class with feudal habits and ideas. Nevertheless it happens that there have arisen, in Australia, exceedingly large estates, and that the proprietors seek to keep them together. And what have we seen happen lately? An Act has been passed which in effect inflicts a fine upon every proprietor who holds a landed estate of more than a certain value. The measure has been severely blamed in England; to Mr. Lowe such a 'concession to the cry for equality' appears, as we might expect, pregnant with warnings. At present I neither praise it nor blame it; I simply count it as one of the votes for equality. And is it not a singular thing, I ask you, that while we have the religion of inequality, and can hardly bear to hear equality spoken of, there should be, among the nations of Europe which have politically most in common with us, and in the United States of America, and in our own colonies, this diseased appetite, as we must think it, for equality? Perhaps Lord Beaconsfield may not have turned your minds to this subject as he turned mine, and what Menander or George Sand happens to have said may not interest you much; yet surely, when you think of it, when you see what a practical revolt against inequality there is amongst so many people not so very unlike to ourselves, you must feel some curiosity to sift the matter a little further, and may be not ill-disposed to follow me while I try to do so.

I have received a letter from Clerkenwell, in which the writer reproaches me for lecturing about equality at this which he calls 'the most aristocratic and exclusive place out'. I am here because your secretary invited me. But I am glad to treat the subject of equality before such an audience as this. Some of you may remember that I have roughly divided our English society into Barbarians, Philistines, Populace, each of them with their prepossessions, and loving to hear what gratifies them. But I remarked at the same time, that scattered throughout all these classes were a certain number of generous and humane souls, lovers of man's perfection, detached from the prepossessions of the class to which they might naturally belong, and desirous that he who speaks to them should, as Plato says, not try to please his fellow-servants, but his true and legitimate master—the heavenly Gods. I feel sure that among the members and frequenters of an institution like this, such humane souls are apt to congregate in numbers. Even from the reproach which my Clerkenwell friend brings against you of being too aristocratic, I derive some comfort. Only I give to the term *aristocratic* a rather wide extension. An accomplished American, much known and much esteemed in this country, the late Mr. Charles Sumner, says that what particularly struck him in England was the large class of gentlemen as distinct from the nobility, and the abundance amongst them of serious knowledge, high accomplishment, and refined taste;—taste fastidious perhaps, says Mr. Sumner, to excess, but erring on virtue's side. And he goes on: 'I do not know that there is much difference between the manners and social observances of the highest classes of England and those of the corresponding classes of France and Germany; but in the rank immediately below the highest,—as among the professions, or military men, or literary men,—there you will find that the Englishmen have the advantage. They are better educated and better bred, more careful in their personal habits and in social conventions, more refined.' Mr. Sumner's remark is just and important; this large class of gentlemen in the professions, the services, literature, politics,—and a good contingent is now added from business also,—this large class, not of the nobility, but with the accomplishments and taste of an upper class, is something peculiar to England. Of this class I may probably assume that my present audience is in large measure composed. It is aristocratic in this sense, that it has the tastes of a cultivated class, a certain high standard of civilisation. Well, it is in its effects upon *civilisation* that equality interests me. And I speak to an audience with a high standard of civilisation. If I say that certain things in certain classes do not come up to a high standard of civilisation, I need not prove how and why they do not; you will feel instinctively whether they do or no. If they do not, I need not prove that this is a bad thing, that a high standard of civilisation is desirable; you will instinctively feel that it is. Instead of calling this 'the most aristocratic and exclusive place out', I conceive of it as a *civilised* place; and in speaking about civilisation half one's labour is saved when one speaks about it among those who are civilised.

Politics are forbidden here; but equality is not a question of English politics. The abstract right to equality may, indeed, be a question of speculative politics. French equality appeals to this abstract natural right as its support. It goes back to a state of nature where all were equal, and supposes that 'the poor consented', as Rousseau says, 'to the existence of rich people', reserving always a natural right to return to the state of nature. It supposes that a child has a natural right to his equal share in his father's goods. The principle of abstract right, says Mr. Lowe, has never been admitted in England, and is false. I so entirely agree with him, that I run no risk of offending by discussing equality upon the basis of this principle. So far as I can sound human consciousness, I cannot, as I have often said, perceive that man is really conscious of any abstract natural rights at all. The natural right to have work found for one to do, the natural right to have food found for one to eat—rights sometimes so confidently and so indignantly asserted—seem to me quite baseless. It cannot be too often repeated: peasants and workmen have no natural rights, not one. Only we ought instantly to add, that kings and nobles have none either. If it is the sound English doctrine that all rights are created by law and are based on expediency, and are alterable as the public advantage may require, certainly that orthodox doctrine is mine. Property is created and maintained by law. It would disappear in that state of private war and scramble which legal society supersedes. Legal society creates, for the common good, the right of property; and for the common good that right is by legal society limitable. That property should exist, and that it should be held with a sense of security and with a power of disposal, may be taken, by us here at any rate, as a settled matter of expediency. With these conditions a good deal of inequality is inevitable. But that the power of disposal should be practically *unlimited*, that the inequality should be *enormous*, or that the degree of inequality admitted at one time should be admitted *always*,—this is by no means so certain. The right of bequest was in early times, as Sir Henry Maine and Mr. Mill have pointed out, seldom recognised. In later times it has been limited in many countries in the way that we have seen; even in England itself it is not formally quite unlimited. The question is one of expediency. It is assumed, I grant, with great unanimity amongst us, that our signal inequality of classes and property is expedient for our civilisation and welfare. But this assumption, of which the distinguished personages who adopt it seem so sure that they think it needless to produce grounds for it, is just what we have to examine.

Now, there is a sentence of Sir Erskine May, whom I have already quoted, which will bring us straight to the

very point that I wish to raise. Sir Erskine May, after
saying, as you have heard, that France has pursued social
equality, and has come to fearful troubles, demoralisation, and intellectual stoppage by doing so, continues
thus: 'Yet is she high, if not the first, in the scale of
civilised nations.' Why, here is a curious thing, surely!
A nation pursues social equality, supposed to be an
utterly false and baneful ideal; it arrives, as might have
been expected, at fearful misery and deterioration by
doing so; and yet, at the same time, it is high, if not the
first, in the scale of civilised nations. What do we mean
by *civilised*? Sir Erskine May does not seem to have asked
himself the question, so we will try to answer it for ourselves. Civilisation is the humanisation of man in society.
To be humanised is to comply with the true law of our
human nature: *servare modum, finemque tenere, Naturamque
sequi*, says Lucan; 'to keep our measure, and to hold fast
our end, and to follow Nature'. To be humanised is to
make progress towards this, our true and full humanity.
And to be civilised is to make progress towards this in
civil society; in that civil society 'without which', says
Burke, 'man could not by any possibility arrive at the
perfection of which his nature is capable, nor even make
a remote and faint approach to it'. To be the most civilised
of nations, therefore, is to be the nation which comes
nearest to human perfection, in the state which that perfection essentially demands. And a nation which has been
brought by the pursuit of social equality to moral
deterioration, intellectual stoppage, and fearful troubles,
is perhaps the nation which has come nearest to human
perfection in that state which such perfection essentially
demands! Michelet himself, who would deny the
demoralisation and the stoppage, and call the fearful
troubles a sublime expiation for the sins of the whole

world, could hardly say more for France than this. Certainly Sir Erskine May never intended to say so much. But into what a difficulty has he somehow run himself, and what a good action would it be to extricate him from it! Let us see whether the performance of that good action may not also be a way of clearing our minds as to the uses of equality.

When we talk of man's advance towards his full humanity, we think of an advance, not along one line only, but several. Certain races and nations, as we know, are on certain lines pre-eminent and representative. The Hebrew nation was pre-eminent on one great line. 'What nation', it was justly asked by their lawgiver, 'hath statutes and judgments so righteous as the law which I set before you this day? Keep therefore and do them; for this is your wisdom and your understanding in the sight of the nations which shall hear all these statutes and say: Surely this great nation is a wise and understanding people!' The Hellenic race was pre-eminent on other lines. Isocrates could say of Athens: 'Our city has left the rest of the world so far behind in philosophy and eloquence, that those educated by Athens have become the teachers of the rest of mankind; and so well has she done her part, that the name of Greeks seems no longer to stand for a race but to stand for intelligence itself, and they who share in our culture are called Greeks even before those who are merely of our own blood.' The power of intellect and science, the power of beauty, the power of social life and manners,— these are what Greece so felt, and fixed, and may stand for. They are great elements in our humanisation. The power of conduct is another great element; and this was so felt and fixed by Israel that we can never with justice refuse to permit Israel, in spite of all his shortcomings, to stand for it.

So you see that in being humanised we have to move along certain lines, and that on certain lines certain nations find their strength and take a lead. We may elucidate the thing yet further. Nations now existing may be said to feel or to have felt the power of this or that element in our humanisation so signally that they are characterised by it. No one who knows this country would deny that it is characterised, in a remarkable degree, by a sense of the power of conduct. Our feeling for religion is one part of this; our industry is another. What foreigners so much remark in us—our public spirit, our love, amidst all our liberty, for public order and for stability,—are parts of it too. Then the power of beauty was so felt by the Italians that their art revived, as we know, the almost lost idea of beauty, and the serious and successful pursuit of it. Cardinal Antonelli, speaking to me about the education of the common people in Rome, said that they were illiterate indeed, but whoever mingled with them at any public show, and heard them pass judgment on the beauty or ugliness of what came before them,—'è brutto', 'è bello',—would find that their judgment agreed admirably, in general, with just what the most cultivated people would say. Even at the present time, then, the Italians are pre-eminent in feeling the power of beauty. The power of knowledge, in the same way, is eminently an influence with the Germans. This by no means implies, as is sometimes supposed, a high and fine general culture. What it implies is a strong sense of the necessity of knowing *scientifically*, as the expression is, the things which have to be known by us; of knowing them systematically, by the regular and right process, and in the only real way. And this sense the Germans especially have. Finally, there is the power of social life and manners. And even the Athenians themselves, perhaps, have hardly felt this power so much as the French.

Voltaire, in a famous passage where he extols the age of Louis the Fourteenth and ranks it with the chief epochs in the civilisation of our race, has to specify the gift bestowed on us by the age of Louis the Fourteenth, as the age of Pericles, for instance, bestowed on us its art and literature, and the Italian Renascence its revival of art and literature. And Voltaire shows all his acuteness in fixing on the gift to name. It is not the sort of gift which we expect to see named. The great gift of the age of Louis the Fourteenth to the world, says Voltaire, was this: *l'esprit de société*, the spirit of society, the social spirit. And another French writer, looking for the good points in the old French nobility, remarks that this at any rate is to be said in their favour: they established a high and charming ideal of social intercourse and manners, for a nation formed to profit by such an ideal, and which has profited by it ever since. And in America, perhaps, we see the disadvantages of having social equality before there has been any such high standard of social life and manners formed.

We are not disposed in England, most of us, to attach all this importance to social intercourse and manners. Yet Burke says: 'There ought to be a system of manners in every nation which a well-formed mind would be disposed to relish.' And the power of social life and manners is truly, as we have seen, one of the great elements in our humanisation. Unless we have cultivated it, we are incomplete. The impulse for cultivating it is not, indeed, a moral impulse. It is by no means identical with the moral impulse to help our neighbour and to do him good. Yet in many ways it works to a like end. It brings men together, makes them feel the need of one another, be considerate of one another, understand one another. But, above all things, it is a promoter of equality. It is by the humanity of their manners that men are made equal. 'A man thinks to show himself my equal,' says Goethe, 'by being *grob*,—that is to say, coarse and rude; he does not show himself my equal, he shows himself *grob*.' But a community having humane manners is a community of equals, and in such a community great social inequalities have really no meaning, while they are at the same time a menace and an embarrassment to perfect ease of social intercourse. A community with the spirit of society is eminently, therefore, a community with the spirit of equality. A nation with a genius for society, like the French or the Athenians, is irresistibly drawn towards equality. From the first moment when the French people, with its congenital sense for the power of social intercourse and manners, came into existence, it was on the road to equality. When it had once got a high standard of social manners abundantly established, and at the same time the natural, material necessity for the feudal inequality of classes and property pressed upon it no longer, the French people introduced equality and made the French Revolution. It was not the spirit of philanthropy which mainly impelled the French to that Revolution, neither was it the spirit of envy, neither was it the love of abstract ideas, though all these did something towards it; but what did most was the spirit of society.

The well-being of the many comes out more and more distinctly, in proportion as time goes on, as the object we must pursue. An individual or a class, concentrating their efforts upon their own well-being exclusively, do but beget troubles both for others and for themselves also. No individual life can be truly prosperous, passed, as

Obermann says, in the midst of men who suffer; *passée au milieu des générations qui souffrent*. To the noble soul, it cannot be happy; to the ignoble, it cannot be secure. Socialistic and communistic schemes have generally, however, a fatal defect; they are content with too low and material a standard of well-being. That instinct of perfection, which is the master-power in humanity, always rebels at this, and frustrates the work. Many are to be made partakers of well-being, true; but the ideal of well-being is not to be, on that account, lowered and coarsened. M. de Laveleye, the political economist, who is a Belgian and a Protestant, and whose testimony therefore we may the more readily take about France, says that France, being the country of Europe where the soil is more divided than anywhere except in Switzerland and Norway, is at the same time the country where material well-being is most widely spread, where wealth has of late years increased most, and where population is least outrunning the limits which, for the comfort and progress of the working classes themselves, seem necessary. This may go for a good deal. It supplies an answer to what Sir Erskine May says about the bad effects of equality upon French prosperity. But I will quote to you from Mr. Hamerton what goes, I think, for yet more. Mr. Hamerton is an excellent observer and reporter, and has lived for many years in France. He says of the French peasantry that they are exceedingly ignorant. So they are. But he adds:

They are at the same time full of intelligence; their manners are excellent, they have delicate perceptions, they have tact, they have a certain refinement which a brutalised peasantry could not possibly have. If you talk to one of them at his own home, or in his field, he will enter into conversation with you quite easily, and sustain his part in a perfectly becoming way, with a pleasant combination of dignity and quiet humour. The interval between him and a Kentish labourer is enormous.

This is indeed worth your attention. Of course all mankind are, as Mr. Gladstone says, of our own flesh and blood. But you know how often it happens in England that a cultivated person, a person of the sort that Mr. Charles Sumner describes, talking to one of the lower class, or even of the middle class, feels, and cannot but feel, that there is somehow a wall of partition between himself and the other, that they seem to belong to two different worlds. Thoughts, feelings, perceptions, susceptibilities, language, manners,—everything is different. Whereas, with a French peasant, the most cultivated man may find himself in sympathy, may feel that he is talking to an equal. This is an experience which has been made a thousand times, and which may be made again any day. And it may be carried beyond the range of mere conversation, it may be extended to things like pleasures, recreations, eating and drinking, and so on. In general the pleasures, recreations, eating and drinking of English people, when once you get below that class which Mr. Charles Sumner calls the class of gentlemen, are to one of that class unpalatable and impossible. In France there is not this incompatibility. Whether he mix with high or low, the gentleman feels himself in a world not alien or repulsive, but a world where people make the same sort of demands upon life, in things of this sort, which he himself does. In all these respects France is the country where the people, as distinguished from a wealthy refined class, most lives what we call a humane life, the life of civilised man.

Of course, fastidious persons can and do pick holes in it. There is just now, in France, a *noblesse* newly revived, full of pretension, full of airs and graces and disdains; but its sphere is narrow, and out of its own sphere no one cares very much for it. There is a general equality in a humane kind of life. This is the secret of the passionate attachment with which France inspires all Frenchmen, in spite of her fearful troubles, her checked prosperity, her disconnected units, and the rest of it. There is so much of the goodness and agreeableness of life there, and for so many. It is the secret of her having been able to attach so ardently to her the German and Protestant people of Alsace, while we have been so little able to attach the Celtic and Catholic people of Ireland. France brings the Alsatians into a social system so full of the goodness and agreeableness of life; we offer to the Irish no such attraction. It is the secret, finally, of the prevalence which we have remarked in other continental countries of a legislation tending, like that of France, to social equality. The social system which equality creates in France is, in the eyes of others, such a giver of the goodness and agreeableness of life, that they seek to get the goodness by getting the equality.

Yet France has had her fearful troubles, as Sir Erskine May justly says. She suffers too, he adds, from demoralisation and intellectual stoppage. Let us admit, if he likes, this to be true also. His error is that he attributes all this to equality. Equality, as we have seen, has brought France to a really admirable and enviable pitch of humanisation in one important line. And this, the work of equality, is so much a good in Sir Erskine May's eyes, that he has mistaken it for the whole of which it is a part, frankly identifies it with civilisation, and is inclined to pronounce France the most civilised of nations.

But we have seen how much goes to full humanisation, to true civilisation, besides the power of social life and manners. There is the power of conduct, the power of intellect and knowledge, the power of beauty. The power of conduct is the greatest of all. And without in the least wishing to preach, I must observe, as a mere matter of natural fact and experience, that for the power of conduct France has never had anything like the same sense which she has had for the power of social life and manners. Michelet, himself a Frenchman, gives us the reason why the Reformation did not succeed in France. It did not succeed, he says, because *la France ne voulait pas de réforme morale*—moral reform France would not have; and the Reformation was above all a moral movement. The sense in France for the power of conduct has not greatly deepened, I think since. The sense for the power of intellect and knowledge has not been adequate either. The sense for beauty has not been adequate. Intelligence and beauty have been, in general, but so far reached, as they can be and are reached by men who, of the elements of perfect humanisation, lay thorough hold upon one only, —the power of social intercourse and manners. I speak of France in general; she has had, and she has, individuals who stand out and who form exceptions. Well then, if a nation laying no sufficient hold upon the powers of beauty and knowledge, and a most failing and feeble hold upon the power of conduct, comes to demoralisation and intellectual stoppage and fearful troubles, we need not be inordinately surprised. What we should rather marvel at is the healing and bountiful operation of Nature, whereby the laying firm hold on one real element in our humanisation has had for France results so beneficent.

And thus, when Sir Erskine May gets bewildered between France's equality and fearful troubles on the one hand, and the civilisation of France on the other, let us suggest to him that perhaps he is bewildered by his data because he combines them ill. France has not exemplary disaster and ruin as the fruits of equality, and at the same time, and independently of this, an exemplary civilisation. She has a large measure of happiness and success as the fruits of equality, and she has a very large measure of dangers and troubles as the fruits of something else.

We have more to do, however, than to help Sir Erskine May out of his scrape about France. We have to see whether the considerations which we have been employing may not be of use to us about England.

We shall not have much difficulty in admitting whatever good is to be said of ourselves, and we will try not to be unfair by excluding all that is not so favourable. Indeed, our less favourable side is the one which we should be the most anxious to note, in order that we may mend it. But we will begin with the good. Our people has energy and honesty as its good characteristics. We have a strong sense for the chief power in the life and progress of man,—the power of conduct. So far we speak of the English people as a whole. Then we have a rich, refined, and splendid aristocracy. And we have, according to Mr. Charles Sumner's acute and true remark, a class of gentlemen, not of the nobility, but well-bred, cultivated, and refined, larger than is to be found in any other country. For these last we have Mr. Sumner's testimony. As to the splendour of our aristocracy, all the world is agreed. Then we have a middle class and a lower class; and they, after all, are the immense bulk of the nation.

Let us see how the civilisation of these classes appears to a Frenchman, who has witnessed, in his own country, the considerable humanisation of these classes by equality. To such an observer our middle class divides itself into a serious portion and gay or rowdy portion; both are a marvel to him. With the gay or rowdy portion we need not much concern ourselves; we shall figure it to our

minds sufficiently if we conceive it as the source of that
war-song produced in these recent days of excitement:

We don't want to fight, but by jingo, if we do,
We've got the ships, we've got the men, and we've got the
money too.

We may also partly judge its standard of life, and the
needs of its nature, by the modern English theatre, perhaps the most contemptible in Europe. But the real
strength of the English middle class is in its serious portion. And of this a Frenchman, who was here some little
time ago as the correspondent, I think, of the *Siècle* newspaper, and whose letters were afterwards published in
a volume, writes as follows. He had been attending some
of the Moody and Sankey meetings, and he says: 'To
understand the success of Messrs. Moody and Sankey,
one must be familiar with English manners, one must
know the mind-deadening influence of a narrow Biblism,
one must have experienced the sense of acute ennui,
which the aspect and the frequentation of this great
division of English society produce in others, the want
of elasticity and the chronic ennui which characterise
this class itself, petrified in a narrow Protestantism and
in a perpetual reading of the Bible.'

You know the French;—a little more Biblism, one may
take leave to say, would do them no harm. But an
audience like this,—and here, as I said, is the advantage
of an audience like this,—will have no difficulty in
admitting the amount of truth which there is in the
Frenchman's pictures. It is the picture of a class which,
driven by its sense for the power of conduct, in the beginning of the seventeenth century entered,—as I have
more than once said, and as I may more than once have
occasion in future to say,—*entered the prison of Puritanism,
and had the key turned upon its spirit there for two hundred years.*

They did not know, good and earnest people as they were, that to the building up of human life there belong all those other powers also,—the power of intellect and knowledge, the power of beauty, the power of social life and manners. And something, by what they became, they gained, and the whole nation with them; they deepened and fixed for this nation the sense of conduct. But they created a type of life and manners, of which they themselves indeed are slow to recognise the faults, but which is fatally condemned by its hideousness, its immense ennui, and against which the instinct of self-preservation in humanity rebels.

Partisans fight against facts in vain. Mr. Goldwin Smith, a writer of eloquence and power, although too prone to acerbity, is a partisan of the Puritan, and of the Nonconformists who are the special inheritors of the Puritan tradition. He angrily resents the imputation upon that Puritan type of life, by which the life of our serious middle class has been formed, that it was doomed to hideousness, to immense ennui. He protests that it had beauty, amenity, accomplishment. Let us go to facts. Charles the First, who, with all his faults, had the just idea that art and letters are great civilisers, made, as you know, a famous collection of pictures,—our first National Gallery. It was, I suppose, the best collection at that time north of the Alps. It contained nine Raphaels, eleven Correggios, twenty-eight Titians. What became of that collection? The journals of the House of Commons will tell you. There you may see the Puritan Parliament disposing of this Whitehall or York House collection as follows: 'Ordered, that all such pictures and statues there as are without any superstitition, shall be forthwith sold. . . . Ordered, that all such pictures there as have the representation of the Second Person in Trinity upon them, shall be forthwith burnt. Ordered, that all such pictures there as have the representation of the Virgin Mary upon them, shall be forthwith burnt'. There we have the weak side of our parliamentary government and our serious middle class. We are incapable of sending Mr. Gladstone to be tried at the Old Bailey because he proclaims his antipathy to Lord Beaconsfield. A majority in our House of Commons is incapable of hailing, with frantic laughter and applause, a string of indecent jests against Christianity and its Founder. But we are not, or were not, incapable of producing a Parliament which burns or sells the masterpieces of Italian art. And one may surely say of such a Puritan Parliament, and of those who determine its line for it, that they had not the spirit of beauty.

What shall we say of amenity? Milton was born a humanist, but the Puritan temper, as we know, mastered him. There is nothing more unlovely and unamiable than Milton the Puritan disputant. Some one answers his *Doctrine and Discipline of Divorce*. 'I mean not', rejoins Milton, 'to dispute philosophy with this pork, who never read any.' However, he does reply to him, and throughout the reply Milton's great joke is, that his adversary, who was anonymous, is a serving-man. 'Finally, he winds up his text with much doubt and trepidation; for it may be his trenchers were not scraped, and that which never yet afforded corn of favour to his noddle,—the salt-cellar,—was not rubbed; and therefore, in this haste, easily granting that his answers fall foul upon each other, and praying you would not think he writes as a prophet, but as a man, he runs to the black jack, fills his flagon, spreads the table, and serves up dinner.' There you have the same spirit of urbanity and amenity, as much of it, and as little, as generally informs the religious controversies of our Puritan middle class to this day.

But Mr. Goldwin Smith insists, and picks out his own exemplar of the Puritan type of life and manners; and even here let us follow him. He picks out the most favourable specimen he can find,—Colonel Hutchinson, whose well-known memoirs, written by his widow, we have all read with interest. 'Lucy Hutchinson', says Mr. Goldwin Smith, 'is painting what she thought a perfect Puritan would be; and her picture presents to us not a coarse, crop-eared, and snuffling fanatic, but a highly accomplished, refined, gallant, and most amiable, though religious and seriously minded, gentleman.' Let us, I say, in this example of Mr. Goldwin Smith's own choosing, lay our finger upon the points where this type deflects from the truly humane ideal.

Mrs. Hutchinson relates a story which gives us a good notion of what the amiable and accomplished social intercourse, even of a picked Puritan family, was. Her husband was governor of Nottingham. He had occasion, she says, 'to go and break up a private meeting in the cannoneer's chamber'; and in the cannoneer's chamber 'were found some notes concerning pædobaptism, which, being brought into the governor's lodgings, his wife having perused them and compared them with the Scriptures, found not what to say against the truths they asserted concerning the misapplication of that ordinance to infants'. Soon afterwards she expects her confinement, and communicates the cannoneer's doubts about pædobaptism to her husband. The fatal cannoneer makes a breach in him too. 'Then he bought and read all the eminent treatises on both sides, which at that time came thick from the presses, and still was cleared in the error of the pædobaptists.' Finally, Mrs. Hutchinson is confined. Then the governor 'invited all the ministers to dinner, and propounded his doubt and the ground thereof to them. None of them could defend their practice with any satisfactory reason, but the tradition of the Church from the primitive times, and their main buckler of federal holiness, which Tombs and Denne had excellently overthrown. He and his wife then, professing themselves unsatisfied, desired their opinions.' With the opinions I will not trouble you, but hasten to the result: 'Whereupon that infant was not baptized.'

No doubt to a large division of English society at this very day, that sort of dinner and discussion, and, indeed, the whole manner of life and conversation here suggested by Mrs. Hutchinson's narrative, will seem both natural and amiable, and such as to meet the needs of man as a religious and social creature. You know the conversation which reigns in thousands of middle-class families at this hour, about nunneries, teetotalism, the confessional, eternal punishment, ritualism, disestablishment. It goes wherever the class goes which is moulded on the Puritan type of life. In the long winter evenings of Toronto Mr. Goldwin Smith has had, probably, abundant experience of it. What is its enemy? The instinct of self-preservation in humanity. Men make crude types and try to impose them, but to no purpose. '*L'homme s'agite, Dieu le mène*', says Bossuet. 'There are many devices in a man's heart; nevertheless the counsel of the Eternal, that shall stand.' Those who offer us the Puritan type of life offer us a religion not true, the claims of intellect and knowledge not satisfied, the claim of beauty not satisfied, the claim of manners not satisfied. In its strong sense for conduct that life touches truth; but its other imperfections hinder it from employing even this sense aright. The type mastered our nation for a time. Then came the reaction. The nation said: 'This type, at any rate, is amiss; we are not going to be all like *that*!' The type retired into our middle class, and fortified itself there. It seeks to endure, to emerge, to deny its own imperfections, to impose itself again:—impossible! If we continue to live, we must outgrow it. The very class in which it is rooted, our middle class, will have to acknowledge the type's inadequacy, will have to acknowledge the hideousness, the immense ennui of the life which this type has created, will have to transform itself thoroughly. It will have to admit the large part of truth which there is in the criticisms of our Frenchman, whom we have too long forgotten.

After our middle class he turns his attention to our lower class. And of the lower and larger portion of this, the portion not bordering on the middle class and sharing its faults, he says: 'I consider this multitude to be absolutely devoid, not only of political principles, but even of the most simple notions of good and evil. Certainly it does not appeal, this mob, to the principles of '89, which you English make game of; it does not insist on the rights of man; what it wants is beer, gin, and *fun*.'[1]

That is a description of what Mr. Bright would call the residuum, only our author seems to think the residuum a very large body. And its condition strikes him with amazement and horror. And surely well it may. Let us recall Mr. Hamerton's account of the most illiterate class in France; what an amount of civilisation they have notwithstanding! And this is always to be understood, in hearing or reading a Frenchman's praise of England. He envies our liberty, our public spirit, our trade, our stability. But there is always a reserve in his mind. He never means for a moment that he would like to change with us. Life seems to him so much better a thing in France for so

---

[1] So in the original.

many more people, that, in spite of the fearful troubles of France, it is best to be a Frenchman. A Frenchman might agree with Mr. Cobden, that life is good in England for those people who have at least £5000 a year. But the civilisation of that immense majority who have not £5000 a year, or £500, or even £100,—of our middle and lower classes,—seems to him too deplorable.

And now what has this condition of our middle and lower class to tell us about equality? How is it, must we not ask, how is it that, being without fearful troubles, having so many achievements to show and so much success, having as a nation a deep sense for conduct, having signal energy and honesty, having a splendid aristocracy, having an exceptionally large class of gentlemen, we are yet so little civilised? How is it that our middle and lower classes, in spite of the individuals among them who are raised by happy gifts of nature to a more humane life, in spite of the seriousness of the middle class, in spite of the honesty and power of true work, the *virtus verusque labor*, which are to be found in abundance throughout the lower, do yet present, as a whole, the characters which we have seen?

And really it seems as if the current of our discourse carried us of itself to but one conclusion. It seems as if we could not avoid concluding, that just as France owes her fearful trouble to other things and her civilisedness to equality, so we owe our immunity from fearful troubles to other things, and our uncivilisedness to inequality. 'Knowledge is easy', says the wise man, 'to him that understandeth'; easy, he means, to him who will use his mind simply and rationally, and not to make him think he can know what he cannot, or to maintain, *per fas et nefas*, a false thesis with which he fancies his interests to be bound up. And to him who will use his mind as the wise man recommends, surely it is easy to see that our short-comings in civilisation are due to our inequality; or in other words, that the great inequality of classes and property, which came to us from the Middle Age and which we maintain because we have the religion of inequality, that this constitution of things, I say, has the natural and necessary effect, under present circumstances, of materialising our upper class, vulgarising our middle class, and brutalising our lower class. And this is to fail in civilisation.

For only just look how the facts combine themselves. I have said little as yet about our aristocratic class, except that it is splendid. Yet these, 'our often very un-happy brethren', as Burke calls them, are by no means matter for nothing but ecstasy. Our charity ought cer-tainly, Burke says, to 'extend a due and anxious sensation of pity to the distresses of the miserable great'. Burke's extremely strong language about their miseries and defects I will not quote. For my part, I am always disposed to marvel that human beings, in a position so false, should be so good as these are. Their reason for existing was to serve as a number of centres in a world disintegrated after the ruin of the Roman Empire, and slowly re-constituting itself. Numerous centres of material force were needed, and these a feudal aristocracy supplied. Their large and hereditary estates served this public end. The owners had a positive function, for which their estates were essential. In our modern world the function is gone; and the great estates, with an infinitely multiplied power of ministering to mere pleasure and indulgence, remain. The energy and honesty of our race does not leave itself without witness in this class, and nowhere are there more conspicuous examples of individuals raised by happy gifts of nature far above their fellows and their

circumstances. For distinction of all kinds this class has
an esteem. Everything which succeeds they tend to wel-
come, to win over, to put on their side; genius may
generally make, if it will, not bad terms for itself with
them. But the total result of the class, its effect on society
at large and on national progress, are what we must
regard. And on the whole, with no necessary function to
fulfil, never conversant with life as it really is, tempted,
flattered, and spoiled from childhood to old age, our
aristocratic class is inevitably materialised, and the more
so the more the development of industry and ingenuity
augments the means of luxury. Every one can see how
bad is the action of such an aristocracy upon the class of
newly enriched people, whose great danger is a material-
istic ideal, just because it is the ideal they can easiest
comprehend. Nor is the mischief of this action now compensated by signal services of a public kind. Turn even
to that sphere which aristocracies think specially their
own, and where they have under other circumstances
been really effective,—the sphere of politics. When there
is need, as now, for any large forecast of the course of
human affairs, for an acquaintance with the ideas which
in the end sway mankind, and for an estimate of their
power, aristocracies are out of their element, and
materialised aristocracies most of all. In the immense
spiritual movement of our day, the English aristocracy,
as I have elsewhere said, always reminds me of Pilate
confronting the phenomenon of Christianity. Nor can
a materialised class have any serious and fruitful sense for
the power of beauty. They may imagine themselves to
be in pursuit of beauty; but how often, alas, does the pursuit come to little more than dabbling a little in what
they are pleased to call art, and making a great deal of
what they are pleased to call love!

Let us return to their merits. For the power of manners an aristocratic class, whether materialised or not, will always, from its circumstances, have a strong sense. And although for this power of social life and manners, so important to civilisation, our English race has no special natural turn, in our aristocracy this power emerges and marks them. When the day of general humanisation comes, they will have fixed the standard of manners. The English simplicity, too, makes the best of the English aristocracy more frank and natural then the best of the like class anywhere else, and even the worst of them it makes free from the incredible fatuities and absurdities of the worst. Then the sense of conduct they share with their countrymen at large. In no class has it such trials to undergo; in none is it more often and more grievously overborne. But really the right comment on this is the comment of Pepys upon the evil courses of Charles the Second and the Duke of York and the court of that day: 'At all which I am sorry; but it is the effect of idleness and having nothing else to employ their great spirits upon.'

Heaven forbid that I should speak in dispraise of that unique and most English class which Mr. Charles Sumner extols—the large class of gentlemen, not of the landed class or of the nobility, but cultivated and refined. They are a seemly product of the energy and of the power to rise in our race. Without, in general, rank and splendour and wealth and luxury to polish them, they have made their own the high standard of life and manners of an aristocratic and refined class. Not having all the dissipations and distractions of this class, they are much more seriously alive to the power of intellect and knowledge, to the power of beauty. The sense of conduct, too, meets with fewer trials in this class. To some extent, however, their contiguousness to the aristocratic class has now the effect of materialising them, as it does the class of newly enriched people. The most palpable action is on the young amongst them, and on their standard of life and enjoyment. But in general, for this whole class, established facts, the materialism which they see regnant, too much block their mental horizon, and limit the possibilities of things to them. They are deficient in openness and flexibility of mind, in free play of ideas, in faith and ardour. Civilised they are, but they are not much of a civilising force; they are somehow bounded and ineffective.

So on the middle class they produce singularly little effect. What the middle class sees is that splendid piece of materialism, the aristocratic class, with a wealth and luxury utterly out of their reach, with a standard of social life and manners, the offspring of that wealth and luxury, seeming utterly out of their reach also. And thus they are thrown back upon themselves—upon a defective type of religion, a narrow range of intellect and knowledge, a stunted sense of beauty, a low standard of manners. And the lower class see before them the aristocratic class, and its civilisation, such as it is, even infinitely more out of *their* reach than out of that of the middle class; while the life of the middle class, with its unlovely types of religion, thought, beauty, and manners, has naturally, in general, no great attractions for them either. And so they too are thrown back upon themselves; upon their beer, their gin, and their *fun*. Now, then, you will understand what I meant by saying that our inequality materialises our upper class, vulgarises our middle class, brutalises our lower.

And the greater the inequality the more marked is its bad action upon the middle and lower classes. In Scotland the landed aristocracy fills the scene, as is well known, still more than in England; the other classes are more squeezed back and effaced. And the social civilisation of the lower middle class and of the poorest class, in Scotland, is an example of the consequences. Compared with the same class even in England, the Scottish lower middle class is most visibly, to vary Mr. Charles Sumner's phrase, *less* well-bred, *less* careful in personal habits and in social conventions, *less* refined. Let any one who doubts it go, after issuing from the aristocratic solitudes which possess Loch Lomond, let him go and observe the shopkeepers and the middle class in Dumbarton, and Greenock, and Gourock, and the places along the mouth of the Clyde. And for the poorest class, who that has seen it can ever forget the hardly human horror, the abjection and uncivilisedness of Glasgow?

What a strange religion, then, is our religion of inequality! Romance often helps a religion to hold its ground, and romance is good in its way; but ours is not even a romantic religion. No doubt our aristocracy is an object of very strong public interest. The *Times* itself bestows a leading article by way of epithalamium on the Duke of Norfolk's marriage. And those journals of a new type, full of talent, and which interest me particularly because they seem as if they were written by the young lion of our youth,—the young lion grown mellow and, as the French say, *viveur*, arrived at his full and ripe knowledge of the world, and minded to enjoy the smooth evenings of his days,—those journals, in the main a sort of social gazette of the aristocracy, are apparently not read by that class only which they most concern, but are read with great avidity by other classes also. And the common people too have undoubtedly, as Mr. Gladstone says, a wonderful preference for a lord. Yet our aristocracy, from the action upon it of the Wars of the Roses, the Tudors, and the political necessities of George the Third, is for the imagination a singularly modern and uninteresting one. Its splendour of station, its wealth, show, and luxury, is then what the other classes really admire in it; and this is not an elevating admiration. Such an admiration will never lift us out of our vulgarity and brutality, if we chance to be vulgar and brutal to start with; it will rather feed them and be fed by them. So that when Mr. Gladstone invites us to call our love of inequality 'the complement of the love of freedom or its negative pole, or the shadow which the love of freedom casts, or the reverberation of its voice in the halls of the constitution', we must surely answer that all this mystical eloquence is not in the least necessary to explain so simple a matter; that our love of inequality is really the vulgarity in us, and the brutality, admiring and worshipping the splendid materiality.

Our present social organisation, however, will and must endure until our middle class is provided with some better ideal of life than it has now. Our present organisation has been an appointed stage in our growth; it has been of good use, and has enabled us to do great things. But the use is at an end, and the stage is over. Ask yourselves if you do not sometimes feel in yourselves a sense, that in spite of the strenuous efforts for good of so many excellent persons amongst us, we begin somehow to flounder and to beat the air; that we seem to be finding ourselves stopped on this line of advance and on that, and to be threatened with a sort of standstill. It is that we are trying to live on with a social organisation of which the day is over. Certainly equality will never of itself alone give us a perfect civilisation. But, with such inequality as ours, a perfect civilisation is impossible.

To that conclusion, facts, and the stream itself of this

discourse, do seem, I think, to carry us irresistibly. We arrive at it because they so choose, not because we so choose. Our tendencies are all the other way. We are all of us politicians, and in one of two camps, the Liberal or the Conservative. Liberals tend to accept the middle class as it is, and to praise the nonconformists; while Conservatives tend to accept the upper class as it is, and to praise the aristocracy. And yet here we are at the conclusion, that whereas one of the great obstacles to our civilisation is, as I have often said, British nonconformity, another main obstacle to our civilisation is British aristocracy! And this while we are yet forced to recognise excellent special qualities as well as the general English energy and honesty, and a number of emergent humane individuals, in both nonconformists and aristocracy. Clearly such a conclusion can be none of our own seeking.

Then again, to remedy our inequality, there must be a change in the law of bequest, as there has been in France; and the faults and inconveniences of the present French law of bequest are obvious. It tends to over-divide property; it is unequal in operation, and can be eluded by people limiting their families; it makes the children, however ill they may behave, independent of the parent. To be sure, Mr. Mill and others have shown that a law of bequest fixing the maximum, whether of land or money, which any one individual may take by bequest or inheritance, but in other respects leaving the testator quite free, has none of the inconveniences of the French law, and is in every way preferable. But evidently these are not questions of practical politics. Just imagine Lord Hartington going down to Glasgow, and meeting his Scotch Liberals there, and saying to them: 'You are ill at ease, and you are calling for change, and very justly. But the cause of your being ill at ease is not what you suppose. The cause of your being ill at ease is the profound imperfectness of your social civilisation. Your social civilisation is indeed such as I forbear to characterise. But the remedy is not disestablishment. The remedy is social equality. Let me direct your attention to a reform in the law of bequest and entail.' One can hardly speak of such a thing without laughing. No, the matter is at present one for the thoughts of those who think. It is a thing to be turned over in the minds of those who, on the one hand, have the spirit of scientific inquirers, bent on seeing things as they really are; and, on the other hand, the spirit of friends of the humane life, lovers of perfection. To your thoughts I commit it. And perhaps, the more you think of it, the more you will be persuaded that Menander showed his wisdom quite as much when he said *Choose equality*, as when he assured us that *Evil communications corrupt good manners*.

LITERATURE AND SCIENCE

(1882)

PRACTICAL people talk with a smile of Plato and of his absolute ideas; and it is impossible to deny that Plato's ideas do often seem unpractical and impracticable, and especially when one views them in connexion with the life of a great work-a-day world like the United States. The necessary staple of the life of such a world Plato regards with disdain; handicraft and trade and the working professions he regards with disdain; but what becomes of the life of an industrial modern community if you take handicraft and trade and the working professions out of it? The base mechanic arts and handicrafts, says Plato, bring about a natural weakness in the principle of excellence in a man, so that he cannot govern the ignoble growths in him, but nurses them, and cannot understand fostering any other. Those who exercise such arts and trades, as they have their bodies, he says, marred by their vulgar businesses, so they have their souls, too, bowed and broken by them. And if one of these uncomely people has a mind to seek self-culture and philosophy, Plato compares him to a bald little tinker, who has scraped together money, and has got his release from service, and has had a bath, and bought a new coat, and is rigged out like a bridegroom about to marry the daughter of his master who has fallen into poor and helpless estate.

Nor do the working professions fare any better than trade at the hands of Plato. He draws for us an inimitable picture of the working lawyer, and of his life of bondage;

he shows how this bondage from his youth up has stunted and warped him, and made him small and crooked of soul, encompassing him with difficulties which he is not man enough to rely on justice and truth as means to encounter, but has recourse, for help out of them, to falsehood and wrong. And so, says Plato, this poor creature is bent and broken, and grows up from boy to man without a particle of soundness in him, although exceedingly smart and clever in his own esteem.

One cannot refuse to admire the artist who draws these pictures. But we say to ourselves that his ideas show the influence of a primitive and obsolete order of things, when the warrior caste and the priestly caste were alone in honour, and the humble work of the world was done by slaves. We have now changed all that; the modern majority consists in work, as Emerson declares; and in work, we may add, principally of such plain and dusty kind as the work of cultivators of the ground, handicraftsmen, men of trade and business, men of the working professions. Above all is this true in a great industrious community such as that of the United States.

Now education, many people go on to say, is still mainly governed by the ideas of men like Plato, who lived when the warrior caste and the priestly or philosophical class were alone in honour, and the really useful part of the community were slaves. It is an education fitted for persons of leisure in such a community. This education passed from Greece and Rome to the feudal communities of Europe, where also the warrior caste and the priestly caste were alone held in honour, and where the really useful and working part of the community, though not nominally slaves as in the pagan world, were practically not much better off than slaves, and not more seriously regarded. And how absurd it is, people end by saying, to inflict this education upon an industrious modern community, where very few indeed are persons of leisure, and the mass to be considered has not leisure, but is bound, for its own great good, and for the great good of the world at large, to plain labour and to industrial pursuits, and the education in question tends necessarily to make men dissatisfied with these pursuits and unfitted for them!

That is what is said. So far I must defend Plato, as to plead that his view of education and studies is in the general, as it seems to me, sound enough, and fitted for all sorts and conditions of men, whatever their pursuits may be. 'An intelligent man', says Plato, 'will prize those studies which result in his soul getting soberness, righteousness, and wisdom, and will less value the others.' I cannot consider *that* a bad description of the aim of education, and of the motives which should govern us in the choice of studies, whether we are preparing ourselves for a hereditary seat in the English House of Lords or for the pork trade in Chicago.

Still I admit that Plato's world was not ours, that his scorn of trade and handicraft is fantastic, that he had no conception of a great industrial community such as that of the United States, and that such a community must and will shape its education to suit its own needs. If the usual education handed down to it from the past does not suit it, it will certainly before long drop this and try another. The usual education in the past has been mainly literary. The question is whether the studies which were long supposed to be the best for all of us are practically the best now; whether others are not better. The tyranny of the past, many think, weighs on us injuriously in the predominance given to letters in education. The question is raised whether, to meet the needs of our modern life, the predominance ought not now to pass from letters to science; and naturally the question is nowhere raised with more energy than here in the United States. The design of abasing what is called 'mere literary instruction and education', and of exalting what is called 'sound, extensive, and practical scientific knowledge', is, in this intensely modern world of the United States, even more perhaps than in Europe, a very popular design, and makes great and rapid progress.

I am going to ask whether the present movement for ousting letters from their old predominance in education, and for transferring the predominance in education to the natural sciences, whether this brisk and flourishing movement ought to prevail, and whether it is likely that in the end it really will prevail. An objection may be raised which I will anticipate. My own studies have been almost wholly in letters, and my visits to the field of the natural sciences have been very slight and inadequate, although those sciences have always strongly moved my curiosity. A man of letters, it will perhaps be said, is not competent to discuss the comparative merits of letters and natural science as means of education. To this objection I reply, first of all, that his incompetence, if he attempts the discussion but is really incompetent for it, will be abundantly visible; nobody will be taken in; he will have plenty of sharp observers and critics to save mankind from that danger. But the line I am going to follow is, as you will soon discover, so extremely simple, that perhaps it may be followed without failure even by one who for a more ambitious line of discussion would be quite incompetent.

Some of you may possibly remember a phrase of mine which has been the object of a good deal of comment; an observation to the effect that in our culture, the aim being *to know ourselves and the world*, we have, as the means to this end, *to know the best which has been thought and said in the world*. A man of science, who is also an excellent writer and the very prince of debaters, Professor Huxley, in a discourse at the opening of Sir Josiah Mason's college at Birmingham, laying hold of this phrase, expanded it by quoting some more words of mine, which are these:

The civilised world is to be regarded as now being, for intellectual and spiritual purposes, one great confederation, bound to a joint action and working to a common result; and whose members have for their proper outfit a knowledge of Greek, Roman, and Eastern antiquity, and of one another. Special local and temporary advantages being put out of account, that modern nation will in the intellectual and spiritual sphere make most progress, which most thoroughly carries out this programme.

Now on my phrase, thus enlarged, Professor Huxley remarks that when I speak of the above-mentioned knowledge as enabling us to know ourselves and the world, I assert *literature* to contain the materials which suffice for thus making us know ourselves and the world. But it is not by any means clear, says he, that after having learnt all which ancient and modern literatures have to tell us, we have laid a sufficiently broad and deep foundation for that criticism of life, that knowledge of ourselves and the world, which constitutes culture. On the contrary, Professor Huxley declares that he finds himself

wholly unable to admit that either nations or individuals will really advance, if their outfit draws nothing from the stores of physical science. An army without weapons of precision, and with no particular base of operations, might more hopefully enter upon a campaign on the Rhine, than a man, devoid of a knowledge of what physical science has done in the last century, upon a criticism of life.

This shows how needful it is for those who are to discuss any matter together, to have a common understanding as to the sense of the terms they employ,—how needful, and how difficult. What Professor Huxley says, implies just the reproach which is so often brought against the study of *belles lettres*, as they are called: that the study is an elegant one, but slight and ineffectual; a smattering of Greek and Latin and other ornamental things, of little use for any one whose object is to get at truth, and to be a practical man. So, too, M. Renan talks of the 'superficial humanism' of a school-course which treats us as if we were all going to be poets, writers, preachers, orators, and he opposes this humanism to positive science, or the critical search after truth. And there is always a tendency in those who are remonstrating against the predominance of letters in education, to understand by letters *belles lettres*, and by *belles lettres* a superficial humanism, the opposite of science or true knowledge.

But when we talk of knowing Greek and Roman antiquity, for instance, which is the knowledge people have called the humanities, I for my part mean a knowledge which is something more than a superficial humanism, mainly decorative. 'I call all teaching *scientific*', says Wolf, the critic of Homer, 'which is systematically laid out and followed up to its original sources. For example: a knowledge of classical antiquity is scientific when the remains of classical antiquity are correctly studied in the original languages.' There can be no doubt that Wolf is perfectly right; that all learning is scientific which is systematically laid out and followed up to its original sources, and that a genuine humanism is scientific.

When I speak of knowing Greek and Roman antiquity, therefore, as a help to knowing ourselves and the world, I mean more than a knowledge of so much vocabulary, so much grammar, so many portions of authors in the Greek and Latin languages. I mean knowing the Greeks and Romans, and their life and genius, and what they were and did in the world; what we get from them, and what is its value. That, at least, is the ideal; and when we talk of endeavouring to know Greek and Roman antiquity, as a help to knowing ourselves and the world, we mean endeavouring so to know them as to satisfy this ideal, however much we may still fall short of it.

The same also as to knowing our own and other modern nations, with the like aim of getting to understand ourselves and the world. To know the best that has been thought and said by the modern nations, is to know, says Professor Huxley, 'only what modern *literatures* have to tell us; it is the criticism of life contained in modern literature'. And yet 'the distinctive character of our times', he urges, 'lies in the vast and constantly increasing part which is played by natural knowledge'. And how, therefore, can a man, devoid of knowledge of what physical science has done in the last century, enter hopefully upon a criticism of modern life?

Let us, I say, be agreed about the meaning of the terms we are using. I talk of knowing the best which has been thought and uttered in the world; Professor Huxley says this means knowing *literature*. Literature is a large word; it may mean everything written with letters or printed in a book. Euclid's *Elements* and Newton's *Principia* are thus literature. All knowledge that reaches us through books is literature. But by literature Professor Huxley means *belles lettres*. He means to make me say, that knowing the best which has been thought and said by the modern nations is knowing their *belles lettres* and no more. And this is no sufficient equipment, he argues, for a criticism of modern life. But as I do not mean, by knowing ancient Rome, knowing merely more or less of Latin *belles lettres*, and taking no account of Rome's military, and political, and legal, and administrative work in the world; and as, by knowing ancient Greece, I understand knowing her as the giver of Greek art, and the guide to a free and right use of reason and to scientific method, and the founder of our mathematics and physics and astronomy and biology,—I understand knowing her as all this, and not merely knowing certain Greek poems, and histories, and treatises, and speeches,—so as to the knowledge of modern nations also. By knowing modern nations, I mean not merely knowing their *belles lettres*, but knowing also what has been done by such men as Copernicus, Galileo, Newton, Darwin. 'Our ancestors learned', says Professor Huxley, 'that the earth is the centre of the visible universe, and that man is the cynosure of things terrestrial; and more especially was it inculcated that the course of nature had no fixed order, but that it could be, and constantly was, altered.' But for us now, continues Professor Huxley, 'the notions of the beginning and the end of the world entertained by our forefathers are no longer credible. It is very certain that the earth is not the chief body in the material universe, and that the world is not subordinated to man's use. It is even more certain that nature is the expression of a definite order, with which nothing interferes.' 'And yet', he cries, 'the purely classical education advocated by the representatives of the humanists in our day gives no inkling of all this!'

In due place and time I will just touch upon that vexed question of classical education; but at present the question is as to what is meant by knowing the best which modern nations have thought and said. It is not knowing their *belles lettres* merely which is meant. To know Italian *belles lettres* is not to know Italy, and to know English *belles lettres* is not to know England. Into knowing Italy and England there comes a great deal more, Galileo and Newton, amongst it. The reproach of being a superficial humanism, a tincture of *belles lettres*, may attach rightly enough to some other disciplines; but to the particular discipline recommended when I proposed knowing the best that has been thought and said in the world, it does not apply. In that best I certainly include what in modern times has been thought and said by the great observers and knowers of nature.

There is, therefore, really no question between Professor Huxley and me as to whether knowing the great results of the modern scientific study of nature is not required as a part of our culture, as well as knowing the products of literature and art. But to follow the processes by which those results are reached, ought, say the friends of physical science, to be made the staple of education for the bulk of mankind. And here there does arise a question between those whom Professor Huxley calls with playful sarcasm 'the Levites of culture', and those whom the poor humanist is sometimes apt to regard as its Nebuchadnezzars.

The great results of the scientific investigation of nature we are agreed upon knowing, but how much of our study are we bound to give to the processes by which those results are reached? The results have their visible bearing on human life. But all the processes, too, all the items of fact, by which those results are reached and established, are interesting. All knowledge is interesting to a wise man, and the knowledge of nature is interesting to all men. It is very interesting to know, that, from the albuminous white of the egg, the chick in the egg gets the materials for its flesh, bones, blood, and feathers; while, from the fatty yolk of the egg, it gets the heat and energy which enable it at length to break its shell and begin the world. It is less interesting, perhaps, but still it is interesting to know that when a taper burns, the wax is converted into carbonic acid and water. Moreover, it is quite true that the habit of dealing with facts, which is given by the study of nature, is, as the friends of physical science praise it for being, an excellent discipline. The appeal, in the study of nature, is constantly to observation and experiment; not only is it said that the thing is so, but we can be made to see that it is so. Not only does a man tell us that when a taper burns the wax is converted into carbonic acid and water, as a man may tell us, if he likes, that Charon is punting his ferry-boat on the river Styx, or that Victor Hugo is a sublime poet, or Mr. Gladstone the most admirable of statesmen; but we are made to see that the conversion into carbonic acid and water does actually happen. This reality of natural knowledge it is, which makes the friends of physical science contrast it, as a knowledge of things, with the humanist's knowledge, which is, say they, a knowledge of words. And hence Professor Huxley is moved to lay it down that, 'for the purpose of attaining real culture, an exclusively scientific education is at least as effectual as an exclusively literary education'. And a certain President of the Section for Mechanical Science in the British Association is, in Scripture phrase, 'very bold', and declares that if a man, in his mental training, 'has substituted literature and history and natural science, he has chosen the less useful alternative'. But whether we go these lengths or not, we must all admit that in natural science the habit gained of dealing with facts is a most valuable discipline, and that every one should have some experience of it.

More than this, however, is demanded by the reformers. It is proposed to make the training in natural science the main part of education, for the great majority of mankind at any rate. And here, I confess, I part company with the friends of physical science, with whom up to this point I have been agreeing. In differing from them, however, I wish to proceed with the utmost caution and diffidence. The smallness of my own acquaintance with the disciplines of natural science is ever before my mind, and I am fearful of doing these disciplines an injustice. The ability and pugnacity of the partisans of natural science makes them formidable persons to contradict. The tone of tentative inquiry, which befits a being of dim faculties and bounded knowledge, is the tone I would wish to take and not to depart from. At present it seems to me, that those who are for giving to natural knowledge, as they call it, the chief place in the education of the majority of mankind, leave one important thing out of their account: the constitution of human nature. But I put this forward on the strength of some facts not at all recondite, very far from it; facts capable of being stated in the simplest possible fashion, and to which, if I so state them, the man of science will, I am sure, be willing to allow their due weight.

Deny the facts altogether, I think, he hardly can. He can hardly deny, that when we set ourselves to enumerate the powers which go to the building up of human life, and say that they are the power of conduct, the power of intellect and knowledge, the power of beauty, and the power of social life and manners,—he can hardly deny that this scheme, though drawn in rough and plain lines enough, and not pretending to scientific exactness, does yet give a fairly true representation of the matter. Human nature is built up by these powers; we have the need for them all. When we have rightly met and adjusted the claims of them all, we shall then be in a fair way for getting soberness and righteousness, with wisdom. This is evident enough, and the friends of physical science would admit it.

But perhaps they may not have sufficiently observed another thing: namely, that the several powers just mentioned are not isolated, but there is, in the generality of mankind, a perpetual tendency to relate them one to another in divers ways. With one such way of relating them I am particularly concerned now. Following our instinct for intellect and knowledge, we acquire pieces of knowledge; and presently, in the generality of men, there arises the desire to relate these pieces of knowledge to our sense for conduct, to our sense for beauty,—and there is weariness and dissatisfaction if the desire is baulked. Now in this desire lies, I think, the strength of that hold which letters have upon us.

All knowledge is, as I said just now, interesting; and even items of knowledge which from the nature of the case cannot well be related, but must stand isolated in our thoughts, have their interest. Even lists of exceptions have their interest. If we are studying Greek accents, it is interesting to know that *pais* and *pas*, and some other monosyllables of the same form of declension, do not take the circumflex upon the last syllable of the genitive plural, but vary, in this respect, from the common rule. If we are studying physiology, it is interesting to know that the pulmonary artery carries dark blood and the pulmonary vein carries bright blood, departing in this respect from the common rule for the division of labour between the veins and the arteries. But every one knows how we seek naturally to combine the pieces of our knowledge together, to bring them under general rules, to relate them to principles; and how unsatisfactory and tiresome it would be to go for ever learning lists of exceptions, or accumulating items of fact which must stand isolated.

Well, that same need of relating our knowledge, which operates here within the sphere of our knowledge itself, we shall find operating, also, outside that sphere. We experience, as we go on learning and knowing,—the vast majority of us experience,—the need of relating what we have learnt and known to the sense which we have in us for conduct, to the sense which we have in us for beauty.

A certain Greek prophetess of Mantineia in Arcadia, Diotima by name, once explained to the philosopher Socrates that love, and impulse and bent of all kinds, is, in fact, nothing else but the desire in men that good should for ever be present to them. This desire for good, Diotima assured Socrates, is our fundamental desire, of which fundamental desire every impulse in us is only some one particular form. And therefore this fundamental desire it is, I suppose,—this desire in men that good should be for ever present to them,—which acts in us when we feel the impulse for relating our knowledge to our sense for conduct and to our sense for beauty. At any rate, with men in general the instinct exists. Such is human nature. And the instinct, it will be admitted, is innocent, and human nature is preserved by our following the lead of its innocent instincts. Therefore, in seeking to gratify this instinct in question, we are following the instinct of self-preservation in humanity.

But, no doubt, some kinds of knowledge cannot be made to directly serve the instinct in question, cannot be

directly related to the sense for beauty, to the sense for
conduct. These are instrument-knowledges; they lead on
to other knowledges, which can. A man who passes his
life in instrument-knowledges is a specialist. They may
be invaluable as instruments to something beyond, for
those who have the gift thus to employ them; and they
may be disciplines in themselves wherein it is useful for
every one to have some schooling. But it is inconceivable
that the generality of men should pass all their mental
life with Greek accents or with formal logic. My friend
Professor Sylvester, who is one of the first mathematicians
in the world, holds transcendental doctrines as to the
virtue of mathematics, but those doctrines are not for
common men. In the very Senate House and heart of our
English Cambridge I once ventured, though not without
an apology for my profaneness, to hazard the opinion
that for the majority of mankind a little of mathematics,
even, goes a long way. Of course this is quite consistent
with their being of immense importance as an instrument
to something else; but it is the few who have the aptitude
for thus using them, not the bulk of mankind.

The natural sciences do not, however, stand on the
same footing with these instrument-knowledges. Experience shows us that the generality of men will find more
interest in learning that, when a taper burns, the wax is
converted into carbonic acid and water, or in learning
the explanation of the phenomenon of dew, or in learning
how the circulation of the blood is carried on, than they
find in learning that the genitive plural of *pais* and *pas*
does not take the circumflex on the termination. And one
piece of natural knowledge is added to another, and
others are added to that, and at last we come to propositions so interesting as Mr. Darwin's famous proposition
that 'our ancestor was a hairy quadruped furnished with

a tail and pointed ears, probably arboreal in his habits'. Or we come to propositions of such reach and magnitude as those which Professor Huxley delivers, when he says that the notions of our forefathers about the beginning and end of the world were all wrong, and that nature is the expression of a definite order with which nothing interferes.

Interesting, indeed, these results of science are, important they are, and we should all of us be acquainted with them. But what I now wish you to mark is, that we are still, when they are propounded to us and we receive them, we are still in the sphere of intellect and knowledge. And for the generality of men there will be found, I say, to arise, when they have duly taken in the proposition that their ancestor was 'a hairy quadruped furnished with a tail and pointed ears, probably arboreal in his habits', there will be found to arise an invincible desire to relate this proposition to the sense in us for conduct, and to the sense in us for beauty. But this the men of science will not do for us, and will hardly even profess to do. They will give us other pieces of knowledge, other facts, about other animals and their ancestors, or about plants, or about stones, or about stars; and they may finally bring us to those great 'general conceptions of the universe, which are forced upon us all', says Professor Huxley, 'by the progress of physical science'. But still it will be *knowledge* only which they give us; knowledge not put for us into relation with our sense for conduct, our sense for beauty, and touched with emotion by being so put; not thus put for us, and therefore, to the majority of mankind, after a certain while, unsatisfying, wearying.

Not to the born naturalist, I admit. But what do we mean by a born naturalist? We mean a man in whom the zeal for observing nature is so uncommonly strong and eminent, that it marks him off from the bulk of mankind. Such a man will pass his life happily in collecting natural knowledge and reasoning upon it, and will ask for nothing or hardly anything, more. I have heard it said that the sagacious and admirable naturalist whom we lost not very long ago, Mr. Darwin, once owned to a friend that for his part he did not experience the necessity for two things which most men find so necessary to them, —religion and poetry; science and the domestic affections, he thought, were enough. To a born naturalist, I can well understand that this should seem so. So absorbing is his occupation with nature, so strong his love for his occupation, that he goes on acquiring natural knowledge and reasoning upon it, and has little time or inclination for thinking about getting it related to the desire in man for conduct, the desire in man for beauty. He relates it to them for himself as he goes along, so far as he feels the need; and he draws from the domestic affections all the additional solace necessary. But then Darwins are extremely rare. Another great and admirable master of natural knowledge, Faraday, was a Sandemanian. That is to say, he related his knowledge to his instinct for conduct and to his instinct for beauty, by the aid of that respectable Scottish sectary, Robert Sandeman. And so strong, in general, is the demand of religion and poetry to have their share in a man, to associate themselves with his knowing, and to relieve and rejoice it, that, probably for one man amongst us with the disposition to do as Darwin did in this respect, there are at least fifty with the disposition to do as Faraday.

Education lays hold upon us, in fact, by satisfying this demand. Professor Huxley holds up to scorn mediæval education, with its neglect of the knowledge of nature, its poverty even of literary studies, its formal logic devoted to 'showing how and why that which the Church said was true must be true'. But the great mediæval Universities were not brought into being, we may be sure, by the zeal for giving a jejune and contemptible education. Kings have been their nursing fathers, and queens have been their nursing mothers, but not for this. The mediæval Universities came into being, because the supposed knowledge, delivered by Scripture and the Church, so deeply engaged men's hearts, by so simply, easily, and powerfully relating itself to their desire for conduct, their desire for beauty. All other knowledge was dominated by this supposed knowledge and was subordinated to it, because of the surpassing strength of the hold which it gained upon the affections of men, by allying itself profoundly with their sense for conduct, their sense for beauty.

But now, says Professor Huxley, conceptions of the universe fatal to the notions held by our forefathers have been forced upon us by physical science. Grant to him that they are thus fatal, that the new conceptions must and will soon become current everywhere, and that every one will finally perceive them to be fatal to the beliefs of our forefathers. The need of humane letters, as they are truly called, because they serve the paramount desire in men that good should be for ever present to them, —the need of humane letters, to establish a relation between the new conceptions, and our instinct for beauty, our instinct for conduct, is only the more visible. The Middle Age could do without humane letters, as it could do without the study of nature, because its supposed knowledge was made to engage its emotions so powerfully. Grant that the supposed knowledge disappears, its power of being made to engage the emotions will of course disappear along with it,—but the emotions themselves, and their claim to be engaged and satisfied, will remain.

Now if we find by experience that humane letters have an undeniable power of engaging the motions, the importance of humane letters in a man's training becomes not less, but greater, in proportion to the success of modern science in extirpating what it calls 'mediæval thinking'.

Have humane letters, then, have poetry and eloquence, the power here attributed to them of engaging the emotions, and do they exercise it? And if they have it and exercise it, *how* do they exercise it, so as to exert an influence upon man's sense for conduct, his sense for beauty? Finally, even if they both can and do exert an influence upon the senses in question, how are they to relate to them the results,—the modern results,—of natural science? All these questions may be asked. First, have poetry and eloquence the power of calling out the emotions? The appeal is to experience. Experience shows that for the vast majority of men, for mankind in general, they have the power. Next do they exercise it? They do. But then, *how* do they exercise it so as to affect man's sense for conduct, his sense for beauty? And this is perhaps a case for applying the Preacher's words: 'Though a man labour to seek it out, yet he shall not find it; yea, farther, though a wise man think to know it, yet shall he not be able to find it.'[1] Why should it be one thing, in its effect upon the emotions, to say, 'Patience is a virtue,' and quite another thing, in its effect upon the emotions, to say with Homer,

τλητὸν γὰρ Μοῖραι θυμὸν θέσαν ἀνθρώποισιν—[2]

'for an enduring heart have the destinies appointed to the children of men?' Why should it be one thing, in its effect

---

[1] *Eccles.* viii. 17.   [2] *Iliad*, xxiv. 49.

upon the emotions, to say with the philosopher Spinoza, *Felicitas in eo consistit quod homo suum esse conservare potest*— 'Man's happiness consists in his being able to preserve his own essence,' and quite another thing, in its effect upon the emotions, to say with the Gospel, 'What is a man advantaged, if he gain the whole world, and lose himself, forfeit himself?' How does this difference of effect arise? I cannot tell, and I am not much concerned to know; the important thing is that it does arise, and that we can profit by it. But how, finally, are poetry and eloquence to exercise the power of relating the modern results of natural science to man's instinct for conduct, his instinct for beauty? And here again I answer that I do not know *how* they will exercise it, but that they can and will exercise it I am sure. I do not mean that modern philosophical poets and modern philosophical moralists are to come and relate for us, in express terms, the results of modern scientific research to our instinct for conduct, our instinct for beauty. But I mean that we shall find, as a matter of experience, if we know the best that has been thought and uttered in the world, we shall find that the art and poetry and eloquence of men who lived, perhaps, long ago, who had the most limited natural knowledge, who had the most erroneous conceptions about many important matters, we shall find that this art, and poetry, and eloquence, have in fact not only the power of refreshing and delighting us, they have also the power,—such is the strength and worth, in essentials, of their author's criticism of life,—they have a fortifying, and elevating, and quickening, and suggestive power, capable of wonderfully helping us to relate the results of modern science to our need for conduct, our need for beauty. Homer's conceptions of the physical universe were, I imagine, grotesque; but really, under the shock of hearing from modern science that 'the world is not subordinated to man's use, and that man is not the synosure of things terrestrial', I could, for my own part, desire no better comfort than Homer's line which I quoted just now,

τλητὸν γὰρ Μοῖραι θυμὸν θέσαν ἀνθρώποισιν—

'for an enduring heart have the destinies appointed to the children of men!'

And the more that men's minds are cleared, the more that the results of science are frankly accepted, the more that poetry and eloquence come to be received and studied as what in truth they really are,—the criticism of life by gifted men, alive and active with extraordinary power at an unusual number of points;—so much the more will the value of humane letters, and of art also, which is an utterance having a like kind of power with theirs, be felt and acknowledged, and their place in education be secured.

Let us therefore, all of us, avoid indeed as much as possible any invidious comparison between the merits of humane letters, as means of education, and the merits of the natural sciences. But when some President of a Section for Mechanical Science insists on making the comparison, and tells us that 'he who in his training has substituted literature and history for natural science has chosen the less useful alternative', let us make answer to him that the student of humane letters only, will, at least, know also the great general conceptions brought in by modern physical science; for science, as Professor Huxley says, forces them upon us all. But the student of the natural sciences only, will, by our very hypothesis, know nothing of humane letters; not to mention that in setting himself to be perpetually accumulating natural knowledge, he sets himself to do what only specialists have in general

the gift for doing genially. And so he will probably be
unsatisfied, or at any rate incomplete, and even
more incomplete than the student of humane letters
only.

I once mentioned in a school-report, how a young man
in one of our English training colleges having to paraphrase the passage in *Macbeth* beginning,

> Can'st thou not minister to a mind diseased?

turned this line into, 'Can you not wait upon the lunatic?'
And I remarked what a curious state of things it would
be, if every pupil of our national schools knew, let us say,
that the moon is two thousand one hundred and sixty
miles in diameter, and thought at the same time that a
good paraphrase for

> Can'st thou not minister to a mind diseased?

was, 'Can you not wait upon the lunatic?' If one is
driven to choose, I think I would rather have a young
person ignorant about the moon's diameter, but aware
that 'Can you not wait upon the lunatic?' is bad, than
a young person whose education had been such as to
manage things the other way.

Or to go higher than the pupils of our national schools.
I have in my mind's eye a member of our British Parliament who comes to travel here in America, who afterwards relates his travels, and who shows a really masterly
knowledge of the geology of this great country and of its
mining capabilities, but who ends by gravely suggesting
that the United States should borrow a prince from our
Royal Family, and should make him their king, and
should create a House of Lords of great landed proprietors
after the pattern of ours; and then America, he thinks,
would have her future happily and perfectly secured.

Surely, in this case, the President of the Section for Mechanical Science would himself hardly say that our member of Parliament, by concentrating himself upon geology and mineralogy, and so on, and not attending to literature and history, had 'chosen the more useful alternative'.

If then there is to be separation and option between humane letters on the one hand, and the natural sciences on the other, the great majority of mankind, all who have not exceptional and overpowering aptitudes for the study of nature, would do well, I cannot but think, to choose to be educated in humane letters rather than in the natural sciences. Letters will call out their being at more points, will make them live more.

I said that before I ended I would just touch on the question of classical education, and I will keep my word. Even if literature is to retain a large place in our education, yet Latin and Greek, say the friends of progress, will certainly have to go. Greek is the grand offender in the eyes of these gentlemen. The attackers of the established course of study think that against Greek, at any rate, they have irresistible arguments. Literature may perhaps be needed in education, they say; but why on earth should it be Greek literature? Why not French or German? Nay, 'has not an Englishman models in his own literature of every kind of excellence?' As before, it is not on any weak pleadings of my own that I rely for convincing the gainsayers; it is on the constitution of human nature itself, and on the instinct of self-preservation in humanity. The instinct for beauty is set in human nature, as surely as the instinct for knowledge is set there, or the instinct for conduct. If the instinct for beauty is served by Greek literature and art as it is served by no other literature and art, we may trust to the instinct of self-preservation in humanity for keeping Greek as part of our culture. We may trust to it for even making the study of Greek more prevalent than it is now. Greek will come, I hope, some day to be studied more rationally than at present; but it will be increasingly studied as men increasingly feel the need in them for beauty, and how powerfully Greek art and Greek literature can serve this need. Women will again study Greek, as Lady Jane Grey did; I believe that in that chain of forts, with which the fair host of the Amazons are now engirdling our English universities, I find that here in America, in colleges like Smith College in Massachusetts, and Vassar College in the State of New York, and in the happy families of the mixed universities out West, they are studying it already.

Defuit una mihi symmetria prisca,—'The antique symmetry was the one thing wanting to me', said Leonardo da Vinci; and he was an Italian. I will not presume to speak for the Americans, but I am sure that, in the Englishman, the want of this admirable symmetry of the Greeks is a thousand times more great and crying than in any Italian. The results of the want show themselves most glaringly, perhaps, in our architecture, but they show themselves, also, in all our art. *Fit details strictly combined, in view of a large general result nobly conceived*; that is just the beautiful *symmetria prisca* of the Greeks, and it is just where we English fail, where all our art fails. Striking ideas we have, and well-executed details we have; but that high symmetry which, with satisfying and delightful effects, combines them, we seldom or never have. The glorious beauty of the Acropolis at Athens did not come from single fine things stuck about on that hill, a statue here, a gateway there;—no, it arose from all things being perfectly combined for a supreme total effect. What must

not an Englishman feel about our deficiencies in this
respect, as the sense for beauty, whereof this symmetry is
an essential element, awakens and strengthens within
him! what will not one day be his respect and desire for
Greece and its *symmetria prisca*, when the scales drop from
his eyes as he walks the London streets, and he sees such
a lesson in meanness as the Strand, for instance, in its
true deformity! But here we are coming to our friend
Mr. Ruskin's province, and I will not intrude upon it,
for he is its very sufficient guardian.

And so we at last find, it seems, we find flowing in
favour of the humanities the natural and necessary
stream of things, which seemed against them when we
started. The 'hairy quadruped furnished with a tail and
pointed ears, probably arboreal in his habits,' this good
fellow carried hidden in his nature, apparently, something
destined to develop into a necessity for humane letters.
Nay, more; we seem finally to be even led to the further
conclusion that our hairy ancestor carried in his nature,
also, a necessity for Greek.

And therefore, to say the truth, I cannot really think
that humane letters are in much actual danger of being
thrust out from their leading place in education, in spite
of the array of authorities against them at this moment.
So long as human nature is what it is, their attractions
will remain irresistible. As with Greek, so with letters
generally: they will some day come, we may hope, to be
studied more rationally, but they will not lose their place.
What will happen will rather be that there will be crowded
into education other matters besides, far too many; there
will be, perhaps, a period of unsettlement and confusion
and false tendency; but letters will not in the end lose
their leading place. If they lose it for a time, they will get
it back again. We shall be brought back to them by our

wants and aspirations. And a poor humanist may possess his soul in patience, neither strive nor cry, admit the energy and brilliancy of the partisans of physical science, and their present favour with the public, to be far greater than his own, and still have a happy faith that the nature of things works silently on behalf of the studies which he loves, and that, while we shall all have to acquaint ourselves with the great results reached by modern science, and to give ourselves as much training in its disciplines as we can conveniently carry, yet the majority of men will always require humane letters; and so much the more, as they have the more and the greater results of science to relate to the need in man for conduct, and to the need in him for beauty.

CULTURE AND ANARCHY

(abridged)

(1869)

I. SWEETNESS AND LIGHT

THE disparagers of culture make its motive curiosity;
sometimes, indeed, they make its motive mere exclusive-
ness and vanity. The culture which is supposed to plume
itself on a smattering of Greek and Latin is a culture
which is begotten by nothing so intellectual as curiosity;
it is valued either out of sheer vanity and ignorance, or
else as an engine of social and class distinction, separating
its holder, like a badge or title, from other people who
have not got it. No serious man would call this *culture*,
or attach any value to it, as culture, at all. To find the
real ground for the very differing estimate which serious
people will set upon culture, we must find some motive
for culture in the terms of which may lie a real ambiguity;
and such a motive the word *curiosity* gives us.

I have before now pointed out that we English do not,
like the foreigners, use this word in a good sense as well as
in a bad sense. With us the word is always used in a
somewhat disapproving sense. A liberal and intelligent
eagerness about the things of the mind may be meant by
a foreigner when he speaks of curiosity, but with us the
word always conveys a certain notion of frivolous and
unedifying activity. In the *Quarterly Review*, some little
time ago, was an estimate of the celebrated French
critic, M. Sainte-Beuve, and a very inadequate estimate

it in my judgment was. And its inadequacy consisted chiefly in this: that in our English way it left out of sight the double sense really involved in the word *curiosity*, thinking enough was said to stamp M. Sainte-Beuve with blame if it was said that he was impelled in his operations as a critic by curiosity, and omitting either to perceive that M. Sainte-Beuve himself, and many other people with him, would consider that this was praiseworthy and not blameworthy, or to point out why it ought really to be accounted worthy of blame and not of praise. For as there is a curiosity about intellectual matters which is futile, and merely a disease, so there is certainly a curiosity,—a desire after the things of the mind simply for their own sakes and for the pleasure of seeing them as they are,—which is, in an intelligent being, natural and laudable. Nay, and the very desire to see things as they are, implies a balance and regulation of minds which is not often attained without fruitful effort, and which is the very opposite of the blind and diseased impulse of mind which is what we mean to blame when we blame curiosity. Montesquieu says: 'The first motive which ought to impel us to study is the desire to augment the excellence of our nature, and to render an intelligent being yet more intelligent'. This is the true ground to assign for the genuine scientific passion, however manifested, and for culture, viewed simply as a fruit of passion; and it is a worthy ground, even though we let the term *curiosity* stand to describe it.

But there is of culture another view, in which not solely the scientific passion, the sheer desire to see things as they are, natural and proper in an intelligent being, appears as the ground of it. There is a view in which all the love of our neighbour, the impulses towards action, help, and beneficence, the desire for removing human error, clearing human confusion, and diminishing human misery, the noble aspiration to leave the world better and happier than we found it,—motives eminently such as are called social,—come in as part of the grounds of culture, and the main and pre-eminent part. Culture is then properly described not as having its origin in curiosity, but as having its origin in the love of perfection; it is *a study of perfection.* It moves by the force, not merely or primarily of the scientific passion for pure knowledge, but also of the moral and social passion for doing good. As, in the first view of it, we took for its worthy motto Montesquieu's words: 'To render an intelligent being yet more intelligent!' so, in the second view of it, there is no better motto which it can have than these words of Bishop Wilson: 'To make reason and the will of God prevail!'

Only, whereas the passion for doing good is apt to be overhasty in determining what reason and the will of God say, because its turn is for acting rather than thinking, and it wants to be beginning to act; and whereas it is apt to take its own conceptions, which proceed from its own state of development and share in all the imperfections and immaturities of this, for a basis of action; what distinguishes culture is, that it is possessed by the scientific passion as well as by the passion of doing good; that it demands worthy notions of reason and the will of God, and does not readily suffer its own crude conceptions to substitute themselves for them. And knowing that no action or institution can be salutary and stable which is not based on reason and the will of God, it is not so bent on acting and instituting, even with the great aim of diminishing human error and misery ever before its thoughts, but that it can remember that acting and instituting are of little use, unless we know how and what we ought to act and to institute.

This culture is more interesting and more far-reaching than that other, which is founded solely on the scientific passion for knowing. But it needs times of faith and ardour, times when the intellectual horizon is opening and widening all round us, to flourish in. And is not the close and bounded intellectual horizon within which we have long lived and moved now lifting up, and are not new lights finding free passage to shine in upon us? For a long time there was no passage for them to make their way in upon us, and then it was of no use to think of adapting the world's action to them. Where was the hope of making reason and the will of God prevail among people who had a routine which they had christened reason and the will of God, in which they were inextricably bound, and beyond which they had no power of looking? But now the iron force of adhesion to the old routine,—social, political, religious,—has wonderfully yielded; the iron force of exclusion of all which is new has wonderfully yielded. The danger now is, not that people should obstinately refuse to allow anything but their old routine to pass for reason and the will of God, but either that they should allow some novelty or other to pass for these too easily, or else that they should underrate the importance of them altogether, and think it enough to follow action for its own sake, without troubling themselves to make reason and the will of God prevail therein. Now, then, is the moment for culture to be of service, culture which believes in making reason and the will of God prevail, believes in perfection, is the study and pursuit of perfection, and is no longer debarred, by a rigid invincible exclusion of whatever is new, from getting acceptance for its ideas, simply because they are new.

The moment this view of culture is seized, the moment it is regarded not solely as the endeavour to see things as they are, to draw towards a knowledge of the universal order which seems to be intended and aimed at in the world, and which it is a man's happiness to go along with or his misery to go counter to,—to learn, in short, the will of God,—the moment, I say, culture is considered not merely as the endeavour to *see* and *learn* this, but as the endeavour, also, to make it *prevail*, the moral, social, and beneficent character of culture becomes manifest. The mere endeavour to see and learn the truth for our own personal satisfaction is indeed a commencement for making it prevail, a preparing the way for this, which always serves this, and is wrongly, therefore, stamped with blame absolutely in itself and not only in its caricature and degeneration. But perhaps it has got stamped with blame, and disparaged with the dubious title of curiosity, because in comparison with this wider endeavour of such great and plain utility it looks selfish, petty, and unprofitable.

And religion, the greatest and most important of the efforts by which the human race has manifested its impulse to perfect itself,—religion, that voice of the deepest human experience,—does not only enjoin and sanction the aim which is the great aim of culture, the aim of setting ourselves to ascertain what perfection is and to make it prevail; but also, in determining generally in what human perfection consists, religion comes to a conclusion identical with that which culture,—culture seeking the determination of this question through *all* the voices of human experience which have been heard upon it, of art, science, poetry, philosophy, history, as well as of religion, in order to give a greater fulness and certainty to its solution,— likewise reaches. Religion says: *The kingdom of God is within you*; and culture, in like manner, places human perfection in an *internal* condition, in the growth and predominance of our humanity proper, as distinguished from our animality. It places it in the ever-increasing efficacy and in the general harmonious expansion of those gifts of thought and feeling which make the peculiar dignity, wealth, and happiness of human nature. As I have said on a former occasion: 'It is in making endless additions to itself, in the endless expansion of its powers, in endless growth in wisdom and beauty, that the spirit of the human race finds its ideal. To reach this ideal, culture is an indispensable aid, and that is the true value of culture.' Not a having and a resting, but a growing and a becoming, is the character of perfection as culture conceives it; and here, too, it coincides with religion.

And because men are all members of one great whole, and the sympathy which is in human nature will not allow one member to be indifferent to the rest or to have a perfect welfare independent of the rest, the expansion of our humanity, to suit the idea of perfection which culture forms, must be a *general* expansion. Perfection, as culture conceives it, is not possible while the individual remains isolated. The individual is required, under pain of being stunted and enfeebled in his own development if he disobeys, to carry others along with him in his march towards perfection, to be continually doing all he can to enlarge and increase the volume of the human stream sweeping thitherward. And here, once more, culture lays on us the same obligation as religion, which says, as Bishop Wilson has admirably put it, that 'to promote the kingdom of God is to increase and hasten one's own happiness'.

But, finally, perfection,—as culture, from a thorough disinterested study of human nature and human experience learns to conceive it,—is a harmonious expansion of *all* the powers which make the beauty and worth of human nature, and is not consistent with the over-development of any one power at the expense of the rest. Here culture goes beyond religion, as religion is generally conceived by us.

If culture, then, is a study of perfection, and of harmonious perfection, general perfection, and perfection which consists in becoming something rather than in having something, in an inward condition of the mind and spirit, not in an outward set of circumstances,—it is clear that culture, instead of being the frivolous and useless thing which Mr. Bright, and Mr. Frederic Harrison, and many other Liberals are apt to call it, has a very important function to fulfil for mankind. And this function is particularly important in our modern world, of which the whole civilisation is, to a much greater degree than the civilisation of Greece and Rome, mechanical and external, and tends constantly to become more so. But above all in our own country has culture a weighty part to perform, because here that mechanical character, which civilisation tends to take everywhere, is shown in the most eminent degree. Indeed nearly all the characters of perfection, as culture teaches us to fix them, meet in this country with some powerful tendency which thwarts them and sets them at defiance. The idea of perfection as an *inward* condition of the mind and spirit is at variance with the mechanical and material civilisation in esteem with us, and nowhere, as I have said, so much in esteem as with us. The idea of perfection as a *general* expansion of the human family is at variance with our strong individualism, our hatred of all limits to the unrestrained swing of the individual's personality, our maxim of 'every man for himself'. Above all the idea of perfection as a *harmonious* expansion of human nature is at variance with our want of flexibility, with our inaptitude for seeing more than one side of a thing, with our intense energetic absorption in the particular pursuit we happen to be following. So culture has a rough task to achieve in this country. Its preachers have, and are likely long to have, a hard time of it, and they will much oftener be regarded, for a great while to come, as elegant or spurious Jeremiahs, than as friends and benefactors. That, however, will not prevent their doing in the end good service if they persevere. And meanwhile, the mode of action they have to pursue, and the sort of habits they must fight against, ought to be made quite clear for every one to see who may be willing to look at the matter attentively and dispassionately.

Faith in machinery is, I said, our besetting danger; often in machinery most absurdly disproportioned to the end which this machinery, if it is to do any good at all, is to serve; but always in machinery, as if it had a value in and for itself. What is freedom but machinery? what is population but machinery? what is coal but machinery? what are railroads but machinery? what is wealth but machinery? what are, even, religious organisations but machinery? Now almost every voice in England is accustomed to speak of these things as if they were precious ends in themselves, and therefore had some of the characters of perfection indisputably joined to them. I have before now noticed Mr. Roebuck's stock argument for proving the greatness and happiness of England as she is and for quite stopping the mouths of all gainsayers. Mr. Roebuck is never weary of reiterating this argument of his, so I do not know why I should be weary of noticing it. 'May not every man in England say what he likes?'— Mr. Roebuck perpetually asks; and that, he thinks, is quite sufficient, and when every man may say what he likes, our aspirations ought to be satisfied. But the aspirations of culture, which is the study of perfection, are not satisfied, unless what men say, when they may say what they like, is worth saying,—has good in it, and more good than bad. In the same way the *Times*, replying to some foreign strictures on the dress, looks, and behaviour of the English abroad, urges that the English ideal is that every one should be free to do and to look just as he likes. But culture indefatigably tries, not to make what each raw person may like, the rule by which he fashions himself; but to draw ever nearer to a sense of what is indeed beautiful, graceful, and becoming, and to get the raw person to like that.

And in the same way with respect to railroads and coal. Every one must have observed the strange language current during the late discussions as to the possible failure of our supplies of coal. Our coal, thousands of people were saying, is the real basis of our national greatness; if our coal runs short, there is an end of the greatness of England. But what *is* greatness?—culture makes us ask. Greatness is a spiritual condition worthy to excite love, interest, and admiration; and the outward proof of possessing greatness is that we excite love, interest, and admiration. If England were swallowed up by the sea to-morrow, which of the two, a hundred years hence, would most excite the love, interest, and admiration of mankind,—would most, therefore, show the evidences of having possessed greatness,—the England of the last twenty years, or the England of Elizabeth, of a time of splendid spiritual effort, but when our coal, and our industrial operations depending on coal, were very little developed? Well, then, what an unsound habit of mind it must be which makes us talk of things like coal or iron as constituting the greatness of England, and how salutary a friend is culture, bent on seeing things as they are, and thus dissipating delusions of this kind and fixing standards of perfection that are real!

Wealth, again, that end to which our prodigious works for material advantage are directed,—the commonest of commonplaces tells us how men are always apt to regard wealth as a precious end in itself; and certainly they have never been so apt thus to regard it as they are in England at the present time. Never did people believe anything more firmly, than nine Englishmen out of ten at the present day believe that our greatness and welfare are proved by our being so very rich. Now, the use of culture is that it helps us, by means of its spiritual standard of perfection, to regard wealth as but machinery, and not only to say as a matter of words that we regard wealth as but machinery, but really to perceive and feel that it is so. If it were not for this purging effect wrought upon our minds by culture, the whole world, the future as well as the present, would inevitably belong to the Philistines. The people who believe most that our greatness and welfare are proved by our being very rich, and who most give their lives and thoughts to becoming rich, are just the very people whom we call Philistines. Culture says: 'Consider these people, then, their way of life, their habits, their manners, the very tones of their voice; look at them attentively; observe the literature they read, the things which give them pleasure, the words which come forth out of their mouths, the thoughts which make the furniture of their minds; would any amount of wealth be worth having with the condition that one was to become just like these people by having it?' And thus culture begets a dissatisfaction which is of the highest possible value in stemming the common tide of men's thoughts in a wealthy and industrial community, and which saves the future, as one may hope, from being vulgarised, even if it cannot save the present.

Population, again, and bodily health and vigour, are things which are nowhere treated in such an unintelligent, misleading, exaggerated way as in England. Both are really machinery; yet how many people all around us do we see rest in them and fail to look beyond them! Why, one has heard people, fresh from reading certain articles of the *Times* on the Registrar-General's returns of marriages and births in this country, who would talk of our large English families in quite a solemn strain, as if they had something in itself beautiful, elevating, and meritorious in them; as if the British Philistine would have only to present himself before the Great Judge with his twelve children, in order to be received among the sheep as a matter of right!

But bodily health and vigour, it may be said, are not to be classed with wealth and population as mere machinery; they have a more real and essential value. True; but only as they are more intimately connected with a perfect spiritual condition than wealth or population are. The moment we disjoin them from the idea of a perfect spiritual condition, and pursue them, as we do pursue them, for their own sake and as ends in themselves, our worship of them becomes as mere worship of machinery, as our worship of wealth or population, and as unintelligent vulgarising a worship as that is. Every one with anything like an adequate idea of human perfection has distinctly marked this subordination to higher and spiritual ends of the cultivation of her bodily vigour and activity. 'Bodily exercise profiteth little; but godliness is profitable unto all things', says the author of the Epistle to Timothy: And the utilitarian Franklin says just as explicitly 'Eat and drink such an exact quantity as suits the constitution of thy body, *in reference to the services of the mind.*' But the point of view of culture, keeping the mark of human perfection simply and broadly in view, and not assigning to this perfection, as religion or

— spiritual/physical are good together

utilitarianism assign to it, a special and limited character,—
this point of view, I say, of culture is best given by these
words of Epictetus:—'It is a sign of ἀφυΐα, says he,—that
is, of a nature not finely tempered,—'to give yourselves
up to things which relate to the body; to make, for
instance, a great fuss about exercise, a great fuss about
eating, a great fuss about drinking, a great fuss about
walking, a great fuss about riding. All these things ought
to be done merely by the way: the formation of the
spirit and character must be our real concern.' This is
admirable; and, indeed, the Greek word εὐφυΐα, a finely
tempered nature, gives exactly the notion of perfection
as culture brings us to conceive it: a harmonious perfection,
a perfection in which the characters of beauty and intelligence are both present, which unites 'the two noblest of
things',—as Swift, who of one of the two, at any rate, had
himself all too little, most happily calls them in his *Battle
of the Books*,—'the two noblest of things, *sweetness and
light*'. The εὐφυής is the man who tends towards sweetness and light; the ἀφυής, on the other hand, is our Philistine. The immense spiritual significance of the Greeks is
due to their having been inspired with this central and
happy idea of the essential character of human perfection; and Mr. Bright's misconception of culture, as a
smattering of Greek and Latin, comes itself, after all,
from this wonderful significance of the Greeks having
affected the very machinery of our education, and is in
itself a kind of homage to it.

In thus making sweetness and light to be characters of
perfection, culture is of like spirit with poetry, follows one
law with poetry. Far more than on our freedom, our population, and our industrialism, many amongst us rely upon
our religious organisations to save us. I have called religion a yet more important manifestation of human nature

religion is higher than poetry

than poetry, because it has worked on a broader scale for perfection, and with greater masses of men. But the idea of beauty and of a human nature perfect on all its sides, which is the dominant idea of poetry, is a true and invaluable idea, though it has not yet had the success that the idea of conquering the obvious faults of our animality, and of a human nature perfect on the moral side,—which is the dominant idea of religion,—has been enabled to have; and it is destined, adding to itself the religious idea of a devout energy, to transform and govern the other.

The best art and poetry of the Greeks, in which religion and poetry are one, in which the idea of beauty and of a human nature perfect on all sides adds to itself a religious and devout energy, and works in the strength of that, is on this account of such surpassing interest and instructiveness for us, though it was,—as, having regard to the human race in general, and, indeed, having regard to the Greeks themselves, we must own,—a premature attempt, an attempt which for success needed the moral and religious fibre in humanity to be more braced and developed than it had yet been. But Greece did not err in having the idea of beauty, harmony, and complete human perfection, so present and paramount. It is impossible to have this idea too present and paramount; only, the moral fibre must be braced too. And we, because we have braced the moral fibre, are not on that account in the right way, if at the same time the idea of beauty, harmony, and complete human perfection, is wanting or misapprehended amongst us; and evidently it *is* wanting or misapprehended at present. And when we rely as we do on our religious organisations, which in themselves do not and cannot give us this idea, and think we have done enough if we make them spread and prevail, then, I say, we fall into our common fault of over-valuing machinery.

Nothing is more common than for people to confound the inward peace and satisfaction which follows the sub-duing of the obvious faults of our animality with what I may call absolute inward peace and satisfaction,—the peace and satisfaction which are reached as we draw near to complete spiritual perfection, and not merely to moral perfection, or rather to relative moral per-fection. No people in the world have done more and struggled more to attain this relative moral perfection than our English race has. For no people in the world has the command to *resist the devil*, to *overcome the wicked one*, in the nearest and most obvious sense of those words, had such a pressing force and reality. And we have had our reward, not only in the great worldly prosperity which our obedience to this command has brought us, but also, and far more, in great inward peace and satis-faction. But to me few things are more pathetic than to see people, on the strength of the inward peace and satisfaction which their rudimentary efforts towards per-fection have brought them, employ, concerning their incomplete perfection and the religious organisations within which they have found it, language which prop-erly applies only to complete perfection, and is a far-off echo of the human soul's prophecy of it. Religion itself, I need hardly say, supplies them in abundance with this grand language. And very freely do they use it; yet it is really the severest criticism of such an incomplete perfection as alone we have yet reached through our religious organisations.

The impulse of the English race towards moral develop-ment and self-conquest has nowhere so powerfully mani-fested itself as in Puritanism. Nowhere has Puritanism found so adequate an expression as in the religious organisation of the Independents. The modern Independents have a newspaper, the *Nonconformist*, written with great sincerity and ability. The motto, the standard, the profession of faith which this organ of theirs carries aloft is, 'The Dissidence of Dissent and the Protestantism of the Protestant religion.' There is sweetness and light, and an ideal of complete harmonious human perfection! One need not go to culture and poetry to find language to judge it. Religion, with its instinct for perfection, supplies language to judge it, language too which is in our mouths every day. 'Finally, be of one mind, united in feeling', says St. Peter. There is an ideal which judges the Puritan ideal: 'The Dissidence of Dissent and the Protestantism of the Protestant religion!' And religious organisations like this are what people believe in, rest in, would give their lives for! Such, I say, is the wonderful virtue of even the beginnings of perfection, of having conquered even the plain faults of our animality, that the religious organisation which has helped us to do it can seem to us something precious, salutary, and to be propagated, even when it wears such a brand of imperfection on its forehead as this. And men have got such a habit of giving to the language of religion a special application, of making it a mere jargon, that for the condemnation which religion itself passes on the shortcomings of their religious organisations they have no ear; they are sure to cheat themselves and to explain this condemnation away. They can only be reached by the criticism which culture, like poetry, speaking a language not to be sophisticated, and resolutely testing these organisations by the ideal of a human perfection complete on all sides, applies to them.

But men of culture and poetry, it will be said, are again and again failing, and failing conspicuously, in the

Puritans are imperfect

necessary first stage to a harmonious perfection, in the subduing of the great obvious faults of our animality, which it is the glory of these religious organisations to have helped us to subdue. True, they do often so fail. They have often been without the virtues as well as the faults of the Puritan; it has been one of their dangers that they so felt the Puritan's faults that they too much neglected the practice of his virtues. I will not, however, exculpate them at the Puritan's expense. They have often failed in morality, and morality is indispensable. And they have been punished for their failure, as the Puritan has been rewarded for his performance. They have been punished wherein they erred; but their ideal of beauty, of sweetness and light, and a human nature complete on all its sides, remains the true ideal of perfection still; just as the Puritan's ideal of perfection remains narrow and inadequate, although for what he did well he has been richly rewarded. Notwithstanding the mighty results of the Pilgrim Fathers' voyage, they and their standard of perfection are rightly judged when we figure to ourselves Shakespeare or Virgil,—souls in whom sweetness and light, and all that in human nature is most humane, were eminent,—accompanying them on their voyage, and think what intolerable company Shakespeare and Virgil would have found them! In the same way let us judge the religious organisations which we see all around us. Do not let us deny the good and the happiness which they have accomplished; but do not let us fail to see clearly that their idea of human perfection is narrow and inadequate, and that the Dissidence of Dissent and the Protestantism of the Protestant religion will never bring humanity to its true goal. As I said with regard to wealth: Let us look at the life of those who live in and for it,—so I say with regard to the religious organisations. Look at the life imaged in such a newspaper as the *Nonconformist*,—a life of jealousy of the Establishment, disputes, tea-meetings, openings of chapels, sermons, and then think of it as an ideal of a human life completing itself on all sides, and aspiring with all its organs and sweetness, light, and perfection!

Another newspaper, representing, like the *Nonconformist*, one of the religious organisations of this country, was a short time ago giving an account of the crowd at Epsom on the Derby day, and of all the vice and hideousness which was to be seen in that crowd; and then the writer turned suddenly round upon Professor Huxley, and asked him how he proposed to cure all this vice and hideousness without religion. I confess I felt disposed to ask the asker this question: and how do you propose to cure it with such a religion as yours? How is the ideal of a life so unlovely, so unattractive, so incomplete, so narrow, so far removed from a true and satisfying ideal of human perfection, as is the life of your religious organisation as you yourself reflect it, to conquer and transform all this vice and hideousness? Indeed, the strongest plea for the study of perfection as pursued by culture, the clearest proof of the actual inadequacy of the idea of perfection held by the religious organisations,—expressing, as I have said, the most wide-spread effort which the human race has yet made after perfection,—is to be found in the state of our life and society with these in possession of it, and having been in possession of it I know not how many hundred years. We are all of us included in some religious organisation or other; we all call ourselves, in the sublime and aspiring language of religion which I have before noticed, *children of God*. Children of God;—it is an immense pretension!—and how are we to justify it? By the works which we do, and the words which we speak. And the

work which we collective children of God do, our grand
centre of life, our *city* which we have builded for us to
dwell in, is London! London, with its unutterable external
hideousness, and with its internal canker of *publicè egestas,
privatim opulentia*,—to use the words which Sallust puts
into Cato's mouth about Rome,—unequalled in the
world! The word, again, which we children of God speak,
the voice which most hits our collective thought, the
newspaper with the largest circulation in England, nay,
with the largest circulation in the whole world, is the
Daily Telegraph! I say that when our religious organisations,—which I admit to express the most considerable
effort after perfection that our race has yet made,—land
us in no better result than this, it is high time to examine
carefully their idea of perfection, to see whether it does
not leave out of account sides and forces of human nature
which we might turn to great use; whether it would not
be more operative if it were more complete. And I say
that the English reliance on our religious organisations
and on their ideas of human perfection just as they stand,
is like our reliance on freedom, on muscular Christianity,
on population, on coal, on wealth,—mere belief in
machinery, and unfruitful; and that it is wholesomely
counteracted by culture, bent on seeing things as they
are, and on drawing the human race onwards to a more
complete, a harmonious perfection.

Culture, however, shows its single-minded love of perfection, its desire simply to make reason and the will of
God prevail, its freedom from fanaticism, by its attitude
towards all this machinery, even while it insists that it *is*
machinery. Fanatics, seeing the mischief men do themselves by their blind belief in some machinery or other,—
whether it is wealth and industrialism, or whether it is
the cultivation of bodily strength and activity, or whether

it is a political organisation,—or whether it is a religious organisation,—oppose with might and main the tendency to this or that political and religious organisation, or to games and athletic exercises, or to wealth and industrialism, and try violently to stop it. But the flexibility which sweetness and light give, and which is one of the rewards of culture pursued in good faith, enables a man to see that a tendency may be necessary, and even, as a preparation for something in the future, salutary, and yet that the generations or individuals who obey this tendency are sacrificed to it, that they fall short of the hope of perfection by following it; and that its mischiefs are to be criticised, lest it should take too firm a hold and last after it has served its purpose.

Mr. Gladstone well pointed out, in a speech at Paris,— and others have pointed out the same thing,—how necessary is the present great movement towards wealth and industrialism, in order to lay broad foundations of material well-being for the society of the future. The worst of these justifications is, that they are generally addressed to the very people engaged, body and soul, in the movement in question; at all events, that they are always seized with the greatest avidity by these people, and taken by them as quite justifying their life; and that thus they tend to harden them in their sins. Now, culture admits the necessity of the movement towards fortune-making and exaggerated industrialism, readily allows that the future may derive benefit from it; but insists, at the same time, that the passing generations of industrialists,—forming for the most part, the stout main body of Philistinism,—are sacrificed to it. In the same way, the result of all the games and sports which occupy the passing generation of boys and young men may be the establishment of a better and sounder physical type for the future

to work with. Culture does not set itself against the games
and sports; it congratulates the future, and hopes it will
make a good use of its improved physical basis; but it
points out that our passing generation of boys and young
men is, meantime, sacrificed. Puritanism was perhaps
necessary to develop the moral fibre of the English race,
Nonconformity to break the yoke of ecclesiastical domina-
tion over men's minds and to prepare the way for freedom
of thought in the distant future; still, culture points out
that the harmonious perfection of generations of Puritans
and Nonconformists has been, in consequence, sacrificed.
Freedom of speech may be necessary for the society of
the future, but the young lions of the *Daily Telegraph* in
the meanwhile are sacrificed. A voice for every man in
his country's government may be necessary for the
society of the future, but meanwhile Mr. Beales and
Mr. Bradlaugh are sacrificed.

Oxford, the Oxford of the past, has many faults; and
she has heavily paid for them in defeat, in isolation, in
want of hold upon the modern world. Yet we in Oxford,
brought up amidst the beauty and sweetness of that
beautiful place, have not failed to seize one truth:—the
truth that beauty and sweetness are essential characters
of a complete human perfection. When I insist on this, I
am all in the faith and tradition of Oxford. I say boldly
that this our sentiment for beauty and sweetness, our
sentiment against hideous and rawness, has been at the
bottom of our attachment to so many beaten causes, of
our opposition to so many triumphant movements. And
the sentiment is true, and has never been wholly defeated,
and has shown its power even in its defeat. We have not
won our political battles, we have not carried our main
points, we have not stopped our adversaries' advance, we
have not marched victoriously with the modern world;

but we have told silently upon the mind of the country, we have prepared currents of feeling which sap our adversaries' position when it seems gained, we have kept up our own communications with the future. Look at the course of the great movement which shook Oxford to its centre some thirty years ago! It was directed, as any one who reads Dr. Newman's *Apology* may see, against what in one word may be called 'Liberalism'. Liberalism prevailed; it was the appointed force to do the work of the hour; it was necessary, it was inevitable that it should prevail. The Oxford movement was broken, it failed; our wrecks are scattered on every shore:

Quæ regio in terris nostri non plena laboris?

But what was it, this Liberalism, as Dr. Newman saw it, and as it really broke the Oxford movement? It was the great middle-class Liberalism, which had for the cardinal points of its belief the Reform Bill of 1832, and local self-government, in politics; in the social sphere, free-trade, unrestricted competition, and the making of large industrial fortunes; in the religious sphere, the Dissidence of Dissent and the Protestantism of the Protestant religion. I do not say that other and more intelligent forces than this were not opposed to the Oxford movement: but this was the force which really beat it; this was the force which Dr. Newman felt himself fighting with; this was the force which till only the other day seemed to be the paramount force in this country, and to be in possession of the future; this was the force whose achievements fill Mr. Lowe with such inexpressible admiration, and whose rule he was so horror-struck to see threatened. And where is this great force of Philistinism now? It is thrust into the second rank, it is become a power of yesterday, it has lost the future. A new power has suddenly appeared, a power which it is impossible yet to judge fully, but which is certainly a wholly different force from middle-class Liberalism; different in its cardinal points of belief, different in its tendencies in every sphere. It loves and admires neither the legislation of middle-class Parliaments, nor the local self-government of middle-class vestries, nor the unrestricted competition of middle-class industrialists, nor the dissidence of middle-class Dissent and the Protestantism of middle-class Protestant religion. I am not now praising this new force, or saying that its own ideals are better; all I say is, that they are wholly different. And who will estimate how much the currents of feeling created by Dr. Newman's movement, the keen desire for beauty and sweetness which it nourished, the deep aversion it manifested to the hardness and vulgarity of middle-class Liberalism, the strong light it turned on the hideous and grotesque illusions of middle-class Protestantism,—who will estimate how much all these contributed to swell the tide of secret dissatisfaction which has mined the ground under the self-confident Liberalism of the last thirty years, and has prepared the way for its sudden collapse and supersession? It is in this manner that the sentiment of Oxford for beauty and sweetness conquers, and in this manner long may it continue to conquer!

In this manner it works to the same end as culture, and there is plenty of work for it yet to do. I have said that the new and more democratic force which is now superseding our old middle-class Liberalism cannot yet be rightly judged. It has its main tendencies still to form. We hear promises of its giving us administrative reform, law reform, reform of education, and I know not what; but those promises come rather from its advocates, wishing to make a good plea for it and to justify it for superseding middle-class Liberalism, than from clear tendencies which it has itself yet developed. But meanwhile it has plenty of well-intentioned friends against whom culture may with advantage continue to uphold steadily its ideal of human perfection; that this is *an inward spiritual activity, having for its characters increased sweetness, increased light, increased life, increased sympathy*. Mr. Bright, who has a foot in both worlds, the world of middle-class Liberalism and the world of democracy, but who brings most of his ideas from the world of middle-class Liberalism in which he was bred, always inclines to inculcate that faith in machinery to which, as we have seen, Englishmen are so prone, and which has been the bane of middle-class Liberalism. He complains with a sorrowful indignation of people who 'appear to have no proper estimate of the value of the franchise'; he leads his disciples to believe,— what the Englishman is always too ready to believe,— that the having a vote, like the having a large family, or a large business, or large muscles, has in itself some edifying and perfecting effect upon human nature. Or else he cries out to democracy,—'the men', as he calls them, 'upon whose shoulders the greatness of England rests',— he cries out to them: 'See what you have done! I look over this country and see the cities you have built, the railroads you have made, the manufactures you have produced, the cargoes which freight the ships of the greatest mercantile navy the world has ever seen! I see that you have converted by your labours what was once a wilderness, these islands, into a fruitful garden; I know that you have created this wealth, and are a nation whose name is a word of power throughout all the world.' Why, this is just the very style of laudation with which Mr. Roebuck or Mr. Lowe debauch the minds of the middle classes, and make such Philistines of them. It is the same fashion of teaching a man to value himself not on what he *is*, not on his progress in sweetness and light, but on the number of the railroads he has constructed, or the bigness of the tabernacle he has built. Only the middle classes are told they have done it all with their energy, self-reliance, and capital, and the democracy are told they have done it all with their hands and sinews. But teaching the democracy to put its trust in achievements of this kind is merely training them to be Philistines to take the place of the Philistines whom they are superseding; and they too, like the middle class, will be encouraged to sit down at the banquet of the future without having on a wedding garment, and nothing excellent can then come from them. Those who know their besetting faults, those who have watched them and listened to them, or those who will read the instructive account recently given of them by one of themselves, the *Journeyman Engineer*, will agree that the idea which culture set before us of perfection,—an increased spiritual activity, having for its characters increased sweetness, increased light, increased life, increased sympathy,—is an idea which the new democracy needs far more than the idea of the blessedness of the franchise, or the wonderfulness of its own industrial performances.

Other well-meaning friends of this new power are for leading it, not in the old ruts of middle-class Philistinism, but in ways which are naturally alluring to the feet of democracy, though in this country they are novel and untried ways. I may call them the ways of Jacobinism. Violent indignation with the past, abstract systems of renovation applied wholesale, a new doctrine drawn up in black and white for elaborating down to the very smallest details a rational society for the future,—these are the ways of Jacobinism. Mr. Frederic Harrison and other disciples of Comte,—one of them, Mr. Congreve, is an old friend of mine, and I am glad to have an opportunity of publicly expressing my respect for his talents and character,—are among the friends of democracy who are for leading it in paths of this kind. Mr. Frederic Harrison is very hostile to culture, and from a natural enough motive; for culture is the eternal opponent of the two things which are the signal marks of Jacobinism,—its fierceness, and its addiction to an abstract system. Culture is always assigning to system-makers and systems a smaller share in the bent of human destiny than their friends like. A current in people's minds sets towards new ideas; people are dissatisfied with their old narrow stock of Philistine ideas, Anglo-Saxon ideas, or any other; and some man, some Bentham or Comte, who has the real merit of having early and strongly felt and helped the new current, but who brings plenty of narrowness and mistakes of his own into his feeling and help of it, is credited with being the author of the whole current, the first person to be entrusted with its regulation and to guide the human race.

The excellent German historian of the mythology of Rome, Preller, relating the introduction at Rome under the Tarquins of the worship of Apollo, the god of light, healing, and reconciliation, will have us observe that it was not so much the Tarquins who brought to Rome the new worship of Apollo, as a current in the mind of the Roman people which set powerfully at that time towards a new worship of this kind, and away from the old run of Latin and Sabine religious ideas. In a similar way, culture directs our attention to the natural current there is in human affairs, and to its continual working, and will not let us rivet our faith upon any one man and his doings. It makes us see, not only his good side, but also how much in him was of necessity limited and transient; nay, it even feels a pleasure, a sense of an increased freedom and of an ampler future, in so doing.

I remember, when I was under the influence of a mind to which I feel the greatest obligations, the mind of a man who was the very incarnation of sanity and clear sense, a man the most considerable, it seems to me, whom America has yet produced,—Benjamin Franklin,—I remember the relief with which, after long feeling the sway of Franklin's imperturbable common-sense, I came upon a project of his for a new version of the Book of Job, to replace the old version, the style of which, says Franklin, has become obsolete, and thence less agreeable. 'I give', he continues, 'a few verses, which may serve as a sample of the kind of version I would recommend.' We all recollect the famous verse in our translation: 'Then Satan answered the Lord and said: "Doth Job fear God for nought?"' Franklin makes this: 'Does Your Majesty imagine that Job's good conduct is the effect of mere personal attachment and affection?' I well remember how when first I read that, I drew a deep breath of relief, and said to myself: 'After all, there is a stretch of humanity beyond Franklin's victorious good sense!' So, after hearing Bentham cried loudly up as the renovator of modern society, and Bentham's mind and ideas proposed as the rulers of our future, I open the *Deontology*. There I read: 'While Xenophon was writing his history and Euclid teaching geometry, Socrates and Plato were talking nonsense under pretence of talking wisdom and morality. This morality of theirs consisted in words; this wisdom of theirs was the denial of matters known to every man's experience.' From the moment of reading that, I am delivered from the bondage of Bentham! the fanaticism of his adherents can touch me no longer; I feel the inadequacy of his mind and ideas for supplying the rule of human society, for perfection.

Culture tends always thus to deal with the men of a system, of disciples, of a school; with men like Comte, or the late Mr. Buckle, or Mr. Mill. However much it may find to admire in these personages, or in some of them, it nevertheless remembers the text: 'Be not ye called Rabbi!' and it soon passes on from any Rabbi. But Jacobinism loves a Rabbi; it does not want to pass on from its Rabbi in pursuit of a future and still unreached perfection; it wants its Rabbi and his ideas to stand for perfection, that they may with the more authority recast the world; and for Jacobinism, therefore, culture,—eternally passing onwards and seeking,—is an impertinence and an offence. But culture, just because it resists this tendency of Jacobinism to impose on us a man with limitations and errors of his own along with the true ideas of which he is the organ, really does the world and Jacobinism itself a service.

So, too, Jacobinism, in its fierce hatred of the past and of those whom it makes liable for the sins of the past, cannot away with the inexhaustible indulgence proper to culture, the consideration of circumstances, the severe judgment of actions joined to the merciful judgment of persons. 'The man of culture is in politics', cries Mr. Frederic Harrison, 'one of the poorest mortals alive!' Mr. Frederic Harrison wants to be doing business, and he complains that the man of culture stops him with a 'turn for small fault-finding, love of selfish ease, and indecision in action'. Of what use is culture, he asks, except for 'a critic of new books or a professor of *belles lettres*?' Why, it is of use because, in presence of the fierce exasperation which breathes, or rather, I may say, hisses, through the whole production in which Mr. Frederick Harrison asks that question, it reminds us that the perfection of human nature is sweetness and light. It is of use because, like religion,—that other effort after perfection,—it testifies that, where bitter envying and strife are, there is confusion and every evil work.

The pursuit of perfection, then, is the pursuit of sweetness and light. He who works for sweetness works in the end for light also; he who works for light works in the end for sweetness also. But he who works for sweetness and light united, works to make reason and the will of God prevail. He who works for machinery, he who works for hatred, works only for confusion. Culture looks beyond machinery, culture hates hatred; culture has one great passion, the passion for sweetness and light. It has one even yet greater!—the passion for making them *prevail*. It is not satisfied till we *all* come to a perfect man; it knows that the sweetness and light of the few must be imperfect until the raw and unkindled masses of humanity are touched with sweetness and light. If I have not shrunk from saying that we must work for sweetness and light, so neither have I shrunk from saying that we must have a broad basis, must have sweetness and light for as many as possible. Again and again I have insisted how those are the happy moments of humanity, how those are the marking epochs of a people's life, how those are the flowering times for literature and art and all the creative power of genius, when there is a *national* glow of life and thought, when the whole of society is in the fullest measure permeated by thought, sensible to beauty, intelligent and alive. Only it must be *real* thought and *real* beauty; *real* sweetness and *real* light. Plenty of people will try to give the masses, as they call them, an intellectual food prepared and adapted in the way they think proper for the actual condition of the masses. The ordinary popular literature is an example of this way of working on the masses. Plenty of people will try to indoctrinate the masses with the set of ideas and judgments constituting the creed of their own profession or party. Our religious and political organisations give an example of this way of working on the masses. I condemn neither way; but culture works differently. It does not try to teach down to the level of inferior classes; it does not try to win them for this or that sect of its own, with ready-made judgments and watchwords. It seeks to do away with classes; to make the best that has been thought and known in the world current everywhere; to make all men live in an atmosphere of sweetness and light, where they may use ideas, as it uses them itself, freely,—nourished and not bound by them.

This is the *social idea*; and the men of culture are the true apostles of equality. The great men of culture are those who have had a passion for diffusing, for making prevail, for carrying from one end of society to the other, the best knowledge, the best ideas of their time; who have laboured to divest knowledge of all that was harsh, uncouth, difficult, abstract, professional, exclusive; to humanise it, to make it efficient outside the clique of the cultivated and learned, yet still remaining the *best* knowledge and thought of the time, and a true source, therefore, of sweetness and light. Such a man was Abelard in the Middle Ages, in spite of all his imperfections; and thence the boundless emotion and enthusiasm which Abelard excited. Such were Lessing and Herder in Germany, at the end of the last century; and their services to Germany were in this way inestimably precious. Generations will pass, and literary monuments will accumulate, and works far more perfect than the works of Lessing and Herder will be produced in Germany; and yet the names of these two men will fill a German with a reverence and enthusiasm such as the names of the most gifted master will hardly awaken. And why? Because they *humanised* knowledge; because they broadened the basis of life and intelligence; because they worked powerfully to diffuse sweetness and light, to make reason and the will of God prevail. With Saint Augustine they said:

Let us not leave Thee alone to make in the secret of thy knowledge, as thou didst before the creation of the firmament, the division of life from darkness; let the children of thy spirit, placed in their firmament, make their light shine upon the earth, mark the division of night and day, and announce the revolution of the times; for the old order is passed, and the new arises; the night is spent, the day is come forth; and thou shalt crown the year with thy blessing, when thou shalt send forth labourers into thy harvest sown by other hands than theirs; when thou shalt send forth new labourers to new seed-times, whereof the harvest shall be not yet.

II. DOING AS ONE LIKES

I HAVE been trying to show that culture is or ought to be, the study and pursuit of perfection; and that of perfection, as pursued by culture, beauty and intelligence, or, in other words, sweetness and light, are the main characters. But hitherto I have been insisting chiefly on beauty, or sweetness, as a character of perfection. To complete rightly my design, it evidently remains to speak also of intelligence, or light, as a character of perfection.

First, however, I ought perhaps to notice that, both here and on the other side of the Atlantic, all sorts of objections are raised against the 'religion of culture', as the objectors mockingly call it, which I am supposed to be promulgating. It is said to be a religion proposing parmaceti, or some scented salve or other, as a cure for human miseries; a religion breathing a spirit of cultivated inaction

making its believer refuse to lend a hand at uprooting the definite evils on all sides of us, and filling him
with antipathy against the reforms and reformers which
try to extirpate them. In general, it is summed up as
being not practical, or,—as some critics familiarly put it,
—all moonshine. That Alcibiades, the editor of the
Morning Star, taunts me, as its promulgator, with living
out of the world and knowing nothing of life and men.
That great austere toiler, the editor of the *Daily Telegraph*, upbraids me,—but kindly, and more in sorrow
than in anger,—for trifling with æsthetics and poetical
fancies, while he himself, in that arsenal of his in Fleet
Street, is bearing the burden and heat of the day. An
intelligent American newspaper, the *Nation*, says that it
is very easy to sit in one's study and find fault with the
course of modern society, but the thing is to propose
practical improvements for it. While, finally, Mr. Frederic
Harrison, in a very good-tempered and witty satire,
which makes me quite understand his having apparently
achieved such a conquest of my young Prussian friend,
Arminius, at last gets moved to an almost stern moral
impatience, to behold, as he says, 'Death, sin, cruelty
stalk among us, filling their maws with innocence and
youth', and me, in the midst of the general tribulation,
handing out my pouncet-box.

It is impossible that all these remonstrances and re-
proofs should not affect me, and I shall try my very best,
in completing my design and in speaking of light as one of
the characters of perfection, and of culture as giving us
light, to profit by the objections I have heard and read,
and to drive at practice as much as I can, by showing
the communications and passages into practical life from
the doctrine which I am inculcating.

It is said that a man with my theories of sweetness and

light is full of antipathy against the rougher or coarser movements going on around him, that he will not lend a hand to the humble operation of uprooting evil by their means, and that therefore the believers in action grow impatient with them. But what if rough and coarse action, ill-calculated action, action with insufficient light, is, and has for a long time been, our bane? What if our urgent want now is, not to act at any price, but rather to lay in a stock of light for our difficulties? In that case, to refuse to lend a hand to the rougher and coarser movements going on round us, to make the primary need, both for oneself and others, to consist in enlightening ourselves and qualifying ourselves to act less at random, is surely the best and in real truth the most practical line our endeavours can take. So that if I can show what my opponents call rough or coarse action, but what I would rather call random and ill-regulated action,—action with insufficient light, action pursued because we like to be doing something and doing it as we please, and do not like the trouble of thinking and the severe constraint of any kind of rule,—if I can show this to be, at the present moment, a practical mischief and dangerous to us, then I have found a practical use for light in correcting this state of things, and have only to exemplify how, in cases which fall under everybody's observation, it may deal with it.

When I began to speak of culture, I insisted on our bondage to machinery, on our proneness to value machinery as an end in itself, without looking beyond it to the end for which alone, in truth, it is valuable. Freedom, I said, was one of those things which we thus worshipped in itself, without enough regarding the ends for which freedom is to be desired. In our common notions and talk about freedom, we eminently show our idolatry of machinery. Our prevalent notion is,—and

I quoted a number of instances to prove it,—that it is a most happy and important thing for a man merely to be able to do as he likes. On what he is to do when he is thus free to do as he likes, we do not lay so much stress. Our familiar praise of the British Constitution under which we live, is that it is a system of checks,— a system which stops and paralyses any power in interfering with the free action of individuals. To this effect Mr. Bright, who loves to walk in the old ways of the Constitution, said forcibly in one of his great speeches, what many other people are every day saying less forcibly, that the central idea of English life and politics is *the assertion of personal liberty*. Evidently this is so; but evidently, also, as feudalism, which with its ideas and habits of subordination was for many centuries silently behind the British Constitution, dies out, and we are left with nothing but our system of checks, and our notion of its being the great right and happiness of an Englishman to do as far as possible what he likes, we are in danger of drifting towards anarchy. We have not the notion, so familiar on the Continent and to antiquity, of *the State*—the nation in its collective and corporate character, entrusted with stringent powers for the general advantage, and controlling individual wills in the name of an interest wider than that of individuals. We say, what is very true, that this notion is often made instrumental to tyranny; we say that a State is in reality made up of the individuals who compose it, and that every individual is the best judge of his own interests. Our leading class is an aristocracy, and no aristocracy likes the notion of a State-authority greater than itself, with a stringent administrative machinery superseding the decorative inutilities of lord-lieutenancy, deputy-lieutenancy, and the *posse comitatûs*, which are all in its own hands. Our middle class, the great representative of trade and Dissent, with its maxims of every man for himself in business, every man for himself in religion, dreads a powerful administration which might somehow interfere with it; and besides, it has its own decorative inutilities of vestrymanship and guardianship, which are to this class what lord-lieutenancy and the county magistracy are to the aristocratic class, and a stringent administration might either take these functions out of its hands, or prevent its exercising them in its own comfortable, independent manner, as at present.

Then as to our working class. This class, pressed constantly by the hard daily compulsion of material wants, is naturally the very centre and stronghold of our national idea, that it is man's ideal right and felicity to do as he likes. I think I have somewhat related how M. Michelet said to me of the people of France, that it was 'a nation of barbarians civilised by the conscription'. He meant that through their military service the idea of public duty and of discipline was brought to the mind of these masses, in other respects so raw and uncultivated. Our masses are quite as raw and uncultivated as the French; and so far from their having the idea of public duty and of discipline, superior to the individual's self-will, brought to their mind by a universal obligation of military service, such as that of the conscription,—so far from their having this, the very idea of a conscription is so at variance with our English notion of the prime right and blessedness of doing as one likes, that I remember the manager of the Clay Cross works in Derbyshire told me during the Crimean war, when our want of soldiers was much felt and some people were talking of a conscription, that sooner than submit to a conscription the population of that district would flee to the mines, and lead a sort of Robin Hood life under ground.

For a long time, as I have said, the strong feudal habits

of subordination and deference continued to tell upon the working class. The modern spirit has now almost entirely dissolved those habits, and the anarchical tendency of our worship of freedom in and for itself, of our superstitious faith, as I say, in machinery, is becoming very manifest. More and more, because of this our blind faith in machinery, because of our want of light to enable us to look beyond machinery to the end for which machinery is valuable, this and that man, and this and that body of men, all over the country, are beginning to assert and put in practice an Englishman's right to do what he likes; his right to march where he likes, meet where he likes, enter where he likes, hoot as he likes, threaten as he likes, smash as he likes. All this, I say, tends to anarchy; and though a number of excellent people, and particularly my friends of the Liberal or progressive party, as they call themselves, are kind enough to reassure us by saying that these are trifles, that a few transient outbreaks of rowdyism signify nothing, that our system of liberty is one which itself cures all the evils which it works, that the educated and intelligent classes stand in overwhelming strength and majestic repose, ready, like our military force in riots, to act at a moment's notice,—yet one finds that one's Liberal friends generally say this because they have such faith in themselves and their nostrums, when they shall return, as the public welfare requires, to place and power. But this faith of theirs one cannot exactly share, when one has so long had them and their nostrums at work, and sees that they have not prevented our coming to our present embarrassed condition. And one finds, also, that the outbreaks of rowdyism tend to become less and less of trifles, to become more frequent rather than less frequent; and that meanwhile our educated and intelligent classes remain in their majestic repose, and somehow or other, whatever happens, their overwhelming strength, like our military force in riots, never does act.

How, indeed, *should* their overwhelming strength act, when the man who gives an inflammatory lecture, or breaks down the park railings, or invades a Secretary of State's office, is only following an Englishman's impulse to do as he likes; and our own conscience tells us that we ourselves have always regarded this impulse as something primary and sacred? Mr. Murphy lectures at Birmingham, and showers on the Catholic population of that town 'words', says the Home Secretary, Mr. Hardy, 'only fit to be addressed to thieves or murderers'. What then? Mr. Murphy has his own reasons of several kinds. He suspects the Roman Catholic Church of designs upon Mrs. Murphy; and he says, if mayors and magistrates do not care for their wives and daughters, he does. But, above all, he is doing as he likes; or, in worthier language, asserting his personal liberty. 'I will carry out my lectures if they walk over my body as a dead corpse; and I say to the Mayor of Birmingham that he is my servant while I am in Birmingham, and as my servant he must do his duty and protect me.' Touching and beautiful words, which find a sympathetic chord in every British bosom! The moment it is plainly put before us that a man is asserting his personal liberty, we are half disarmed; because we are believers in freedom, and not in some dream of a right reason to which the assertion of our freedom is to be subordinated. Accordingly, the Secretary of State had to say that although the lecturer's language was 'only fit to be addressed to thieves or murderers', yet, 'I do not think he is to be deprived, I do not think that anything I have said could justify the inference that he is to be deprived, of the right of protection in a place built by him for the purpose of these lectures; because the language was not language which afforded grounds for a criminal prosecution.' No, nor to be silenced by Mayor, or Home Secretary, or any administrative authority on earth, simply on their notion of what is discreet and reasonable! This is in perfect consonance with our public opinion, and with our national love for the assertion of personal liberty.

In quite another department of affairs, an experienced and distinguished Chancery Judge relates an incident which is just to the same effect as this of Mr. Murphy. A testator bequeathed 300*l.* a year, to be for ever applied as a pension to some person who had been unsuccessful in literature, and whose duty should be to support and diffuse, by his writings, the testator's own views, as enforced in the testator's publications. The views were not worth a straw and the bequest was appealed against in the Court of Chancery on the ground of its absurdity; but, being only absurd, it was upheld, and the so-called charity was established. Having, I say, at the bottom of our English hearts a very strong belief in freedom, and a very weak belief in right reason, we are soon silenced when a man pleads the prime right to do as he likes, because this is the prime right for ourselves too; and even if we attempt now and then to mumble something about reason, yet we have ourselves thought so little about this and so much about liberty, that we are in conscience forced, when our brother Philistine with whom we are meddling turns boldly round upon us and asks: *Have you any light?*—to shake our heads ruefully, and to let him go his own way after all.

There are many things to be said on behalf of this exclusive attention of ours to liberty, and of the relaxed habits of government which it has engendered. It is very easy to mistake or to exaggerate the sort of anarchy from which we are in danger through them. We are not in danger from Fenianism, fierce and turbulent as it may show itself; for against this our conscience is free enough to let us act resolutely and put forth our overwhelming strength the moment there is any real need for it. In the first place, it was never any part of our creed that the great right and blessedness of an Irishman, or, indeed, of anybody on earth except an Englishman, is to do as he likes; and we can have no scruple at all about abridging, if necessary, a non-Englishman's assertion of personal liberty. The British Constitution, its checks, and its prime virtues, are for Englishmen. We may extend them to others out of love and kindness; but we find no real divine law written on our hearts constraining us so to extend them. And then the difference between an Irish Fenian and an English rough is so immense, and the case, in dealing with the Fenian, so much more clear! He is so evidently desperate and dangerous, a man of a con-quered race, a Papist, with centuries of ill-usage to inflame him against us, with an alien religion established in his country by us at his expense, with no admiration of our institutions, no love of our virtues, no talents for our business, no turn for our comfort! Show him our symbolical Truss Manufactory on the finest site in Europe, and tell him that British industrialism and individualism can bring a man to that, and he remains cold! Evidently, if we deal tenderly with a sentimentalist like this, it is out of pure philanthropy.

But with the Hyde Park rioter how different! He is our own flesh and blood; he is a Protestant; he is framed by nature to do as we do, hate what we hate, love what we love; he is capable of feeling the symbolical force of the Truss Manufactory; the question of questions, for him, is a wages question. That beautiful sentence Sir Daniel

Gooch quoted to the Swindon workmen, and which I treasure as Mrs. Gooch's Golden Rule, or the Divine Injunction 'Be ye Perfect' done into British,—the sentence Sir Daniel Gooch's mother repeated to him every morning when he was a boy going to work: '*Ever remember, my dear Dan, that you should look forward to being some day manager of that concern!*'—this fruitful maxim is perfectly fitted to shine forth in the heart of the Hyde Park rough also, and to be his guiding-star through life. He has no visionary schemes of revolution and transformation, though of course he would like his class to rule, as the aristocratic class like their class to rule, and the middle class theirs. But meanwhile our social machine is a little out of order; there are a good many people in our paradisiacal centres of industrialism and individualism taking the bread out of one another's mouths. The rough has not yet quite found his groove and settled down to his work, and so he is just asserting his personal liberty a little, going where he likes, assembling where he likes, bawling as he likes, hustling as he likes. Just as the rest of us,—as the country squires in the aristocratic class, as the political dissenters in the middle class,—he has no idea of a *State*, of the nation in its collective and corporate character controlling, as government, the free swing of this or that one of its members in the name of the higher reason of all of them, his own as well as that of others. He sees the rich, the aristocratic class, in occupation of the executive government, and so if he is stopped from making Hyde Park a bear-garden or the streets impassable, he says he is being butchered by the aristocracy.

His apparition is somewhat embarrassing, because too many cooks spoil the broth; because, while the aristocratic and middle classes have long been doing as they like with great vigour, he has been too undeveloped and submissive hitherto to join in the game; and now, when he does come, he comes in immense numbers, and is rather raw and rough. But he does not break many laws, or not many at one time; and, as our laws were made for very different circumstances from our present (but always with an eye to Englishmen doing as they like), and as the clear letter of the law must be against our Englishman who does as he likes and not only the spirit of the law and public policy, and as Government must neither have any discretionary power nor act resolutely on its own interpretation of the law if any one disputes it, it is evident our laws give our playful giant, in doing as he likes, considerable advantage. Besides, even if he can be clearly proved to commit an illegality in doing as he likes, there is always the resource of not putting the law in force, or of abolishing it. So he has his way, and if he has his way he is soon satisfied for the time. However, he falls into the habit of taking it oftener and oftener, and at last begins to create by his operations a confusion of which mischievous people can take advantage, and which at any rate, by troubling the common course of business throughout the country, tends to cause distress, and so to increase the sort of anarchy and social disintegration which had previously commenced. And thus that profound sense of settled order and security, without which a society like ours cannot live and grow at all, sometimes seems to be beginning to threaten us with taking its departure.

Now, if culture, which simply means trying to perfect oneself, and one's mind as part of oneself, brings us light, and if light shows us that there is nothing so very blessed in merely doing as one likes, that the worship of the mere freedom to do as one likes is worship of machinery, that the really blessed thing is to like what right reason ordains and to follow her authority, when we have got a practical benefit out of culture. We have got a much wanted principle, a principle of authority, to counteract the tendency to anarchy which seems to be threatening us.

But how to organise this authority, or to what hands to entrust the wielding of it? How to get your *State*, summing up the right reason of the community, and giving effect to it, as circumstances may require, with vigour? And here I think I see my enemies waiting for me with a hungry joy in their eyes. But I shall elude them.

The *State*, the power most representing the right reason of the nation, and most worthy, therefore, of ruling,—of exercising, when circumstances require it, authority over us all,—is for Mr. Carlyle the aristocracy. For Mr. Lowe, it is the middle class with its incomparable Parliament. For the Reform League, it is the working class, the class with 'the brightest powers of sympathy and readiest powers of action'. Now, culture, with its disinterested pursuit of perfection, culture, simply trying to see things as they are, in order to seize on the best and to make it prevail, is surely well fitted to help us to judge rightly, by all the aids of observing, reading, and thinking, the qualifications and titles to our confidence of these three candidates for authority, and can thus render us a practical service of no mean value.

So when Mr. Carlyle, a man of genius to whom we have all at one time or other been indebted for refreshment and stimulus, says we should give rule to the aristocracy, mainly because of its dignity and politeness, surely culture is useful in reminding us, that in our idea of perfection the characters of beauty and intelligence are both of them present, and sweetness and light, the two noblest of things, are united. Allowing, therefore, with Mr. Carlyle, the aristocratic class to possess sweetness,

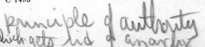

- principle of authority is reason which gets rid of anarchy

culture insists on the necessity of light also, and shows us that aristocracies, being by the very nature of things inaccessible to ideas, unapt to see how the world is going, must be somewhat wanting in light, and must therefore be, at a moment when light is our great requisite, inadequate to our needs. Aristocracies, those children of the established fact, are for epochs of concentration. In epochs of expansion, epochs such as that in which we now live, epochs when always the warning voice is again heard: *Now is the judgment of this world*—in such epochs aristocracies with their natural clinging to the established fact, their want of sense for the flux of things, for the inevitable transitoriness of all human institutions, are bewildered and helpless. Their serenity, their high spirit, their power of haughty resistance,—the great qualities of an aristocracy, and the secret of its distinguished manners and dignity,—these very qualities, in an epoch of expansion, turn against their possessors. Again and again I have said how the refinement of an aristocracy may be precious and educative to a raw nation as a kind of shadow of true refinement; how its serenity and dignified freedom from petty cares may serve as a useful foil to set off the vulgarity and hideousness of that type of life which a hard middle class tends to establish, and to help people to see this vulgarity and hideousness in their true colours. From such an ignoble spectacle as that of poor Mrs. Lincoln, —a spectacle to vulgarise a whole nation,—aristocracies undoubtedly preserve us. But the true grace and serenity is that of which Greece and Greek art suggest that admirable ideals of perfection,— a serenity which comes from having made order among ideas and harmonised them; whereas the serenity of aristocracies, at least the peculiar serenity of aristocracies of Teutonic origin, appears to come from their never having had any ideas to trouble them. And so, in a time of expansion like the present, a time for ideas, one gets, perhaps, in regarding an aristocracy, even more than the idea of serenity, the idea of futility and sterility.

One has often wondered whether upon the whole earth there is anything so unintelligent, so unapt to perceive how the world is really going, as an ordinary young Englishman of our upper class. Ideas he has not, and neither has he that seriousness of our middle class which is, as I have often said, the great strength of this class, and may become its salvation. Why, a man may hear a young Dives of the aristocratic class, when the whim take him to sing the praises of wealth and material comfort, sing them with a cynicism from which the conscience of the veriest Philistine of our industrial middle class would recoil in affright. And when, with the natural sympathy of aristocracies for firm dealing with the multitude, and his uneasiness at our feeble dealing with it at home, an unvarnished young Englishman of our aristocratic class applauds the absolute rulers on the Continent, he in general manages completely to miss the grounds of reason and intelligence which alone can give any colour of justification, any possibility of existence, to those rulers, and applauds them on grounds which it would make their own hair stand on end to listen to.

And all this time we are in an epoch of expansion; and the essence of an epoch of expansion is a movement of ideas, and the one salvation of an epoch of expansion is a harmony of ideas. The very principle of the authority which we are seeking as a defence against anarchy is right reason, ideas, light. The more, therefore, an aristocracy calls to its aid its innate forces,—its impenetrability, its high spirit, its power of haughty resistance,—to deal with an epoch of expansion, the graver is the danger, the greater the certainty of explosion, the surer the aristocracy's defeat; for it is trying to do violence to nature instead of working along with it. The best powers shown by the best men of an aristocracy at such an epoch are, it will be observed, non-aristocratical powers, powers of industry, powers of intelligence; and these powers, thus exhibited, tend really not to strengthen the aristocracy, but to take their owners out of it, to expose them to the dissolving agencies of thought and change, to make them men of the modern spirit and of the future. If, as sometimes happens, they add to their non-aristocratical qualities of labour and thought, a strong dose of aristocratical qualities also,—of pride, defiance, turn for resistance— this truly aristocratical side of them, so far from adding any strength to them, really neutralises their force and makes them impracticable and ineffective.

Knowing myself to be indeed sadly to seek, as one of my many critics says, in 'a philosophy with coherent, interdependent, subordinate and derivative principles', I continually have recourse to a plain man's expedient of trying to make what few simple notions I have, clearer and more intelligible to myself, by means of example and illustration. And having been brought up at Oxford in the bad old times, when we were stuffed with Greek and Aristotle, and thought nothing of preparing ourselves by the study of modern languages,—as after Mr. Lowe's great speech at Edinburgh we shall do,—to fight the battle of life with the waiters in foreign hotels, my head is still full of a lumber of phrases we learnt at Oxford from Aristotle, about virtue being in a mean, and about excess and defect, and so on. Once when I had had the advantage of listening to the Reform debates in the House of Commons, having heard a number of interesting speakers, and among them Lord Elcho and Sir Thomas

Bateson, I remember it struck me, applying Aristotle's machinery of the mean to my ideas about our aristocracy, that Lord Elcho was exactly the perfection, or happy mean, or virtue, of aristocracy, and Sir Thomas Bateson the excess; and I fancied that by observing these two we might see both the inadequacy of aristocracy to supply the principle of authority needful for our present wants, and the danger of its trying to supply it when it was not really competent for the business. On the one hand, in Lord Elcho, showing plenty of high spirit, but remarkable, far above and beyond his gift of high spirit, for the fine tempering of his high spirit, for ease, serenity, politeness, —the great virtues, as Mr. Carlyle says, of aristocracy,— in this beautiful and virtuous mean, there seemed evidently some insufficiency of light; while, on the other hand, Sir Thomas Bateson, in whom the high spirit of aristocracy, its impenetrability, defiant courage, and pride of resistance, were developed even in excess, was manifestly capable, if he had his way given him, of causing us great danger, and, indeed, of throwing the whole commonwealth into confusion. Then I reverted to that old fundamental notion of mine about the grand merit of our race being really our honesty. And the very helplessness of our aristocratic or governing class in dealing with our perturbed social condition gave me a sort of pride and satisfaction; because I saw they were, as a whole, too honest to try and manage a business for which they did not feel themselves capable.

Surely, now, it is no inconsiderable boon which culture confers upon us, if in embarrassed times like the present it enables us to look at the ins and the outs of things in this way, without hatred and without partiality, and with a disposition to see the good in everybody all round. And I try to follow just the same course with our middle class as with our aristocracy. Mr. Lowe talks to us of this strong middle part of the nation, of the unrivalled deeds of our Liberal middle-class Parliament, of the noble, the heroic work it has performed in the last thirty years; and I begin to ask myself if we shall not, then, find in our middle class the principle of authority we want, and if we had not better take administration as well as legislation away from the weak extreme which now administers for us, and commit both to the strong middle part. I observe, too, that the heroes of middle-class Liberalism, such as we have hitherto known it, speak with a kind of prophetic anticipation of the great destiny which awaits them, and as if the future was clearly theirs. The advanced party, the progressive party, the party in alliance with the future, are the names they like to give themselves. 'The principles which will obtain recognition in the future', says Mr. Miall, a personage of deserved eminence among the political Dissenters, as they are called, who have been the backbone of middle-class Liberalism— 'the principles which will obtain recognition in the future are the principles for which I have long and zealously laboured. I qualified myself for joining in the work of harvest by doing to the best of my ability the duties of seed time.' These duties, if one is to gather them from the works of the great Liberal party in the last thirty years, are, as I have elsewhere summed them up, the advocacy of free-trade, of parliamentary reform, of abolition of church-rates, of voluntaryism in religion and education, of non-interference of the State between employers and employed, and of marriage with one's deceased wife's sister.

Now I know, when I object that all this is machinery, the great Liberal middle class has by this time grown cunning enough to answer that it always meant more by these things than meets the eye; that it has had that within which passes show, and that we are soon going to see, in a Free Church and all manner of good things, what it was. But I have learned from Bishop Wilson (if Mr. Frederic Harrison will forgive my again quoting that poor old hierophant of a decayed superstition): 'If we would really know our heart let us impartially view our actions'; and I cannot help thinking that if our Liberals had had so much sweetness and light in their inner minds as they allege, more of it must have come out in their sayings and doings.

An American friend of the English Liberals says, indeed, that their Dissidence of Dissent has been a mere instrument of the political Dissenters for making reason and the will of God prevail (and no doubt he would say the same of marriage with one's deceased wife's sister); and that the abolition of a State Church is merely the Dissenter's means to this end, just as culture is mine. Another American defender of theirs says just the same of their industrialism and free-trade; indeed, this gentleman, taking the bull by the horns, proposes that we should for the future call industrialism culture, and the industrialists the men of culture, and then of course there can be no longer any misapprehension about their true character; and besides the pleasure of being wealthy and comfortable, they will have authentic recognition as vessels of sweetness and light.

All this is undoubtedly specious; but I must remark that the culture of which I talked was an endeavour to come at reason and the will of God by means of reading, observing, and thinking; and that whoever calls anything else culture, may, indeed, call it so if he likes, but then he talks of something quite different from what I talked of. And, again, as culture's way of working for reason and the will of God is by directly trying to know more about them, while the Dissidence of Dissent is evidently in itself no effort of this kind, nor is its Free Church, in fact, a church with worthier conceptions of God and the ordering of the world than the State Church professes, but with mainly the same conceptions of these as the State Church has, only that every man is to comport himself as he likes in professing them,—this being so, I cannot at once accept the Non-conformity any more than the industrialism and the other great works of our Liberal middle class as proof positive that this class is in possession of light, and that here is the true seat of authority for which we are in search; but I must try a little further, and seek for other indications which may enable me to make up my mind.

Why should we not do with the middle class as we have done with the aristocratic class,—find in it some representative men who may stand for the virtous mean of this class, for the perfection of its present qualities and mode of being, and also for the excess of them. Such men must clearly not be men of genius like Mr. Bright; for, as I have formerly said, so far as a man has genius he tends to take himself out of the category of class altogether, and to become simply a man. Mr. Bright's brother, Mr. Jacob Bright, would, perhaps, be more to the purpose; he seems to sum up very well in himself, without disturbing influences, the general liberal force of the middle class, the force by which it has done its great works of free-trade, parliamentary reform, voluntaryism, and so on, and the spirit in which it has done them. Now it is clear, from what has been already said, that there has been at least an apparent want of light in the force and spirit through which these great works have been done, and that the works have worn in consequence too much a look of machinery. But this will be clearer still if we take, as the happy mean of the middle class, not Mr. Jacob Bright, but his colleague in the representation of Manchester, Mr. Bazley. Mr. Bazley sums up for us, in general, the middle class, its spirit and its works, at least as well as Mr. Jacob Bright; and he has given us, moreover, a famous sentence, which bears directly on the resolution of our present question,—whether there is light enough in our middle class to make it the proper seat of the authority we wish to establish. When there was a talk some little while ago about the state of middle-class education, Mr. Bazley, as the representative of that class, spoke some memorable words: 'There had been a cry that middle class education ought to receive more attention. He confessed himself very much surprised by the clamour that was raised. He did not think that class need excite the sympathy either of the legislature or the public.' Now this satisfaction of Mr. Bazley with the mental state of the middle class was truly representative, and makes good his claim to stand as the beautiful and virtuous mean of that class. But it is obviously at variance with our definition of culture, or the pursuit of light and perfection, which made light and perfection consist, not in resting and being, but in growing and becoming, in a perpetual advance in beauty and wisdom. So the middle class is by its essence, as one may say, by its incomparable self-satisfaction decisively expressed through its beautiful and virtuous mean, self-excluded from wielding an authority of which light is to be the very soul.

Clear as this is, it will be made clearer still if we take some representative man as the excess of the middle class, and remember that the middle class, in general, is to be conceived as a body swaying between the qualities of its mean and its excess, and on the whole, of course, as

Aristotle π

human nature is constituted, inclining rather towards the excess than the mean. Of its excess no better representative can possibly be imagined than the Rev. W. Cattle, a Dissenting minister from Walsall, who came before the public in connection with the proceedings at Birmingham of Mr. Murphy, already mentioned. Speaking in the midst of an irritated population of Catholics, the Rev. W. Cattle exclaimed: 'I say, then, away with the Mass! It is from the bottomless pit; and in the bottomless pit shall all liars have their part, in the lake that burneth with fire and brimstone.' And again: 'When all the praties were black in Ireland, why didn't the priests say the hocus-pocus over them, and make them all good again?' He shared, too, Mr. Murphy's fears of some invasion of his domestic happiness: 'What I wish to say to you as Protestant husbands is, *Take care of your wives*!' And, finally, in the true vein of an Englishman doing as he likes, a vein of which I have at some length pointed out the present dangers, he recommended for imitation the example of some churchwardens at Dublin, among whom, said he, 'there was a Luther and also a Melancthon', who had made very short work with some ritualist or other, hauled him down from his pulpit, and kicked him out of church. Now it is manifest, as I said in the case of Sir Thomas Bateson, that if we let this excess of the sturdy English middle class, this conscientious Protestant Dissenter, so strong, so self-reliant, so fully persuaded in his own mind, have his way, he would be capable, with his want of light—or, to use the language of the religious world, with his zeal without knowledge—of stirring up strife which neither he nor any one else could easily compose.

And then comes in, as it did also with the aristocracy, the honesty of our race, and by the voice of another middle-class man, Alderman Wilson, Alderman of the City of London and Colonel of the City of London Militia, proclaims that it has twinges of conscience, and that it will not attempt to cope with our social disorders, and to deal with a business which it feels to be too high for it. Every one remembers how this virtuous Alderman-Colonel, or Colonel-Alderman, led his militia through the London streets; how the bystanders gathered to see him pass; how the London roughs, asserting an Englishman's best and most blissful right of doing what he likes, robbed and beat the bystanders; and how the blameless warrior-magistrate refused to let his troops interfere. 'The crowd', he touchingly said afterwards, 'was mostly composed of fine healthy strong men, bent on mischief; if he had allowed his soldiers to interfere they might have been overpowered, their rifles taken from them and used against them by the mob; a riot, in fact, might have ensued, and been attended with bloodshed, compared with which the assaults and loss of property that actually occurred would have been as nothing'. Honest and affecting testimony of the English middle class to its own inadequacy for the authoritative part one's admiration would sometimes incline one to assign to it! 'Who are we,' they say by the voice of their Alderman-Colonel, 'that we should not be overpowered if we attempt to cope with social anarchy, our rifles taken from us and used against us by the mob, and we, perhaps, robbed and beaten ourselves? Or what light have we, beyond a freeborn Englishman's impulse to do as he likes, which could justify us in preventing, at the cost of bloodshed, other free-born Englishmen from doing as they like, and robbing and beating us as much as they please?'

This distrust of themselves as an adequate centre of authority does not mark the working class, as was shown by their readiness the other day in Hyde Park to take upon themselves all the functions of government. But this comes from the working class being as I have often said, still an embryo, of which no one can yet quite foresee the final development; and from its not having the same experience and self-knowledge as the aristocratic and middle classes. Honesty it no doubt has, just like the other classes of Englishmen, but honesty in an inchoate and untrained state; and meanwhile its powers of action, which are, as Mr. Frederic Harrison says, exceedingly ready, easily run away with it. That it cannot at present have a sufficiency of light which comes by culture,—that is, by reading, observing, and thinking,—is clear from the very nature of its condition; and, indeed, we saw that Mr. Frederic Harrison, in seeking to make a free stage for its bright powers of sympathy and ready powers of action, had to begin by throwing overboard culture, and flouting it as only fit for a professor of *belles lettres*. Still, to make it perfectly manifest that no more in the working class than in the aristocratic and middle classes can one find an adequate centre of authority,—that is, as culture teaches us to conceive our required authority, of light,— let us again follow, with this class, the method we have followed with the aristocratic and middle classes, and try to bring before our minds representative men, who may figure to us its virtue and its excess.

We must not take, of course, men like the chiefs of the Hyde Park demonstration, Colonel Dickson or Mr. Beales; because Colonel Dickson, by his martial profession and dashing exterior, seems to belong properly, like Julius Cæsar and Mirabeau and other great popular leaders, to the aristocratic class, and to be carried into the popular ranks only by his ambition or his genius; while Mr. Beales belongs to our solid middle class, and, perhaps, if he had not been a great popular leader, would have been a Philistine. But Mr. Odger, whose speeches we have all read, and of whom his friends relate, besides, much that is favourable, may very well stand for the beautiful and virtuous mean of our present working class; and I think everybody will admit that in Mr. Odger, as in Lord Elcho, there is manifestly, with all his good points, some insufficiency of light. The excess of the working class, in its present state of development, is perhaps best shown in Mr. Bradlaugh, the iconoclast, who seems to be almost for baptizing us all in blood and fire into his new social dispensation, and to whose reflections, now that I have once been set going on Bishop Wilson's track, I cannot forbear commending this maxim of the good old man: 'Intemperance in talk makes a dreadful havoc in the heart.' Mr. Bradlaugh, like Sir Thomas Bateson and the Rev. W. Cattle, is evidently capable, if he had his head given him, of running us all into great dangers and confusion. I conclude, therefore—what, indeed, few of those who do me the honour to read this disquisition are likely to dispute,—that we can as little find in the working class as in the aristocratic or in the middle class our much-wanted source of authority, as culture suggests it to us.

Well, then, what if we tried to rise above the idea of class to the idea of the whole community, *the State*, and to find our centre of light and authority there? Every one of us has the idea of country, as a sentiment; hardly any one of us has the idea of *the State*, as a working power. And why? Because we habitually live in our ordinary selves, which do not carry us beyond the ideas and wishes of the class to which we happen to belong. And we are all afraid of giving to the State too much power, because we only conceive of the State as something equivalent to the class in occupation of the executive government, and are afraid of that class abusing power to its own purposes. If we strengthen the State with the aristocratic class in occupation of the executive government, we imagine we are delivering ourselves up captive to the ideas and wishes of our fierce aristocratical baronet Sir Thomas Bateson; if with the middle class in occupation of the executive government, to those of our truculent middle-class Dissenting minister, the Rev. W. Cattle; if with the working class, to those of its notorious tribune, Mr. Bradlaugh. And with much justice; owing to the exaggerated notion which we English, as I have said, entertain of the right and blessedness of the mere doing as one likes, of the affirming oneself, and oneself just as it is. People of the aristocratic class want to affirm their ordinary selves, their likings and dislikings; people of the middle class the same, people of the working class the same. By our every-day selves, however, we are separate, personal, at war; we are only safe from one another's tyranny when no one has any power; and this safety, in its turn, cannot save us from anarchy. And when, therefore, anarchy presents itself as a danger to us, we know not where to turn.

But by our *best self* we are united, impersonal, at harmony. We are in no peril from giving authority to this, because it is the truest friend we all of us can have; and when anarchy is a danger to us, to this authority we may turn with sure trust. Well, and this is the very self which culture, or the study of perfection, seeks to develop in us; at the expense of our old untransformed self, taking pleasure only in doing what it likes or is used to do, and exposing us to the risk of clashing with every one else who is doing the same! So that our poor culture, which is flouted as so unpractical, leads us to the very ideas capable of meeting the great want of our present embarrassed times! We want an authority, and we find nothing but jealous classes, checks, and a deadlock; culture suggests the idea of *the State*. We find no basis for a firm State-power in our ordinary selves; culture suggests one to us in our *best self*.

It cannot but acutely try a tender conscience to be accused, in a practical country like ours, of keeping aloof from the work and hope of a multitude of earnest-hearted men, and of merely toying with poetry and æsthetics. So it is with no little sense of relief that I find myself thus in the position of one who makes a contribution in aid of the practical necessities of our times. The great thing, it will be observed, is to find our *best* self, and to seek to affirm nothing but that; not,—as we English with our over-value for merely being free and busy have been so accustomed to do,—resting satisfied with a self which comes uppermost long before our best self, and affirming that with blind energy. In short,—to go back yet once more to Bishop Wilson,—of these two excellent rules of Bishop Wilson's for a man's guidance: 'Firstly, never go against the best light you have; secondly, take care that your light be not darkness', we English have followed with praiseworthy zeal the first rule, but we have not given so much heed to the second. We have gone manfully, the Rev. W. Cattle and the rest of us, according to the best light we have; but we have not taken enough care that this should be really the best light possible for us, that it should not be darkness. And, our honesty being very great, conscience has whispered to us that the light we were following, our ordinary self, was, indeed, perhaps, only an inferior self, only darkness; and that it would not do to impose this seriously on all the world.

But our best self inspires faith, and is capable of affording a serious principle of authority. For example. We are on our way to what the late Duke of Wellington, with his strong sagacity, foresaw and admirably described as 'a revolution by due course of law'. This is undoubtedly, —if we are still to live and grow, and this famous nation is not to stagnate and dwindle away on the one hand, or, on the other, to perish miserably in mere anarchy and confusion,—what we are on the way to. Great changes there must be, for a revolution cannot accomplish itself without great changes; yet order there must be, for without order a revolution cannot accomplish itself by due course of law. So whatever brings risk of tumult and disorder, multitudinous processions in the streets of our crowded towns, multitudinous meetings in their public places and parks,—demonstrations perfectly unnecessary in the present course of our affairs,—our best self, or right reason, plainly enjoins us to set our faces against. It enjoins us to encourage and uphold the occupants of the executive power, whoever they may be, in firmly prohibiting them. But it does this clearly and resolutely, and is thus a real principle of authority, because it does it with a free conscience; because in thus provisionally strengthening the executive power, it knows that it is not doing this merely to enable Sir Thomas Bateson to affirm himself as against Mr. Bradlaugh, or the Rev. W. Cattle to affirm himself as against both. It knows that it is stablishing *the State*, or organ of our collective best self, of our national right reason; and it has the testimony of conscience that it is stablishing the State on behalf of whatever great changes are needed, just as much as on behalf of order; stablishing it to deal just as stringently, when the time comes, with Sir Thomas Bateson's Protestant ascendency, or with the Rev. W. Cattle's sorry education of his children, as it deals with Mr. Bradlaugh's street-processions.

III. BARBARIANS, PHILISTINES, POPULACE

FROM a man without a philosophy no one can expect philosophical completeness. Therefore I may observe without shame, that in trying to get a distinct notion of our aristocratic, our middle, and our working class, with a view of testing the claims of each of these classes to become a centre of authority, I have omitted, I find, to complete the old-fashioned analysis which I had the fancy of applying, and have not shown in these classes, as well as the virtuous mean and the excess, the defect also. I do not know that the omission very much matters. Still, as clearness is the one merit which a plain, unsystematic writer, without a philosophy, can hope to have, and as our notion of the three great English classes may perhaps be made clearer if we see their distinctive qualities in the defect, as well as in the excess and in the mean, let us try, before proceeding further, to remedy this omission.

It is manifest, if the perfect and virtuous mean of that fine spirit which is the distinctive quality of aristocracies, is to be found in Lord Elcho's chivalrous style, and its excess in Sir Thomas Bateson's turn for resistance, that its defect must lie in a spirit not bold and high enough, and in an excessive and pusillanimous unaptness for resistance. If, again, the perfect and virtuous mean of that force by which our middle class has done its great works, and of that self-reliance with which it contemplates itself and them, is to be seen in the performances and speeches of Mr. Bazley, and the excess of that force and of that self-reliance in the performances and speeches of the Rev. W. Cattle, then it is manifest that their defect must lie in a helpless inaptitude for the great works of the middle class, and in a poor and despicable lack of its self-satisfaction.

To be chosen to exemplify the happy mean of a good quality, or set of good qualities, is evidently a praise to a man; nay, to be chosen to exemplify even their excess, is a kind of praise. Therefore I could have no hesitation in taking Lord Elcho and Mr. Bazley, the Rev. W. Cattle and Sir Thomas Bateson, to exemplify, respectively, the mean and the excess of aristocratic and middle-class qualities. But perhaps there might be a want of urbanity in singling out this or that personage as the representative of defect. Therefore I shall leave the defect of aristocracy unillustrated by any representative man. But with oneself one may always, without impropriety, deal quite freely; and, indeed, this sort of plain-dealing with oneself has in it, as all the moralists tell us, something very wholesome. So I will venture to humbly offer myself as an illustration of defect in those forces and qualities which make our middle class what it is. The too well-founded reproaches of my opponents declare how little I have lent a hand to the great works of the middle class; for it is evidently these works, and my slackness at them, which are meant, when I am said to 'refuse to lend a hand to the humble operation of uprooting certain definite evils' (such as church-rates and others), and that therefore 'the believers in action grow impatient' with me. The line, again, of a still unsatisfied seeker which I have followed, the idea of self-transformation, of growing towards some measure of sweetness and light not yet reached, is evidently at clean variance with the perfect self-satisfaction current in my class, the middle class, and may serve to indicate in me, therefore, the extreme defect of this feeling. But these confessions, though salutary, are bitter and unpleasant.

To pass, then, to the working class. The defect of this class would be the falling short in what Mr. Frederic

Harrison calls those 'bright powers of sympathy and ready powers of action', of which we saw in Mr. Odger the virtous mean, and in Mr. Bradlaugh the excess. The working class is so fast growing and rising at the present time, that instances of this defect cannot well be now very common. Perhaps Canning's 'Needy Knife-Grinder' (who is dead, and therefore cannot be pained at my taking him for an illustration) may serve to give us the notion of defect in the essential quality of a working class; or I might even cite (since, though he is alive in the flesh, he is dead to all heed of criticism) my poor old poaching friend, Zephaniah Diggs, who, between his hare-snaring and his gin-drinking, has got his powers of sympathy quite dulled and his powers of action in any great movement of his class hopelessly impaired. But examples of this defect belong, as I have said, to a bygone age rather than to the present.

The same desire for clearness, which has led me thus to extend a little of my first analysis of the three great classes of English society, prompts me also to improve my nomenclature for them a little, with a view to making it thereby more manageable. It is awkward and tiresome to be always saying the aristocratic class, the middle class, the working class. For the middle class, for that great body which, as we know, 'has done all the great things that have been done in all departments', and which is to be conceived as moving between its two cardinal points of Mr. Bazley, our commercial member of Parliament, and the Rev. W. Cattle, our fanatical Protestant Dissenter,— for this class we have a designation which now has become pretty well known, and which we may as well still keep for them, the designation of Philistines. What this term means I have so often explained that I need not repeat it here. For the aristocratic class, conceived mainly as a body moving between the two cardinal points of our chivalrous Lord Elcho and our defiant baronet, Sir Thomas Bateson, we have as yet got no special designation. Almost all my attention has naturally been concentrated on my own class, the middle class, with which I am in closest sympathy, and which has been, besides, the great power of our day, and has had its praises sung by all speakers and newspapers.

Still the aristocratic class is so important in itself, and the weighty functions which Mr. Carlyle proposes at the present critical time to commit to it must add so much to its importance, that it seems neglectful, and a strong instance of that want of coherent philosophic method for which Mr. Frederic Harrison blames me, to leave the aristocratic class so much without notice and denomination. It may be thought that the characteristic which I have occasionally mentioned as proper to aristocracies,— their natural inaccessibility, as children of the established fact, to ideas,—points to our extending to this class also the designation of Philistines; the Philistine being, as is well known, the enemy of the children of light or servants of the idea. Nevertheless, there seem to be an inconvenience in thus giving one and the same designation to two very different classes; and besides, if we look into the thing closely, we shall find that the term Philistine conveys a sense which makes it more peculiarly appropriate to our middle class than to our aristocratic. For *Philistine* gives the notion of something particularly stiff-necked and perverse in the resistance to light and its children; and therein it specially suits our middle class, who not only do not pursue sweetness and light, but who even prefer to them that sort of machinery of business, chapels, tea-meetings, and addresses from Mr. Murphy and the Rev. W. Cattle, which makes up the dismal and illiberal life on which I have so often touched. But the aristocratic class has actually, as we have seen, in its well-known politeness, a kind of image or shadow of sweetness; and as for light, if it does not pursue light, it is not that it perversely cherishes some dismal and illiberal existence in preference to light, but it is lured off from following light by those mighty and eternal seducers of our race which weave for this class their most irresistible charms, —by worldly splendour, security, power and pleasure. These seducers are exterior goods, but in a way they are goods; and he who is hindered by them from caring for light and ideas, is not so much doing what is perverse as what is too natural.

Keeping this in view, I have in my own mind often indulged myself with the fancy of employing, in order to designate our aristocratic class, the name of *The Barbarians.* The Barbarians, to whom we all owe so much, and who reinvigorated and renewed our worn-out Europe, had, as is well known, eminent merits; and in this country, where we are for the most part sprung from the Barbarians, we have never had the prejudice against them which prevails among the races of Latin origin. The Barbarians brought with them that staunch individualism, as the modern phrase is, and that passion for doing as one likes, for the assertion of personal liberty, which appears to Mr. Bright the central idea of English life, and of which we have, at any rate, a very rich supply. The stronghold and natural seat of this passion was in the nobles of whom our aristocratic class are the inheritors; and this class, accordingly, have signally manifested it, and have done much by their example to recommend it to the body of the nation, who already, indeed, had it in their blood. The Barbarians, again, had the passion for field-sports; and they have handed it on to our aristocratic class, who of this passion too, as of the passion for asserting one's personal liberty, are the great natural stronghold. The care of the Barbarians for the body, and for all manly exercises; the vigour, good looks, and fine complexion which they acquired and perpetuated in their families by these means,—all this may be observed still in our aristocratic class. The chivalry of the Barbarians, with its characteristics of high spirit, choice manners, and distinguished bearing,—what is this but the attractive commencement of the politeness of our aristocratic class? In some Barbarian noble, no doubt, one would have admired, if one could have been then alive to see it, the rudiments of Lord Elcho. Only, all this culture (to call it by that name) of the Barbarians was an exterior culture mainly. It consisted principally in outward gifts and graces, in looks, manners, accomplishments, prowess. The chief inward gifts which had part in it were the most exterior, so to speak, of inward gifts, those which come nearest to outward ones; they were courage, a high spirit, self-confidence. Far within, and unawakened, lay a whole range of powers of thought and feeling, to which these interesting productions of nature had, from the circumstances of their life, no access. Making allowances for the difference of the times, surely we can observe precisely the same thing now in our aristocratic class. In general its culture is exterior chiefly; all the exterior graces and accomplishments, and the more external of the inward virtues, seem to be principally its portion. It now, of course, cannot but be often in contact with those studies by which, from the world of thought and feeling, true culture teaches us to fetch sweetness and light; but its hold upon these very studies appears remarkably external, and unable to exert any deep power upon its spirit. Therefore the one insufficiency which we noted in the

perfect mean of this class, Lord Elcho, was an insufficiency of light. And owing to the same causes, does not
a subtle criticism lead us to make, even on the good looks
and politeness of our aristocratic class, and of even the
most fascinating half of that class, the feminine half, the
one qualifying remark, that in these charming gifts there
should perhaps be, for ideal perfection, a shade more *soul*?

I often, therefore, when I want to distinguish clearly
the aristocratic class from the Philistines proper, or middle
class, name the former, in my own mind, *the Barbarians*.
And when I go through the country, and see this and that
beautiful and imposing seat of theirs crowning the land-
scape, 'There', I say to myself, 'is a great fortified post of
the Barbarians.'

It is obvious that part of the working class which, working diligently by the light of Mrs. Gooch's Golden Rule,
looks forward to the happy day when it will sit on thrones
with Mr. Bazley and other middle-class potentates, to
survey, as Mr. Bright beautifully says, 'the cities it has
built, the railroads it has made, the manufactures it has
produced, the cargoes which freight the ships of the
greatest mercantile navy the world has ever seen',—it is
obvious, I say, that this part of the working class is, or is
in a fair way to be, one in spirit with the industrial middle
class. It is notorious that our middle-class Liberals have
long looked forward to this consummation, when the
working class shall join forces with them, aid them heartily to carry forward their great works, go in a body to their
tea-meetings, and, in short, enable them to bring about
their millennium. That part of the working class, therefore, which does really seem to lend itself to these great
aims, may, with propriety, be numbered by us among
the Philistines. That part of it, again, which so much
occupies the attention of philanthropists at present,—the

part which gives all its energies to organising itself, through trades' unions and other means, so as to constitute, first, a great working-class power, independent of the middle and aristocratic classes, and then, by dint of numbers, give the law to them, and itself reign absolutely, —this lively and interesting part must also, according to our definition, go with the Philistines; because it is its class and its class-instinct which it seeks to affirm, its ordinary self, not its best self; and it is a machinery, an industrial machinery, and power and pre-eminence and other external goods, which fill its thoughts, and not an inward perfection. It is wholly occupied, according to Plato's subtle expression, with the things of itself and not its real self, with the things of the State and not the real State. But that vast portion, lastly, of the working class which, raw and half-developed, has long lain half-hidden amidst its poverty and squalor, and is now issuing from its hiding-place to assert an Englishman's heaven-born privilege of doing as he likes, and is beginning to perplex us by marching where it likes, meeting where it likes, bawling what it likes, breaking what it likes,—to this vast residuum we may with great propriety give the name of *Populace*.

Thus we have got three distinct terms, *Barbarians*, *Philistines*, *Populace*, to denote roughly the three great classes into which our society is divided; and though this humble attempt at a scientific nomenclature falls, no doubt, very far short in precision of what might be required from a writer equipped with a complete and coherent philosophy, yet, from a notoriously unsystematic and unpretending writer, it will, I trust, be accepted as sufficient.

But in using this new, and, I hope, convenient division of English society, two things are to be borne in mind.

The first is, that since, under all our class divisions, there is a common basis of human nature, therefore, in every one of us, whether we be properly Barbarians, Philistines, or Populace, there exists, sometimes only in germ and potentially, sometimes more or less developed, the same tendencies and passions which have made our fellow-citizens of other classes what they are. This consideration is very important, because it has great influence in begetting that spirit of indulgence which is a necessary part of sweetness, and which, indeed, when our culture is complete, is, as I have said, inexhaustible. Thus, an English Barbarian who examines himself will, in general, find himself to be not so entirely a Barbarian, but that he has in him, also, something of the Philistine, and even something of the Populace as well. And the same with Englishmen of the two other classes.

This is an experience which we may all verify every day. For instance, I myself (I again take myself as a sort of *corpus vile* to serve for illustration in a matter where serving for illustration may not by every one be thought agreeable), I myself am properly a Philistine,—Mr. Swinburne would add, the son of a Philistine. And although, through circumstances which will perhaps one day be known if ever the affecting history of my conversion comes to be written, I have, for the most part, broken with the ideas and the tea-meetings of my own class, yet I have not, on that account, been brought much the nearer to the ideas and works of the Barbarians or of the Populace. Nevertheless, I never take a gun or a fishing-rod in my hands without feeling that I have in the ground of my nature the self-same seeds which, fostered by circumstances, do so much to make the Barbarian; and that, with the Barbarian's advantages, I might have rivalled him. Place me in one of his great fortified ports, with these seeds of a love for field-sports sown in my nature, with all the means of developing them, with all pleasures at my command, with most whom I met deferring to me, every one I met smiling on me, and with every appearance of permanence and security before me and behind me,—then I too might have grown, I feel, into a very passable child of the established fact, of commendable spirit and politeness, and, at the same time, a little inaccessible to ideas and light; not, of course, with either the eminent fine spirit of Lord Elcho, or the eminent power of resistance of Sir Thomas Bateson, but, according to the measure of the common run of mankind, something between the two. And as to the Populace, who, whether he be Barbarian or Philistine, can look at them without sympathy, when he remembers how often,—every time that we snatch up a vehement opinion in ignorance and passion, every time that we long to crush an adversary by sheer violence, every time that we are envious, every time that we are brutal, every time that we adore mere power or success, every time that we add our voice to swell a blind clamour against some unpopular personage, every time that we trample savagely on the fallen,—he has found in his own bosom the eternal spirit of the Populace, and that there needs only a little help from circumstances to make it triumph in him untameably?

The second thing to be borne in mind I have indicated several times already. It is this. All of us, so far as we are Barbarians, Philistines, or Populace, imagine happiness to consist in doing what one's ordinary self likes. What one's ordinary self likes differs according to the class to which one belongs, and has its severer and its lighter side; always, however, remaining machinery, and nothing more. The graver self of the Barbarian likes honours and consideration; his more relaxed self, field-sports and pleasure. The graver self of one kind of Philistine likes fanaticism, business, and money-making; his more relaxed self, comfort and tea-meetings. Of another kind of Philistine, the graver self likes rattening; the relaxed self, deputations, or hearing Mr. Odger speak. The sterner self of the Populace likes bawling, hustling, and smashing; the lighter self, beer. But in each class there are born a certain number of natures with a curiosity about their best self, with a bent for seeing things as they are, for disentangling themselves from machinery, for simply concerning themselves with reason and the will of God, and doing their best to make these prevail;—for the pursuit, in a word, of perfection. To certain manifestations of this love for perfection mankind have accustomed themselves to give the name of genius; implying, by this name, something original and heaven-bestowed in the passion. But the passion is to be found far beyond those manifestations of it to which the world usually gives the name of genius, and in which there is, for the most part, a *talent* of some kind or other, a special and striking faculty of execution, informed by the heaven-bestowed ardour, or genius. It is to be found in many manifestations besides these, and may best be called, as we have called it, the love and pursuit of perfection; culture being the true nurse of the pursuing love, and sweetness and light the true character of the pursued perfection. Natures with this bent emerge in all classes,—among the Barbarians, among the Philistines, among the Populace. And this bent always tends to take them out of their class, and to make their distinguishing characteristic not their Barbarianism or their Philistinism, but their *humanity*. They have, in general, a rough time of it in their lives; but they are sown more abundantly than one might think, they appear where and when one least expects it, they set up a fire which enfilades, so to speak, the class with which they are ranked; and, in general, by the extrication of their best self as the self to develop, and by the simplicity of the ends fixed by them as paramount, they hinder the unchecked predominance of that class-life which is the affirmation of our ordinary self, and seasonably disconcert mankind in their worship of machinery.

Therefore, when we speak of ourselves as divided into Barbarians, Philistines, and Populace, we must be understood always to imply that within each of these classes there are a certain number of *aliens*, if we may so call them,—persons who are mainly led, not by their class spirit, but by a general *humane* spirit, by the love of human perfection; and that this number is capable of being diminished or augmented. I mean, the number of those who will succeed in developing this happy instinct will be greater or smaller, in proportion both to the force of the original instinct within them, and to the hindrance or encouragement which it meets with from without. In almost all who have it, it is mixed with some infusion of the spirit of ordinary self, some quantity of class-instinct, and even, as has been shown, of more than one class-instinct at the same time; so that, in general, the extrication of the best self, the predominance of the *humane* instinct, will very much depend upon its meeting, or not, with what is fitted to help and elicit it. At a moment, therefore, when it is agreed that we want a source of authority, and when it seems probable that the right source is our best self, it becomes of vast importance to see whether or not the things around us are, in general, such as to help and elicit our best self, and if they are not, to see why they are not, and the most promising way of mending them.

Now, it is clear that the very absence of any powerful

authority amongst us, and the prevalent doctrine of the duty and happiness of doing as one likes, and asserting our personal liberty, must tend to prevent the erection of any very strict standard of excellence, the belief in any very paramount authority of right reason, the recognition of our best self as anything very recondite and hard to come at. It may be, as I have said, a proof of our honesty that we do not attempt to give to our ordinary self, as we have it in action, predominant authority, and to impose its rule upon other people. But it is evident, also, that it is not easy, with our style of proceeding, to get beyond the notion of an ordinary self at all, or to get the paramount authority of a commanding best self, or right reason, recognised. The learned Martinus Scriblerus well says: 'The taste of the bathos is implanted by nature itself in the soul of man; till, perverted by custom or example, he is taught, or rather compelled, to relish the sublime.' But with us everything seems directed to prevent any such perversion of us by custom or example as might compel us to relish the sublime; by all means we are encouraged to keep our natural taste for the bathos unimpaired.

I have formerly pointed out how in literature the absence of any authoritative centre, like an Academy, tends to do this. Each section of the public has its own literary organ, and the mass of the public is without any suspicion that the value of these organs is relative to their being nearer a certain ideal centre of correct information, taste, and intelligence, or farther away from it. I have said that within certain limits, which any one who is likely to read this will have no difficulty in drawing for himself, my old adversary, the *Saturday Review*, may, on matters of literature and taste, be fairly enough regarded, relatively to the mass of newspapers which treat these matters, as a kind of organ of reason. But I remember

once conversing with a company of Nonconformist admirers of some lecturer who had let off a great firework,
which the *Saturday Review* said was all noise and false
lights, and feeling my way as tenderly as I could about
the effect of this unfavourable judgment upon those with
whom I was conversing. 'Oh,' said one who was their
spokesman, with the most tranquil air of conviction, 'it
is true the *Saturday Review* abuses the lecture, but the
British Banner' (I am not quite sure it was the *British
Banner*, but it was some newspaper of that stamp) 'says
that the *Saturday Review* is quite wrong.' The speaker had
evidently no notion that there was a scale of value for
judgments on these topics, and that the judgments of the
Saturday Review ranked high on this scale, and those of the
British Banner low; the taste of the bathos implanted by
nature in the literary judgments of man had never, in
my friend's case, encountered any let or hindrance.

Just the same in religion as in literature. We have most
of us little idea of a high standard to choose our guides
by, of a great and profound spirit, which is an authority,
while inferior spirits are none. It is enough to give importance to things that this or that person says them decisively, and has a large following of some strong kind when
he says them. This habit of ours is very well shown in that
able and interesting work of Mr. Hepworth Dixon's,
which we were all reading lately, *The Mormons, by One of
Themselves*. Here, again, I am not quite sure that my
memory serves me as to the exact title, but I mean the
well-known book in which Mr. Hepworth Dixon described
the Mormons, and other similar religious bodies in
America, with so much detail and such warm sympathy.
In this work it seems enough for Mr. Dixon that this or
that doctrine has its Rabbi, who talks big to him, has
a staunch body of disciples, and, above all, has plenty of

rifles. That there are any further stricter tests to be applied to a doctrine, before it is pronounced important, never seems to occur to him. 'It is easy to say', he writes of the Mormons, 'that these saints are dupes and fanatics, to laugh at Joe Smith and his church, but what then? *The great facts remain.* Young and his people are at Utah; a church of 200,000 souls; an army of 20,000 rifles.' But if the followers of a doctrine are really dupes, or worse, and its promulgators are really fanatics, or worse, it gives the doctrine no seriousness or authority the more that there should be found 200,000 souls,—200,000 of the innumerable multitude with a natural taste for the bathos,—to hold it, and 20,000 rifles to defend it. And again, of another religious organisation in America: 'A fair and open field is not to be refused when hosts so mighty throw down wager of battle on behalf of what they hold to be true, however strange their faith may seem.' A fair and open field is not to be refused to any speaker; but this solemn way of heralding him is quite out of place, unless he has, for the best reason and spirit of man, some significance. 'Well, but', says Mr. Hepworth Dixon, 'a theory which has been accepted by men like Judge Edmonds, Dr. Hare, Elder Frederick, and Professor Bush!' And again: 'Such are, in brief, the bases of what Newman Weeks, Sarah Horton, Deborah Butler, and the associated brethren, proclaimed in Rolt's Hall as the new covenant!' If he was summing up an account of the doctrine of Plato or of St. Paul, and of its followers, Mr. Hepworth Dixon could not be more earnestly reverential. But the question is, Have personages like Judge Edmonds, and Newman Weeks, and Elderess Polly, and Elderess Antoinette, and the rest of Mr. Hepworth Dixon's heroes and heroines, anything of the weight and significance for the best reason and spirit of man that Plato and St. Paul have?

Evidently they, at present, have not; and a very small
taste of them and their doctrine ought to have convinced
Mr. Hepworth Dixon that they never could have. 'But',
says he, 'the magnetic power which Shakerism is exercising on American thought would of itself compel us',—
and so on. Now as far as real thought is concerned,—
thought which affects the best reason and spirit of man,
the scientific or the imaginative thought of the world,
the only thought which deserves speaking of in this solemn
way,—America has up to the present time been hardly
more than a province of England, and even now would
not herself claim to be more than abreast of England;
and of this only real human thought, English thought
itself is not just now, as we must all admit, the most significant factor. Neither, then, can American thought be;
and the magnetic power which Shakerism exercises on
American thought is about as important, for the best
reason and spirit of man, as the magnetic power which
Mr. Murphy exercises on Birmingham Protestantism.
And as we shall never get rid of our natural taste for the
bathos in religion,—never get access to a best self and
right reason which may stand as a serious authority,—
by treating Mr Murphy as his own disciples treat him,
seriously, and as if he was as much an authority as any
one else: so we shall never get rid of it while our able and
popular writers treat their Joe Smiths and Deborah
Butlers, with their so many thousand souls and so many
thousand rifles, in the like exaggerated and misleading
manner, and so do their best to confirm us in a bad
mental habit to which we are already too prone.

If our habits make it hard for us to come at the idea of
a high best self, of a paramount authority, in literature or
religion, how much more do they make this hard in the
sphere of politics! In other countries the governors, not

depending so immediately on the favour of the governed, have everything to urge them, if they know anything of right reason (and it is at least supposed that governors should know more of this than the mass of the governed), to set it authoritatively before the community. But our whole scheme of government being representative, every one of our governors has all possible temptation, instead of setting up before the governed who elect him, and on whose favour he depends, a high standard of right reason, to accommodate himself as much as possible to their natural taste for the bathos; and even if he tries to go counter to it, to proceed in this with so much flattering and coaxing, that they shall not suspect their ignorance and prejudices to be anything very unlike right reason, or their natural taste for the bathos to differ much from a relish for the sublime. Every one is thus in every possible way encouraged to trust in his own heart; but 'he that trusteth in his own heart', says the Wise Man, 'is a fool'; and at any rate this, which Bishop Wilson says, is undeniably true: 'The number of those who need to be awakened is far greater than that of those who need comfort.'

But in our political system everybody is comforted. Our guides and governors who have to be elected by the influence of the Barbarians, and who depend on their favour, sing the praises of the Barbarians, and say all the smooth things that can be said of them. With Mr. Tennyson, they celebrate 'the great broad-shouldered genial Englishman', with his 'sense of duty', his 'reverence for the laws', and his 'patient force', who saves us from the 'revolts, republics, revolutions, most no graver than a schoolboy's barring out', which upset other and less broad-shouldered nations. Our guides who are chosen by the Philistines and who have to look to their favour, tell the Philistines how 'all the world knows that the great middle class of this country supplies the mind, the will, and the power requisite for all the great and good things that have to be done', and congratulate them on their 'earnest good sense, which penetrates through sophisms, ignores commonplaces, and gives to conventional illusions their true value'. Our guides who look to the favour of the Populace, tell them that 'theirs are the brightest powers of sympathy, and the readiest powers of action'.

Harsh things are said too, no doubt, against all the great classes of the community; but these things so evidently come from a hostile class, and are so manifestly dictated by the passions and prepossessions of a hostile class, and not by right reason, that they make no serious impression on those at whom they are launched, but slide easily off their minds. For instance, when the Reform League orators inveigh against our cruel and bloated aristocracy, these invectives so evidently show the passions and point of view of the Populace, that they do not sink into the minds of those at whom they are addressed, or awaken any thought or self-examination in them. Again, when Sir Thomas Bateson describes the Philistines and the Populace as influenced with a kind of hideous mania for emasculating the aristocracy, that reproach so clearly comes from the wrath and excited imagination of the Barbarians, that it does not much set the Philistines and the Populace thinking. Or when Mr. Lowe calls the Populace drunken and venal, he so evidently calls them this in an agony of apprehension for his Philistine or middle-class Parliament, which has done so many great and heroic works, and is now threatened with mixture and debasement, that the Populace do not lay his words seriously to heart.

So the voice which makes a permanent impression on each of our classes is the voice of its friends, and this is from the nature of things, as I have said, a comforting voice. The Barbarians remain in the belief that the great broad-shouldered genial Englishman may be well satisfied with himself; the Philistines remain in the belief that the great middle class of this country, with its earnest common-sense penetrating through sophisms and ignoring commonplaces, may be well satisfied with itself; the Populace, that the working man with his bright powers of sympathy and ready powers of action, may be well satisfied with himself. What hope, at this rate, of extinguishing the taste of the bathos implanted by nature itself in the soul of man, or of inculcating the belief that excellence dwells among high and steep rocks, and can only be reached by those who sweat blood to reach her?

But it will be said, perhaps, that candidates for political influence and leadership, who thus caress the self-love of those whose suffrages they desire, know quite well that they are not saying the sheer truth as reason sees it, but that they are using a sort of conventional language, or what we call clap-trap, which is essential to the working of representative institutions. And therefore, I suppose, we ought rather to say with Figaro: *Qui est-ce qu'on trompe ici?* Now, I admit that often, but not always, when our governors say smooth things to the self-love of the class whose political support they want, they know very well that they are overstepping, by a long stride, the bounds of truth and soberness; and while they talk, they in a manner, no doubt, put their tongue in their cheek. Not always; because, when a Barbarian appeals to his own class to make him their representative and give him political power, he, when he pleases their self-love by extolling broad-shouldered genial Englishmen with their sense of duty, reverence for the laws, and patient force, pleases his own self-love and extols himself, and is, therefore, himself ensnared by his own smooth words. And so, too, when a Philistine wants to be sent to Parliament by his brother Philistines, and extols the earnest good sense which characterises Manchester and supplies the mind, the will, and the power, as the *Daily News* eloquently says, requisite for all the great and good things that have to be done, he intoxicates and deludes himself as well as his brother Philistines who hear him.

But it is true that a Barbarian often wants the political support of the Philistines; and he unquestionably, when he flatters the self-love of Philistinism, and extols, in the approved fashion, its energy, enterprise, and self-reliance, knows that he is talking clap-trap, and so to say, puts his tongue in his cheek. On all matters where Nonconformity and its catchwords are concerned, this insincerity of Barbarians needing Nonconformist support, and, therefore, flattering the self-love of Nonconformity and repeating its catchwords without the least real belief in them, is very noticeable. When the Nonconformists, in a transport of blind zeal, threw out Sir James Graham's useful Education Clauses in 1843, one-half of their parliamentary advocates, no doubt, who cried aloud against 'trampling on the religious liberty of the Dissenters by taking the money of Dissenters to teach the tenets of the Church of England', put their tongue in their cheek while they so cried out. And perhaps there is even a sort of motion of Mr. Frederic Harrison's tongue towards his cheek when he talks of 'the shriek of superstition', and tells the working class that 'theirs are the brightest powers of sympathy and the readiest powers of action'. But the point on which I would insist is, that this involuntary tribute to truth and soberness on the part of certain of our governors and guides never reaches at all the mass of us governed, to serve as a lesson to us, to abate our self-love, and to awaken in us a suspicion that our favourite prejudices may be, to a higher reason, all nonsense. Whatever by-play goes on among the more intelligent of our leaders, we do not see it; and we are left to believe that, not only in our own eyes, but in the eyes of our representative and ruling men, there is nothing more admirable than our ordinary self, whatever our ordinary self happens to be, Barbarian, Philistine, or Populace.

Thus everything in our political life tends to hide from us that there is anything wiser than our ordinary selves, and to prevent our getting the notion of a paramount right reason. Royalty itself, in its idea the expression of the collective nation, and a sort of constituted witness to its best mind, we try to turn into a kind of grand advertising van, meant to give publicity and credit to the inventions, sound or unsound, of the ordinary self of individuals.

I remember, when I was in North Germany, having this very strongly brought to my mind in the matter of schools and their institution. In Prussia, the best schools are Crown patronage schools, as they are called; schools which have been established and endowed (and new ones are to this day being established and endowed) by the Sovereign himself out of his own revenues, to be under the direct control and management of him or of those representing him, and to serve as types of what schools should be. The Sovereign, as his position raises him above many prejudices and littlenesses, and as he can always have at his disposal the best advice, has evident advantages over private founders in well planning and directing a school; while at the same time his great means and his great influence secure, to a well-planned school of his, credit and authority. This is what, in North Germany,

ideal education

the governors do in the matter of education for the governed; and one may say that they thus give the governed a lesson, and draw out in them the idea of a right reason higher than the suggestions of an ordinary man's ordinary self.

But in England how different is the part which in this matter our governors are accustomed to play! The Licensed Victuallers or the Commercial Travellers propose to make a school for their children; and I suppose, in the matter of schools, one may call the Licensed Victuallers or the Commercial Travellers ordinary men, with their natural taste for the bathos still strong; and a Sovereign with the advice of men like Wilhelm von Humboldt or Schleiermacher may, in this matter, be a better judge, and nearer to right reason. And it will be allowed, probably, that right reason would suggest that, to have a sheer school of Licensed Victuallers' children, or a sheer school of Commercial Travellers' children, and to bring them all up, not only at home but at school too, in a kind of odour of licensed victualism or of bagmanism, is not a wise training to give to these children. And in Germany, I have said, the action of the national guides or governors is to suggest and provide a better. But, in England, the action of the national guides or governors is, for a Royal Prince or a great Minister to go down to the opening of the Licensed Victuallers' or of the Commercial Travellers' school, to take the chair, to extol the energy and self-reliance of the Licensed Victuallers or the Commercial Travellers, to be all of their way of thinking, to predict full success to their schools, and never so much as to hint to them that they are probably doing a very foolish thing, and that the right way to go to work with their children's education is quite different. And it is the same in almost every department of affairs. While, on the Continent, the idea prevails that it is the business of the heads and representatives of the nation, by virtue of their superior means, power, and information, to set an example and to provide suggestions of right reason, among us the idea is that the business of the heads and representatives of the nation is to do nothing of the kind, but to applaud the natural taste for the bathos showing itself vigorously in any part of the community, and to encourage its works.

Now I do not say that the political system of foreign countries has not inconveniences which may outweigh the inconveniences of our own political system; nor am I the least proposing to get rid of our own political system and to adopt theirs. But a sound centre of authority being what, in this disquisition, we have been led to seek, and right reason, or our best self, appearing alone to offer such a sound centre of authority, it is necessary to take note of the chief impediments which hinder, in this country, the extrication or recognition of this right reason as a paramount authority, with a view to afterwards trying in what way they can best be removed.

This being borne in mind, I proceed to remark how not only do we get no suggestions of right reason, and no rebukes of our ordinary self, from our governors, but a kind of philosophical theory is widely spread among us to the effect that there is no such thing at all as a best self and a right reason having claim to paramount authority, or, at any rate, no such thing ascertainable and capable of being made use of; and that there is nothing but an infinite number of ideas and works of our ordinary selves, and suggestions of our natural taste for the bathos, pretty nearly equal in value, which are doomed either to an irreconcilable conflict, or else to a perpetual give and take; and that wisdom consists in choosing the give and take rather than the conflict, and in sticking to our choice with patience and good humour.

And, on the other hand, we have another philosophical theory rife among us, to the effect that without the labour of perverting ourselves by custom or example to relish right reason, but by continuing all of us to follow freely our natural taste for the bathos, we shall, by the mercy of Providence, and by a kind of natural tendency of things, come in due time to relish and follow right reason.

The great promoters of these philosophical theories are our newspapers, which, no less than our parliamentary representatives, may be said to act the part of guides and governors to us; and these favourite doctrines of theirs I call,—or should call, if the doctrines were not preached by authorities I so much respect,—the first, a peculiarly British form of Atheism, the second, a peculiarly British form of Quietism. The first-named melancholy doctrine is preached in the *Times* with great clearness and force of style; indeed, it is well known, from the example of the poet Lucretius and others, what great masters of style the atheistic doctrine has always counted among its promulgators. 'It is of no use', says the *Times*, 'for us to attempt to force upon our neighbours our several likings and dislikings. We must take things as they are. Everybody has his own little vision of religious or civil perfection. Under the evident impossibility of satisfying everybody, we agree to take our stand on equal laws and on a system as open and liberal as is possible. The result is that everybody has more liberty of action and of speaking here than anywhere else in the Old World'. We come again here upon Mr. Roebuck's celebrated definition of happiness, on which I have so often commented: 'I look around me and ask what is the state of England? Is not every man able to say what he likes? I ask you whether the world over, or in past history, there is anything like it? Nothing. I pray that our unrivalled happiness may last.' This is the old story of our system of checks and every Englishman doing as he likes, which we have already seen to have been convenient enough so long as there were only the Barbarians and the Philistines to do what they liked, but to be getting inconvenient, and productive of anarchy, now that the Populace wants to do what it likes too.

But for all that, I will not at once dismiss this famous doctrine, but will first quote another passage from the *Times*, applying the doctrine to a matter of which we have just been speaking,—education. 'The difficulty here' (in providing a national system of education), says the *Times*, 'does not reside in any removable arrangements. It is inherent and native in the actual and inveterate state of things in this country. All these powers and personages, all these conflicting influences and varieties of character, exist, and have long existed among us; they are fighting it out, and will long continue to fight it out, without coming to that happy consummation when some one element of the British character is to destroy or to absorb all the rest.' There it is; the various promptings of the natural taste for the bathos in this man and that amongst us are fighting it out; and the day will never come (and, indeed, why should we wish it to come?) when one man's particular sort of taste for the bathos shall tyrannise over another man's; nor when right reason (if that may be called an element of the British character) shall absorb and rule them all. 'The whole system of this country, like the constitution we boast to inherit, and are glad to up-hold, is made up of established facts, prescriptive authori-ties, existing usages, powers that be, persons in possession, and communities or classes that have won dominion for themselves, and will hold it against all comers.' Every force in the world, evidently, except the one reconciling force, right reason! Sir Thomas Bateson here, the Rev. W. Cattle on this side, Mr. Bradlaugh on that!—pull devil, pull baker! Really, presented with the mastery of style of our leading journal, the sad picture, as one gazes upon it, assumes the iron and inexorable solemnity of tragic Destiny.

After this, the milder doctrine of our other philosophical teacher, the *Daily News*, has, at first, something very attractive and assuaging. The *Daily News* begins, indeed, in appearance, to weave the iron web of necessity round us like the *Times*. 'The alternative is between a man's doing what he likes and his doing what some one else, probably not one whit wiser than himself, likes.' This points to the tacit compact, mentioned in my last paper, between the Barbarians and the Philistines, and into which it is hoped that the Populace will one day enter; the compact, so creditable to English honesty, that since each class has only the ideas and aims of its ordinary self to give effect to, none of them shall, if it exercise power, treat its ordinary self too seriously, or attempt to impose it on others; but shall let these others,—the Rev. W. Cattle, for instance, in his Papist-baiting, and Mr. Bradlaugh in his Hyde Park anarchy-mongering,—have their fling. But then the *Daily News* suddenly lights up the gloom of necessitarianism with bright beams of hope. 'No doubt,' it says, 'the common reason of society ought to check the aberrations of individual eccentricity.' This common reason of society looks very like our best self or right reason, to which we want to give authority, by making the action of the *State*, or nation in its collective character, the expression of it. But of this project of ours, the *Daily News*, with its subtle dialectics, makes havoc. 'Make the State the organ of the common reason?'—it says. 'You may make it the organ of something or other, but how can you be certain that reason will be the quality which will be embodied in it?' You cannot be certain of it, undoubtedly, if you never try to bring the thing about; but the question is, the action of the State being the action of the collective nation and the action of the collective nation carrying naturally great publicity, weight, and force of example with it, whether we should not try to put into the action of the State as much as possible of right reason, or our best self, which may, in this manner, come back to us with new force and authority; may have visibility, form, and influence; and help to confirm us, in the many moments when we are tempted to be our ordinary selves merely, in resisting our natural taste of the bathos rather than in giving way to it?

But no! says our teacher: 'It is better there should be an infinite variety of experiments in human action, because, as the explorers multiply, the true track is more likely to be discovered. The common reason of society can check the aberrations of individual eccentricity only by acting on the individual reason; and it will do so in the main sufficiently, if left to this natural operation.' This is what I call the specially British form of Quietism, or a devout, but excessive reliance on an over-ruling Providence. Providence, as the moralists are careful to tell us, generally works in human affairs by human means; so when we want to make right reason act on individual inclination, our best self on our ordinary self, we seek to give it more power of doing so by giving it public recognition and authority, and embodying it so far as we can, in the State. It seems too much to ask of Providence, that while we, on our part, leave our congenital taste for the bathos to its natural operation and its infinite variety of experiments, Providence should mysteriously guide it into the true track, and compel it to relish the sublime. At any rate, great men and great institutions have hitherto seemed necessary for producing any considerable effect of this kind. No doubt we have an infinite variety of experiments, and an ever-multiplying multitude of explorers. Even in these few chapters I have enumerated many: the *British Banner*, Judge Edmonds, Newman Weeks, Deborah Butler, Elderess Polly, Brother Noyes, the Rev. W. Cattle, the Licensed Victuallers, the Commercial Travellers, and I know not how many more; and the members of the noble army are swelling every day. But what a depth of Quietism, or rather, what an over-bold call on the direct interposition of Providence, to believe that these interesting explorers will discover the true track, or at any rate, 'will do so in the main well enough' (whatever that may mean) if left to their natural operation; that is, by going on as they are! Philosophers say, indeed, that we learn virtue by performing acts of virtue; but to say that we shall learn virtue by performing any acts to which our natural taste for the bathos carries us, that the Rev. W. Cattle comes at his best self by Papist-baiting, or Newman Weeks and Deborah Butler at right reason by following their noses, this certainly does appear over sanguine.

It is true, what we want is to make right reason act on individual reason, the reason of individuals; all our search for authority has that for its end and aim. The *Daily News* says, I observe, that all my argument for authority 'has a non-intellectual root'; and from what I know of my own mind and its poverty I think this so probable that I should be inclined easily to admit it, if it were not that, in the first place, nothing of this kind, perhaps, should be admitted without examination; and, in the second, a way of accounting for the charge being made, in this particular instance, without good grounds, appears to present itself. What seems to me to account here, perhaps, for the charge, is the want of flexibility of our race, on which I have so often remarked. I mean, it being admitted that the conformity of the individual reason of the Rev. W. Cattle or Mr. Bradlaugh with right reason is our true object, and not the mere restraining them, by the strong arm of the State, from Papist-baiting or railing-breaking,—admitting this, we English have so little flexibility that we cannot readily perceive that the State's restraining them from these indulgences may yet fix clearly in their minds that, to the collective nation, these indulgences appear irrational and unallowable, may make them pause and reflect, and may contribute to bringing, with time, their individual reason into harmony with right reason. But in no country, owing to the want of intellectual flexibility above mentioned, is the leaning which is our natural one, and, therefore, needs no recommending to us, so sedulously recommended, and the leaning which is not our natural one, and, therefore does not need dispraising to us, so sedulously dispraised, as in ours. To rely on the individual being, with us, the natural leaning, we will hear of nothing but the good of relying on the individual; to act through the collective nation on the individual being not our natural leaning, we will hear nothing in recommendation of it. But the wise know that we often need to hear most of that to which we are least inclined, and even to learn to employ, in certain circumstances, that which is capable, if employed amiss, of being a danger to us.

Elsewhere this is certainly better understood than here. In a recent number of the *Westminster Review*, an able writer, but with precisely our national want of flexibility of which I have been speaking, has unearthed, I see, for our present needs, an English translation, published some years ago, of Wilhelm von Humboldt's book, *The Sphere and Duties of Government*. Humboldt's object in this book is to show that the operation of government ought to be severely limited to what directly and immediately relates to the security of person and property. Wilhelm von Humboldt, one of the most beautiful souls that have ever existed, used to say that one's business in life was first to perfect oneself by all the means in one's power, and secondly to try and create in the world around one an aristocracy the most numerous that one possibly could, of talents and characters. He saw, of course, that, in the end, everything comes to this,—that the individual must act for himself, and must be perfect in himself; and he lived in a country, Germany, where people were disposed to act too little for themselves, and to rely too much on the Government. But even thus, such was his flexibility, so little was he in bondage to a mere abstract maxim, that he saw very well that for his purpose itself, of enabling the individual to stand perfect on his own foundations and to do without the State, the action of the State would for long, long years be necessary. And soon after he wrote his book on *The Sphere and Duties of Government*, Wilhelm von Humboldt became Minister of Education in Prussia; and from his ministry all the great reforms which give the control of Prussian education to the State,—the transference of the management of public schools from their old boards of trustees to the State, the obligatory State-examination for schools, the obligatory State-examination for schoolmasters, and the foundation of the great State-University of Berlin,—take their origin. This his English reviewer says not a word of. But, writing for a people whose dangers lie, as we have seen, on the side of their unchecked and unguided individual action, whose dangers none of them like on the side of an over-reliance on the State, he quotes just so much of Wilhelm von Humboldt's example as can flatter them in their propensities, and do them no good; and just what might make them think, and be of use to them, he leaves on one side. This precisely recalls the manner, it will be observed, in which we have seen that our royal and noble personages proceed with the Licensed Victuallers.

In France the action of the State on individuals is yet more preponderant than in Germany; and the need which friends of human perfection feel for what may enable the individual to stand perfect on his own foundations is all the stronger. But what says one of the staunchest of these friends, M. Renan, on State action; and even State action in that very sphere where in France it is most excessive, the sphere of education? Here are his words: 'A Liberal believes in liberty, and liberty signifies the non-intervention of the State. *But such an ideal is still a long way off from us, and the very means to remove it to an indefinite distance would be precisely the State's withdrawing its action too soon.*' And this, he adds, is even truer of education than of any other department of public affairs.

RELIGION GIVEN

(1873)

See Contents, p. v

I HAVE said elsewhere how much it has contributed to the misunderstanding of St. Paul, that terms like *grace*, *new birth*, *justification*,—which he used in a fluid and passing way, as men use terms in common discourse or in eloquence and poetry, to describe approximately, but only approximately, what they have present before their mind but do not profess that their mind does or can grasp exactly or adequately,—that such terms people have blunderingly taken in a fixed and rigid manner, as if they were symbols with as definite and fully grasped a meaning as the names *line* or *angle*, and proceeded to use them on this supposition. Terms, in short, which with St. Paul are *literary* terms, theologians have employed as if they were *scientific* terms.

But if one desires to deal with this mistake thoroughly, one must observe it in that supreme term with which religion is filled,—the term *God*. The seemingly incurable ambiguity in the mode of employing this word is at the root of all our religious differences and difficulties. People use it as if it stood for a perfectly definite and ascertained idea, from which we might, without more ado, extract propositions and draw inferences, just as we should from any other definite and ascertained idea. For instance, I open a book which controverts what its author thinks dangerous views about religion, and I read: 'Our sense of morality tells us so-and-so; our sense of God, on the other hand, tells us so-and-so.' And again, 'the impulse in man to seek God' is distinguished, as if the distinction were self-evident and explained itself, from 'the impulse in man to seek his highest perfection'. Now, *morality* represents for everybody a thoroughly definite and ascertained idea:—the idea of human conduct regulated in a certain manner. Everybody, again, understands distinctly enough what is meant by man's perfection:—his reaching the best which his powers and circumstances allow him to reach. And the word 'God' is used, in connexion with both these words, morality and perfection, as if it stood for just as definite and ascertained an idea as they do; an idea drawn from experience, just as the ideas are which they stand for; an idea about which everyone was agreed, and from which we might proceed to argue and to make inferences, with the certainty that, as in the case of morality and perfection, the basis on which we were going everyone knew and granted. But, in truth, the word 'God' is used in most cases as by no means a term of science or exact knowledge, but a term of poetry and eloquence, a term *thrown out*, so to speak, at a not fully grasped object of the speaker's consciousness, a literary term, in short; and mankind mean different things by it as their consciousness differs.

The first question, then, is, how people are using the word; whether in this literary way, or in a scientific way. The second question is, what, supposing them to use the term as one of poetry and eloquence, and to import into it, therefore, a great deal of their own individual feelings and character, is yet the common substratum of idea on which, in using it, they all rest. For this will then be, for them, and for us in dealing with them, the real sense of the word; the sense in which we can use it for purposes of argument and inference without ambiguity.

Strictly and formally the word 'God', so some philologists tell us, means, like its kindred Aryan words, *Theos*, *Deus*, and *Deva*, simply *shining* or *brilliant*. In a certain narrow way, therefore, this would be (if the etymology is right) the one exact and scientific sense of the word. It was long thought, however, to mean *good*, and so Luther took it to mean *the best that man knows or can know*; and in this sense, as a matter of fact and history, mankind constantly use the word. This is the common substratum of idea on which men in general, when they use the word *God*, rest; and we can take this as the word's real sense fairly enough, only it does not give us anything very precise.

But then there is also the scientific sense held by theologians, deduced from the ideas of substance, identity, causation, design, and so on; but taught, they say, or at least implied, in the Bible, and on which they all the Bible rests. According to this scientific and theological sense,—which has all the outward appearances, at any rate, of great precision,—God is an infinite and eternal substance, and at the same time a person, the great first cause, the moral and intelligent governor of the universe; Jesus Christ is consubstantial with him; and the Holy Ghost is a person proceeding from the other two. This is the sense for which, or for portions of which, the Bishops of Winchester and Gloucester are so zealous to do something.

Other people, however, who fail to perceive the force of such a deduction from the abstract ideas above mentioned, who indeed think it quite hollow, but who are told that this sense is in the Bible, and that they must receive it if they receive the Bible, conclude that in that case they had better receive neither the one nor the other. Something of this sort it was, no doubt, which made Professor Huxley tell the London School Board lately, that 'if these islands had no religion at all, it would not enter into his mind to introduce the religious idea by the agency of the Bible'. Of such people there are now a great many; and indeed there could hardly, for those who value the Bible, be a greater example of the sacrifices one is sometimes called upon to make for the truth, than to find that for the truth as held by the Bishops of Winchester and Gloucester, if it is the truth, one must sacrifice the allegiance of so many people to the Bible.

But surely, if there be anything with which metaphysics have nothing to do, and where a plain man, without skill to walk in the arduous paths of abstruse reasoning, may yet find himself at home, it is religion. For the object of religion is *conduct*; and conduct is really, however men may overlay it with philosophical disquisitions, the simplest thing in the world. That is to say, it is the simplest thing in the world as far as *understanding* is concerned; as regards *doing*, it is the hardest thing in the world. Here is the difficulty,—to *do* what we very well know ought to be done; and instead of facing this, men have searched out another with which they occupy themselves by preference,—the origin of what is called the moral sense, the genesis and physiology of conscience, and so on. No one denies that here, too, is difficulty, or that the difficulty is a proper object for the human faculties to be exercised upon; but the difficulty here is speculative. It is not the difficulty of religion, which is a practical one; and it often tends to divert the attention from this. Yet surely the difficulty of religion is great enough by itself, if men would but consider it, to satisfy the most voracious appetite for difficulties. It extends to rightness in the whole range of what we call *conduct*; in three-fourths, therefore, at the very lowest computation, of human life. The only doubt is whether we ought not to make the range of conduct wider still, and to say it is four-fifths of human life, or five-sixths. But it is better to be under the mark as over it; so let us be content with reckoning conduct as three-fourths of human life.

And to recognise in what way conduct is this, let us eschew all school-terms, like *moral sense*, and *volitional*, and *altruistic*, which philosophers employ, and let us help ourselves by the most palpable and plain examples. When the rich man in the Bible-parable says: 'Soul, thou hast much goods laid up for many years; take thine ease, eat, drink, and be merry!'[1]—those *goods* which he thus assigns as the stuff with which human life is mainly concerned (and so in practice it really is),—those goods and our dealings with them,—our taking our ease, eating, drinking, being merry, are the matter of *conduct*, the range where it is exercised. Eating, drinking, ease, pleasure, money, the intercourse of the sexes, the giving free swing to one's temper and instincts,—these are the matters with which conduct is concerned, and with which all mankind know and feel it to be concerned.

Or, when Protagoras points out of what things we are, from childhood till we die, being taught and admonished, and says (but it is lamentable that here we have not at hand Mr. Jowett, who so excellently introduces the enchanter Plato and his personages, but must use our own words): 'From the time he can understand what is said to him, nurse, and mother, and teacher, and father too, are bending their efforts to this end,—to make the child *good*; teaching and showing him, as to everything he has to do or say, how this is right and that not right, and this is honourable and that vile, and this is holy and that unholy, and this do and that do not';—Protagoras, also, when he says this, bears his testimony to the scope

---

[1] Luke xii. 19.

and nature of *conduct*, tells us what conduct is. Or, once more, when M. Littré (and we hope to make our peace with the Comtists by quoting an author of theirs in preference to those authors whom all the British public is now reading and quoting),—when M. Littré, in a most ingenious essay on the origin of morals, traces up, better, perhaps, than anyone else, all our impulses into two elementary instincts, the instinct of self-preservation and the reproductive instinct,—then we take his theory and we say, that all the impulses which can be conceived as derivable from the instinct of self-preservation in us and from the reproductive instinct, these terms being applied in their ordinary sense, are the matter of *conduct*. It is evident this includes, to say no more, every impulse relating to temper, every impulse relating to sensuality; and we all know how much that is.

How we deal with these impulses is the matter of *conduct*, —how we obey, regulate, or restrain them; that, and nothing else. Not whether M. Littré's theory is true or false; for whether it be true or false, there the impulses confessedly now are, and the business of conduct is to deal with them. But it is evident, if conduct deals with these, both how important a thing conduct is, and how simple a thing. Important, because it covers so large a portion of human life, and the portion common to all sorts of people; simple, because, though there needs perpetual admonition to form conduct, the admonition is needed not to determine what we ought to do, but to make us do it.

And as to this simplicity, all moralists are agreed. 'Let any plain honest man,' says Bishop Butler, 'before he engages in any course of action' (he means action of the very kind we call *conduct*), 'ask himself: Is this I am going about right or is it wrong? is it good or is it evil? I do not in the least doubt but that this question would be answered agreeably to truth and virtue by *almost any fair man in almost any circumstance.*' And Bishop Wilson says: 'Look up to God' (by which he means just this: Consult your conscience) 'at all times, and you will, *as in a glass,* discover what is fit to be done.' And the Preacher's well-known sentence is exactly to the same effect: 'God *made man upright*; but they have sought out many inventions',[1] —or, as it more correctly is, '*many abstruse reasonings*'. Let us hold fast to this, and we shall find we have a stay by the help of which even poor weak men, with no pretensions to be logical athletes, may stand firmly.

And so, when we are asked, what is the object of religion?—let us reply: *Conduct*. And when we are asked further, what is conduct?—let us answer: *Three-fourths of life*.

2

And certainly we need not go far about to prove that conduct, or 'righteousness', which is the object of religion, is in a special manner the object of Bible-religion. The word 'righteousness' is the master-word of the Old Testament. *Keep judgment and do righteousness! Cease to do evil, learn to do well!*[2] these words being taken in their plainest sense of conduct. *Offer the sacrifice*, not of victims and ceremonies, as the way of the world in religion then was, but: Offer the sacrifice of *righteousness!*[3] The great concern of the New Testament is likewise righteousness, but righteousness reached through particular means, righteousness by the means of Jesus Christ. A sentence which sums up the New Testament and assigns the ground whereon the Christian Church stands, is, as we

---

[1] Eccles. vii. 29.   [2] Isa. lvi. 1; i. 16, 17.   [3] Ps. iv. 5.

have elsewhere said,[1] this: *Let every one that nameth the name
of Christ depart from iniquity!*[2] If we are to take a sentence
which in like manner sums up the Old Testament, such
a sentence is this: *O ye that love the Eternal, see that ye hate
the thing which is evil! to him that ordereth his conversation right
shall be shown the salvation of God.*[3]

But instantly there will be raised the objection that this
is morality, not religion; morality, ethics, conduct, being
by many people, and above all by theologians, carefully
contradistinguished from religion, which is supposed in
some special way to be connected with propositions about
the Godhead of the Eternal Son, or propositions about
the personality of God, or about election, or justification.
Religion, however, means simply either a binding to
righteousness, or else a serious attending to righteousness
and dwelling upon it. Which of these two it most nearly
means, depends upon the view we take of the word's
derivation; but it means one of them, and they are really
much the same. And the antithesis between *ethical* and
religious is thus quite a false one. Ethical means *practical*,
it relates to practice or conduct passing into habit or
disposition. Religious also means *practical*, but practical
in a still higher degree; and the right antithesis to both
ethical and religious, is the same as the right antithesis
to practical: namely, *theoretical*.

Now, propositions about the Godhead of the Eternal
Son are theoretical, and they therefore are very properly
opposed to propositions which are moral or ethical; but
they are with equal propriety opposed to propositions
which are religious. They differ in kind from what is
religious, while what is ethical agrees in kind with it.
But is there, therefore, no difference between what is

---

[1] *St. Paul and Protestantism.*   [2] 2 Tim. ii. 19.
[3] Ps. xcvii. 10; l. 23.

ethical, or morality, and religion? There *is* a difference; a difference of degree. Religion, if we follow the intention of human thought and human language in the use of the word, is ethics heightened, enkindled, lit up by feeling; the passage from morality to religion is made when to morality is applied emotion. And the true meaning of religion is thus, not simply *morality*, but *morality touched by emotion*. And this new elevation and inspiration of morality is well marked by the word 'righteousness'. Conduct is the word of common life, morality is the word of philosophical disquisition, righteousness is the word of religion.

Some people, indeed, are for calling all high thought and feeling by the name of religion; according to that saying of Goethe: 'He who has art and science, has also religion.' But let us use words as mankind generally use them. We may call art and science touched by emotion *religion*, if we will; as we may make the instinct of self-preservation, into which M. Littré traces up all our private affections, include the perfecting ourselves by the study of what is beautiful in art; and the reproductive instinct, into which he traces up all our social affections, include the perfecting mankind by political science. But men have not yet got to that stage, when we think much of either their private or their social affections at all, except as exercising themselves in conduct; neither do we yet think of religion as otherwise exercising itself. When mankind speak of religion, they have before their mind an activity engaged, not with the whole of life, but with that three-fourths of life which is *conduct*. This is wide enough range for one word, surely; but at any rate, let us at present limit ourselves in the use of the word *religion* as mankind do.

And if some one now asks: But what *is* this application of emotion to morality, and by what marks may we know it?—we can quite easily satisfy him; not, indeed, by any disquisition of our own, but in a much better way, by examples. 'By the dispensation of Providence to mankind', says Quintilian, 'goodness gives men most satisfaction.[1] That is morality. 'The path of the just is as the shining light which shineth more and more unto the perfect day.'[2] That is morality touched with emotion, or religion. 'Hold off from sensuality,' says Cicero; 'for, if you have given yourself up to it, you will find yourself unable to think of anything else.'[3] That is morality. 'Blessed are the pure in heart,' says Jesus Christ; 'for they shall see God.'[4] That is religion. 'We all want to live honestly, but cannot', says the Greek maxim-maker.[5] That is morality. 'O wretched man that I am, who shall deliver me from the body of this death!' says St. Paul.[6] That is religion. 'Would thou wert of as good conversation in deed as in word!'[7] is morality. 'Not every one that saith unto me, Lord, Lord, shall enter into the kingdom of Heaven, but he that doeth the will of my Father which is in Heaven',[8] is religion. 'Live as you were meant to live!'[9] is morality. 'Lay hold on eternal life!'[10] is religion.

Or we may take the contrast within the bounds of the Bible itself. 'Love not sleep, lest thou come to poverty', is morality. But: 'My meat is to do the will of him that sent me, and to finish his work', is religion.[11] Or we may even observe a third stage between these two stages, which shows to us the transition from one to the other. 'If thou givest thy soul the desires that please her, she will

---

[1] Dedit hoc Providentia hominibus munus, ut honesta magis juvarent.
[2] Prov. iv. 18.
[3] Sis a venereis amoribus aversus; quibus si te dedideris, non aliud quidquam possis cogitare quam illud quod diligis.
[4] Matt. v. 8.　　[5] Θέλομεν καλῶς ζῆν πάντες, ἀλλ' οὐ δυνάμεθα.
[6] Rom. vii. 24.　　[7] Εἴθ' ἦσθα σώφρων ἔργα τοῖς λόγοις ἴσα.
[8] Matt. vii. 21.　　[9] Ζῆσον κατὰ φύσιν.　　　　[10] 1 Tim. vi. 12.
[11] Prov. xx. 13; John iv. 34.

make thee a laughing stock to thine enemies';[1]—that is morality. 'He that resisteth pleasure crowneth his life';[2] —that is morality with the tone heightened, passing, or trying to pass, into religion. 'Flesh and blood cannot inherit the kingdom of God';[3]—there the passage is made, and we have religion. Our religious examples are here all taken from the Bible, and from the Bible such examples can best be taken; but we might also find them elsewhere. 'Oh that my lot might lead me in the path of holy innocence of thought and deed, the path which august laws ordain, laws which in the highest heaven had their birth, neither did the race of mortal man beget them, nor shall oblivion ever put them to sleep; the power of God is mighty in them, and groweth not old!' That is from Sophocles, but it is as much religion as any of the things which we have quoted as religious. Like them, it is not the mere enjoining of conduct, but it is this enjoining touched, strengthened, and almost transformed, by the addition of feeling.

So what is meant by the application of emotion to morality has now, it is to be hoped, been made clear. The next question will probably be: But how does one get the application made? Why, how does one get to feel much about any matter whatever? By dwelling upon it, by staying our thoughts upon it, by having it perpetually in our mind. The very words *mind, memory, remain*, come, probably, all from the same root, from the notion of staying, attending. Possibly even the word *man* comes from the same; so entirely does the idea of humanity, of intelligence, of looking before and after, of raising oneself out of the flux of things, rest upon the idea of steadying oneself, concentrating oneself, making order in the chaos of one's impression, by attending to one impression

[1] Eccles. xviii. 35.   [2] Eccles. xix. 5.   [3] 1 Cor. xv. 50.

rather than the other. The rules of conduct, of morality, were themselves, philosophers suppose, reached in this way;—the notion of a whole self as opposed to a partial self, a best self to an inferior self, to a momentary self a permanent self requiring the restraint of impulses a man would naturally have indulged;—because, by *attending* to his life, man found it had a scope beyond the wants of the present moment. Suppose it was so; then the first man who, as 'a being', comparatively, 'of a large discourse, looking before and after', controlled the native, instantaneous, mechanical impulses of the instinct of self-preservation, controlled the native, instantaneous, mechanical impulses of the reproductive instinct, had morality revealed to him.

But there is a long way from this to that habitual dwelling on the rules thus reached, that constant turning them over in the mind, that near and lively experimental sense of their beneficence, which communicates emotion to our thought of them, and thus incalculably heightens their power. And the more mankind attended to the claims of that part of our nature which does *not* belong to conduct or morality, properly so called (and we have seen that, after all, about one-fourth of our nature is in this case), the more they would have distractions to take off their thoughts from those moral conclusions which all races of men, one may say, seem to have reached, and to prevent these moral conclusions from being quickened by emotion, and thus becoming religious.

3

Only with one people,—the people from whom we get the Bible,—these distractions did not so much happen.

The Old Testament, nobody will ever deny, is filled with the word and thought of righteousness. 'In the way of righteousness is life, and in the pathway thereof is no death'; 'Righteousness tendeth to life'; 'He that pursueth evil pursueth it to his own death'; 'The way of transgressors is hard';—nobody will deny that those texts may stand for the fundamental and ever-recurring idea of the Old Testament.[1] No people ever felt so strongly as the people of the Old Testament, the Hebrew people, that conduct is three-fourths of our life and its largest concern. No people ever felt so strongly that succeeding, going right, hitting the mark in this great concern, was *the way of peace*, the highest possible satisfaction. 'He that keepeth the law, happy is he; its ways are ways of pleasantness, and all its paths are peace; if thou hadst walked in its ways, thou shouldst have dwelt in peace for ever!'[2] Jeshurun, one of the ideal names of their race, is the *upright*; Israel, the other and greater, is the *wrestler with God*, he who has known the contention and strain it costs to stand upright. That mysterious personage by whom their history first touches the hill of Sion, is Melchisedek, the *righteous* king. Their holy city, Jerusalem, is the foundation, or vision, or inheritance, of that which righteousness achieves,—*peace*. The law of righteousness was such an object of attention to them, that its words were to 'be in their heart, and thou shalt teach them diligently unto thy children, and shalt talk of them when thou sittest in thine house, and when thou walkest by the way, and when thou liest down, and when thou risest up'.[3] That they might keep them ever in mind, they wore them, went about with them, made talismans of them: 'Bind them upon thy fingers, bind them about thy neck;

[1] Prov. xii. 28; xi. 19; xiii. 15.
[2] Prov. xxix. 18; iii. 17. Baruch iii. 13.   [3] Deut. vi. 6, 7.

write them upon the table of thine heart!'[1] 'Take fast hold of her,' they said of the doctrine of conduct, or righteousness, 'let her not go! keep her, for *she is thy life!*'[2]

People who thus spoke of righteousness could not but have had their minds long and deeply engaged with it; much more than the generality of mankind, who have nevertheless, as we saw, got as far as the notion of morals or conduct. And, if they were so deeply attentive to it, one thing could not fail to strike them. It is this: the very great part in righteousness which belongs, we may say, to *not ourselves*. In the first place, we did not make ourselves and our nature, or conduct as the object of three-fourths of that nature; we did not provide that happiness should follow conduct, as it undeniably does; that the sense of succeeding, going right, hitting the mark, in conduct, should give satisfaction, and a very high satisfaction, just as really as the sense of doing well in his work gives pleasure to a poet or painter, or accomplishing what he tries gives pleasure to a man who is learning to ride or to shoot; or as satisfying his hunger, also, gives pleasure to a man who is hungry.

All this we did not make; and, in the next place, our dealing with it at all, when it is made, is not wholly, or even nearly wholly, in our own power. Our conduct is capable, irrespective of what we can ourselves certainly answer for, of almost infinitely different degrees of force and energy in the performance of it, of lucidity and vividness in the perception of it, of fulness in the satisfaction from it; and these degrees may vary from day to day, and quite incalculably. Facilities and felicities,—whence do they come? suggestions and stimulations,—where do they tend? hardly a day passes but we have some experience

[1] Prov. vii. 3; iii. 3.   [2] Prov. iv. 13.

of them. And so Henry More was led to say, that 'there was something about us that knew better, often, what we would be at than we ourselves'. For instance: everyone can understand how health and freedom from pain may give energy for conduct, and how a neuralgia, suppose, may diminish it. It does not depend on ourselves, indeed, whether we have the neuralgia or not, but we can understand its impairing our spirit. But the strange thing is, that with the same neuralgia we may find ourselves one day without spirit and energy for conduct, and another day with them. So that we may most truly say, with the author of the *Imitation*: 'Left to ourselves, we sink and perish; visited, we lift up our heads and live.'[1] And we may well give ourselves, in grateful and devout self-surrender, to that by which we are thus visited. So much is there incalculable, so much that belongs to *not ourselves*, in conduct; and the more we attend to conduct, and the more we value it, the more we shall feel this.

The *not ourselves*, which is in us and in the world around us, has almost everywhere, as far as we can see, struck the minds of men as they awoke to consciousness, and has inspired them with awe. Everyone knows how the mighty natural objects which most took their regards became the objects to which this awe addressed itself. Our very word *God* is, perhaps, a reminiscence of these times, when men invoked 'The Brilliant on high', *sublime hoc candens quod invocant omnes Jovem*, as the power representing to them that which transcended the limits of their narrow selves, and by which they lived and moved and had their being. Everyone knows of what differences of operation men's dealing with this power has in different places and times shown itself capable; how here they have been moved by

---

[1] Relicti mergimur et perimus, visitati vero erigimur et vivimus.

the *not ourselves* to a cruel terror, there to a timid religiosity, there again to a play of imagination; almost always, however, connecting with it, by some string or other, conduct.

But we are not writing a history of religion; we are only tracing its effect on the language of the men from whom we get the Bible. At the time they produced those documents which give to the Old Testament its power and its true character, the *not ourselves* which weighed upon the mind of Israel, and engaged its awe, was the *not ourselves* by which we get the sense for *righteousness*, and whence we find the help to *do right*. This conception was indubitably what lay at the bottom of that remarkable change which under Moses, at a certain stage of their religious history, befell the Hebrew people's mode of naming God.[1] This was what they intended in that name, which we wrongly convey, either without translation, by *Jehovah*, which gives us the notion of a mere mythological deity, or by a wrong translation, *Lord*, which gives us the notion of a magnified and non-natural man. The name they used was: *The Eternal*.

Philosophers dispute whether moral ideas, as they call them, the simplest ideas of conduct and righteousness which now seem instinctive, did not all grow, were not once inchoate, embryo, dubious, unformed.[2] That may have been so; the question is an interesting one for science. But the interesting question for conduct is whether those ideas are unformed or formed *now*. They are formed now; and they were formed when the Hebrews named the power, not of their own making, which pressed upon their spirit: *The Eternal*. Probably the life of

[1] See Exod. iii. 14.
[2] 'Qu'est-ce que la nature?' says Pascal; 'Peut-être une première coutume, comme la coutume est une seconde nature.'

Abraham, *the friend of God*, however imperfectly the Bible traditions by themselves convey it to us, was a decisive step forwards in the development of these ideas of righteousness. Probably this was the moment when such ideas became fixed and ruling for the Hebrew people, and marked it permanently off from all other peoples who had not made the same step. But long before the first beginnings of recorded history, long before the oldest word of Bible literature, these ideas must have been at work. We know it by the result, although they may have for a long while been but rudimentary. In Israel's earliest history and earliest utterances, under the name of Eloah, Elohim, *The Mighty*, there may have lain and matured, there did lie and mature, ideas of God more as a moral power, more as a power connected, above everything, with conduct and righteousness, than were entertained by other races. Not only can we judge by the result that this must have been so, but we can see that it was so. Still their name, *The Mighty*, does not in itself involve any true and deep religious ideas, any more than our Aryan name, *Deva Deus, The Shining*. With *The Eternal* it is otherwise. For what did they mean by the Eternal; the Eternal *what*? The Eternal *cause*? Alas, these poor people were not Archbishops of York. They meant the Eternal *righteous*, who loveth *righteousness*. They had dwelt upon the thought of conduct, and of right and wrong, until the *not ourselves*, which is in us and all around us, became to them adorable eminently and altogether as *a power which makes for righteousness*; which makes for it unchangeably and eternally, and is therefore called *The Eternal*.

There is not a particle of metaphysics in their use of this name, any more than in their conception of the *not ourselves* to which they attached it. Both came to them not from abstruse reasoning but from experience, and from experience in the plain region of conduct. Theologians with metaphysical heads render Israel's *Eternal* by *the self-existent*, and Israel's *not ourselves* by *the absolute*, and attribute to Israel their own subtleties. According to them, Israel had his head full of the necessity of a first cause, and therefore said, *The Eternal*; as, again, they imagine him looking out into the world, noting everywhere the marks of design and adaptation to his wants, and reasoning out and inferring thence the fatherhood of God. All these fancies come from an excessive turn for reasoning, and from a neglect of observing men's actual course of thinking and way of using words. Israel, at this stage when *The Eternal* was revealed to him, inferred nothing, reasoned out nothing; he felt and experienced. When he begins to speculate, in the schools of Rabbinism, he quickly shows how much less native talent than the Bishops of Winchester and Gloucester he has for this perilous business. Happily, when *The Eternal* was revealed to him, he had not yet begun to speculate.

Israel personified, indeed, his Eternal, for he was strongly moved, he was an orator and poet. *Man never knows how anthropomorphic he is*, says Goethe; and so man tends always to represent everything under his own figure. In poetry and eloquence man may and must follow this tendency, but in science it often leads him astray. Israel, however, did not scientifically predicate *personality* of God; he would not even have had a notion what was meant by it. He called him the maker of all things, who gives drink to all out of his pleasures as out of a river; but he was led to this by no theory of a first cause. The grandeur of the spectacle given by the world, the grandeur of the sense of its all being *not ourselves*, being above and beyond ourselves and immeasurably dwarfing us, a man of imagination instinctively personifies as a single,

mighty, living and productive power; as Goethe tells us
that the words which rose naturally to his lips, when he
stood on the top of the Brocken, were: 'Lord, what is
man, that thou mindest him, or the son of man, that thou
makest account of him?'[1] But Israel's confessing and
extolling of this power came not even from his imaginative feeling, but came first from his gratitude for righteousness. To one who knows what conduct is, it is a joy to be
alive; and the *not ourselves*, which by bringing forth for us
righteousness makes our happiness, working just in the
same sense, brings forth this glorious world to be righteous
in. That is the notion at the bottom of a Hebrew's praise
of a Creator; and if we attend, we can see this quite
clearly. Wisdom and understanding mean, for Israel, the
love of order, of righteousness. Righteousness, order, conduct, is for Israel at once the source of all man's happiness,
and at the same time the very essence of *The Eternal*. The
great work of the Eternal is the foundation of this order
in man, the implanting in mankind of his own love of
righteousness, his own spirit, his own wisdom and understanding; and it is only as a farther and natural working
of this energy that Israel conceives the establishment of
order in the world, or creation. 'To depart from evil, *that*
is the understanding! Happy is the man that findeth
wisdom, and the man that getteth understanding! *The
Eternal by wisdom hath founded the earth, by understanding
hath he established the heavens*';[2] and so the Bible-writer
passes into the account of creation. It all comes to him
from the idea of righteousness.

And it is the same with all the language our Hebrew
religionist uses. God is a father, because the power in and
around us, which makes for righteousness, is indeed best
described by the name of this authoritative but yet tender

[1] Ps. cxlix. 3.   [2] Prov. iii. 13–20.

and protecting relation. So, too, with the intense fear and
abhorrence of idolatry. Conduct, righteousness, is, above
all, a matter of inward motion and rule. No sensible
forms can represent it, or help us to it; such attempts at
representation can only distract us from it. So, too, with
the sense of the oneness of God. 'Hear, O Israel! The
Lord our God is one Lord.'[1] People think that in this
unity of God,—this monotheistic idea, as they call it,—
they have certainly got metaphysics at last. They have
got nothing of the kind. The monotheistic idea of Israel
is simply *seriousness*. There are, indeed, many aspects of
the *not ourselves*; but Israel regarded one aspect of it only,
that by which it makes for righteousness. He had the
advantage, to be sure, that with this aspect three-fourths
of human life is concerned. But there are other aspects
which may be set in view. 'Frail and striving mortality,'
says the elder Pliny in a noble passage, 'mindful of its
own weakness, has distinguished these aspects severally,
so as for each man to be able to attach himself to the
divine by this or that part, according as he has most need.'[2]
That is an apology for polytheism, as answering to man's
many-sidedness. But Israel felt that being thus many-
sided degenerates into an imaginative play, and bewilders
what Israel recognised as our sole *religious* consciousness,
—the consciousness of right. 'Let thine eyelids look right
on, and let thine eyelids look straight before thee; turn not
to the right hand nor to the left; remove thy foot from evil!'[3]

For does not Ovid say,[4] in excuse for the immorality of

---

[1] Deut. vi. 4.

[2] Fragilis et laboriosa mortalitas in partes ista digessit, infirmitatis suæ
memor, ut portionibus coleret quisque, quo maxime indigeret. *Nat. Hist.*
ii. 5. [3] Prov. iv. 25, 27.

[4] *Tristia*, ii. 287:

> Quis locus est templis augustior? hæc quoque vitet,
> In culpam si qua est ingeniosa suam.

See the whole passage.

his verses, that the sight and mention of the gods them-selves,—the rulers of human life,—often raised immoral thoughts? And so the sight and mention of *all* aspects of the *not ourselves* must. Yet how tempting are many of these aspects! Even at this time of day, the grave authori-ties of the University of Cambridge are so struck by one of them, that of pleasure, life and fecundity,—of the *hominum divomque voluptas, alma Venus,*—that they set it publicly up as an object for their scholars to fix their minds upon, and to compose verses in honour of. That is all very well at present; but with this natural bent in the authorities of the University of Cambridge, and in the Indo-European race to which they belong, where would they be now if it had not been for Israel, and for the stern check which Israel put upon the glorification and divinisa-tion of this natural bent of mankind, this attractive aspect of the *not ourselves*? Perhaps going in procession, Vice-Chancellor, bedels, masters, scholars, and all, in spite of their Professor of Moral Philosophy, to the temple of Aphrodite! Nay, and very likely Mr. Birks himself, his brows crowned with myrtle and scarcely a shade of melancholy on his countenance, would have been going along with them! It is Israel and his *seriousness* that have saved the authorities of the University of Cambridge from carrying their divinisation of pleasure to these lengths, or from making more of it, indeed, than a mere passing intellectual play; and even this play Israel would have beheld with displeasure, saying: *O turn away mine eyes lest they behold vanity, but quicken Thou me in thy way!*[1] So earnestly and exclusively were Israel's regards bent on one aspect of the *not ourselves*: its aspect as a power making for conduct, for righteousness. Israel's Eternal was the Eternal which says: 'Be ye *holy*, for I am *holy*!'

[1] Ps. cxix. 37.

Now, as righteousness is but a heightened conduct, so holiness is but a heightened righteousness; a more finished, entire, and awe-filled righteousness. It was such a righteousness which was Israel's ideal; and therefore it was that Israel said, not indeed what our Bibles make him say, but this: 'Hear, O Israel! *The Eternal is our God, The Eternal alone.*'

And in spite of his turn for personification, his want of a clear boundary-line between poetry and science, his inaptitude to express even abstract notions by other than highly concrete terms,—in spite of these scientific disadvantages, or rather, perhaps, because of them, because he had no talent for abstruse reasoning to lead him astray,—the spirit and tongue of Israel kept a propriety, a reserve, a sense of the inadequacy of language in conveying man's ideas of God, which contrast strongly with the licence of affirmation in our Western theology. 'The high and holy One that inhabiteth eternity, whose name is holy',[1] is far more proper and felicitous language than 'the moral and intelligent Governor of the universe', just because it far less attempts to be precise, but keeps to the language of poetry and does not essay the language of science. As he had developed his idea of God from personal experience, Israel knew what we, who have developed our idea from his words about it, so often are ignorant of: that his words were but *thrown out* at a vast object of consciousness, which he could not fully grasp, and which he apprehended clearly by one point alone,—that it made for the great concern of life, *conduct.* How little we know of it besides, how impenetrable is the course of its ways with us, how we are baffled in our attempts to name and describe it, how, when we personify it and call it 'the moral and intelligent Governor of the universe', we

[1] Ps. lvii. 15.

presently find it not to be a person as man conceives of persons, nor moral as man conceives of moral, nor intelligent as man conceives of intelligent, nor a governor as man conceives of governors,—all this, which scientific theology loses sight of, Israel, who had but poetry and eloquence, and no system, and who did not mind contradicting himself, knew. 'Is it any pleasure to the Almighty, that thou art righteous?'[1] What a blow to our ideal of that magnified and non-natural man, 'the moral and intelligent Governor'! Say what we can about God, say our best, we have yet, Israel knew, to add instantly: 'Lo, these are *fringes* of his ways; *but how little a portion is heard of him!*'[2] Yes, indeed, Israel remembered that, far better than our bishops do. 'Canst thou by searching find out God; canst thou find out the perfection of the Almighty? It is more high than heaven, what canst thou do? deeper than hell, what canst thou know?'[3]

Will it be said, experience might also have shown to Israel a *not ourselves* which did not make for his happiness, but rather made against it, baffled his claims to it? But no man, as I have elsewhere remarked,[4] who simply follows his own consciousness, is aware of any *claims*, any *rights*, whatever; what he gets of good makes him thankful, what he gets of ill seems to him natural. His simple spontaneous feeling is well expressed by that saying of Izaak Walton: 'Every misery that I miss is a new mercy, and therefore let us be thankful.' It is true, the *not ourselves* of which we are thankfully conscious we inevitably speak of and speak to as a man; for 'man never knows how anthropomorphic he is.' And as time proceeds, imagination and reasoning keep working upon this substructure, and build from it a magnified and non-natural man. Attention is then drawn, afterwards, to causes

[1] Job xxii. 3.   [2] Job xxvi. 14.   [3] Job xi. 7.   [4] *Culture and Anarchy.*

outside ourselves which seem to make for sin and suffering; and then either these causes have to be reconciled by some highly ingenious scheme with the magnified and non-natural man's power, or a second magnified and non-natural man has to be supposed, who pulls the contrary way to the first. So arise Satan and his angels. But all this is secondary, and comes much later. Israel, the founder of our religion, did not begin with this. He began with experience. He knew from thankful experience the *not ourselves* which makes for righteousness, and knew how little we know about God besides.

4

The language of the Bible, then, is literary, not scientific language; language *thrown out* at an object of consciousness not fully grasped, which inspired emotion. Evidently, if the object be one not fully to be grasped, and one to inspire emotion, the language of figure and feeling will satisfy us better about it, will cover more of what we seek to express, than the language of literal fact and science. The language of science about it will be *below* what we feel to be the truth.

The question however has risen and confronts us: what was the scientific basis of fact for this consciousness? When we have once satisfied ourselves both as to the tentative, poetic way in which the Bible-authors used language, and also as to their having no pretensions to metaphysics at all, let us, therefore, when there is this question raised as to the scientific account of what they had before their minds, be content with a very unpretending answer. And in this way such a phrase as that which I have formerly used concerning God, and have been much blamed for using,—the phrase, namely, that, 'for science, God is simply *the stream of tendency by which all things seek to fulfil the law of their being'*,—may be allowed, and may even prove useful. Certainly it is inadequate; certainly it is a less proper phrase than, for instance: 'Clouds and darkness are round about him, righteousness and judgment are the habitation of his seat.'[1] But then it is, in however humble a degree and with however narrow a reach, a *scientific* definition, which the other is not. The phrase, 'A personal First Cause, the moral and intelligent Governor of the universe', has also, when applied to God, the character, no doubt, of a scientific definition. But then it goes far beyond what is admittedly certain and verifiable, which is what we mean by scientific. It attempts far too much. If we want here, as we do want, to have what is admittedly certain and verifiable, we must content ourselves with very little. No one will say, that it is admittedly certain and verifiable, that there is a personal first cause, the moral and intelligent governor of the universe, whom we may call *God* if we will. But that all things seem to us to have what we call a law of their being, and to tend to fulfil it, is certain and admitted; though whether we will call this *God* or not, is a matter of choice. Suppose, however, we call it *God*, we then give the name of *God* to a certain admitted reality; this, at least, is an advantage.

And the notion of our definition does, in fact, enter into the term *God*, in men's common use of it. To please God, to serve God, to obey God's will, means to follow a law of things which is found in conscience, and which is an indication, irrespective of our arbitrary wish and

---

[1] Ps. xcvii. 2. It has been urged that if the personifying mode of expression is more proper, it must, also, be more scientifically exact. But surely it will on reflexion appear that this is by no means so. Wordsworth calls the earth 'the mighty mother of mankind', and the geographers call her 'an oblate spheroid'; Wordsworth's expression is more proper and adequate to convey what men feel about the earth, but it is not therefore the more scientifically exact.

fancy, of what we ought to do. There *is*, then, a real power which makes for righteousness; and it is the greatest of realities for us.[1] When St. Paul says, that our business is 'to serve the spirit of God', 'to serve the living and true God';[2] and when Epictetus says: 'What do I want?—to acquaint myself with the natural order of things, and comply with it',[3] they both mean, so far, the same, in that they both mean we should obey a tendency, which is *not ourselves*, but which appears in our consciousness, by which we and other things fulfil the real law of our being.

It is true, the *not ourselves*, by which things fulfil the real law of their being, extends a great deal beyond that sphere where alone we usually think of it. That is, a man may disserve God, disobey indications, not of our own making, but which appear, if we attend, in our consciousness,—he may disobey, I say, such indications of the real law of our being, in other spheres besides the sphere of conduct. He does disobey them, when he sings a hymn like: *My Jesus to know, and feel his blood flow*,—or, indeed, like nine-tenths of our hymns,—or when he frames and maintains a blundering and miserable constitution of society, as well as when he commits some plain breach of the moral law. That is, he may disobey them in art and science as well as in conduct. But he attends, and the generality of men attend, almost solely to the indications of a true law of our being as to *conduct*; and hardly at all to indications, though they as really exist, of a true law of our being on its æsthetic and intelligential side. The

---

[1] Prayer, about which so much has often been said unadvisedly and ill, deals with this reality. All good and beneficial prayer is in truth, however men may describe it, at bottom nothing else than an energy of aspiration towards the eternal *not ourselves* that makes for righteousness,—of aspiration towards it, and of co-operation with it. Nothing, therefore, can be more efficacious, more right, and more real.

[2] Phil. iii. 3 (in the reading of the Vatican manuscript); 1 Thess. i. 9.

[3] τί βούλομαι; καταμαθεῖν τὴν φύσιν καὶ ταύτῃ ἕπεσθαι.

reason is, that the moral side, though not more real, is so much larger; taking in, as we have said, at least three-fourths of life. Now, the indications on this *moral* side of that tendency, not of our making, by which things fulfil the law of their being, we do very much mean to denote and to sum up when we speak of *the will of God, pleasing God, serving God*. Let us keep firm footing on this basis of plain fact, narrow though it may be.

To feel that one is fulfilling in any way the law of one's being, that one is succeeding and hitting the mark, brings, as we know, happiness; to feel this in regard to so great a thing as conduct, brings, of course, happiness proportionate to the thing's greatness. We have already had Quintilian's witness, how right conduct gives joy. Who could value knowledge more than Goethe? but he marks it as being without question a lesser source of joy than conduct. Conduct he ranks with health as beyond all compare primary. 'Nothing, *after* health and *virtue*,' he says, 'can give so much satisfaction as learning and knowing.' Nay, and Bishop Butler, at the view of the happiness from conduct, breaks free from all that hesitancy and depression which so commonly hangs on his masterly thinking. 'Self-love, methinks, should be alarmed! May she not pass over greater pleasures than those she is so wholly taken up with?' And Bishop Wilson, always hitting the right nail on the head in matters of this sort, remarks that, 'if it were not for the practical difficulties attending it, *virtue would hardly be distinguishable from a kind of sensuality*'. The practical difficulties are, indeed, exceeding great. Plain as is the course and high the prize, we all find ourselves daily led to say with the *Imitation*: 'Would that for one single day we had lived in this world as we ought!' Yet the course is so evidently plain, and the prize so high, that the same *Imitation* cries out presently: 'If a man would but take notice, what peace he brings to himself, and what joy to others, merely by managing himself right!' And for such happiness, since certainly we ourselves did not make it, we instinctively feel *grateful*; according to that remark of one of the wholesomest and truest of moralists, Barrow: 'He is not a man, who doth not delight to make some returns thither whence he hath found great kindness.' And this sense of gratitude, again, is itself an addition to our happiness! So strong, altogether, is the witness and sanction *happiness* gives to going right in conduct, to fulfilling, so far as conduct is concerned, the law indicated to us of our being. Now, there can be no sanction to compare, for force, with the strong sanction of happiness, if it be true what Bishop Butler, who is here but the mouthpiece of humanity itself, says so irresistibly: 'It is manifest that nothing can be of consequence to mankind, or any creature, but happiness.' But we English are taunted with our proneness to an unworthy eudæmonism, and an Anglican bishop may perhaps be a suspected witness. Let us call, then, a glorious father of the Catholic Church, the great Augustine himself. Says St. Augustine: 'Act we *must* in pursuance of what gives us most delight; *quod amplius nos delectat, secundum id operemur* necesse est.'

And now let us see how exactly Israel's perceptions about God follow and confirm this simple line, which we have here reached quite independently. First: 'It is *joy* to the just to do judgment.'[1] Then: 'It becometh well the just to be *thankful*.'[2] Finally: 'A *pleasant* thing it is to be thankful.'[3] What can be simpler than this, and at the same time more solid? But again: 'The statutes of the *Eternal* rejoice the heart.'[4] And then: 'I will give thanks

[1] Prov. xxi. 15. [2] Ps. xxxiii. 1. [3] Ps. cxlvii. 1.
[4] Ps. xix. 8.

unto thee, O *Eternal*, with my whole heart; at midnight will I rise to give thanks unto thee because of thy righteous judgments!'[1] And lastly: 'It is a good thing to give thanks unto the *Eternal*; it is a good thing to sing praises unto our *God*!'[2] Why, these are the very same propositions as the preceding, only with a power and depth of emotion added! Emotion has been applied to morality.

God or *Eternal* is here really, at bottom, nothing but a deeply moved way of saying 'the power that makes for *conduct* or *righteousness*'. 'Trust in *God*' is, in a deeply moved way of expression, the trust in the law of conduct; 'delight in *the Eternal*' is, in a deeply moved way of expression, the happiness we all feel to spring from conduct. Attending to conduct, to judgment, makes the attender feel that it is joy to do it. Attending to it more still, makes him feel that it is the commandment of the Eternal, and that the joy got from it is joy from fulfilling the commandment of the Eternal. The thankfulness for this joy is thankfulness to the Eternal; and to the Eternal, again, is due that further joy which comes from this thankfulness. 'The fear of the Eternal, that is wisdom; and to depart from evil, that is understanding.'[3] '*The fear of the Eternal*' and '*To depart from evil*' here mean, and are put to mean, and by the very laws of Hebrew composition which make the second phrase in a parallelism repeat the first in other words, they *must* mean, just the same thing. Yet what man of soul, after he had once risen to feel that to depart from evil was to walk in awful observance of an enduring clue, within us and without us, which leads to happiness, but would prefer to say, instead of 'to depart from evil', 'the fear of the Eternal'?

Henceforth, then, Israel transferred to this Eternal all his obligations. Instead of saying: 'Whoso keepeth the

[1] Ps. cxxxviii. 1; cxix. 62.   [2] Ps. xcii. 1; cxlvii. 1.   [3] Job xxviii. 28.

commandment keepeth his own soul',[1] he rather said, 'My soul, wait thou only upon *God*, for of him cometh my salvation!'[2] Instead of saying: 'Bind them (the laws of righteousness) continually upon thine heart, and tie them about thy neck!'[3] he rather said, 'Have I not remembered *Thee* on my bed, and thought upon *Thee* when I was waking?'[4] The obligation of a grateful and devout self-surrender to the Eternal replaced all sense of obligation to one's own better self, one's own permanent interest. The moralist's rule: 'Take thought for your permanent, not your momentary, well-being', became now: 'Honour *the Eternal*, not doing thine own ways, nor finding thine own pleasure, nor speaking thine own words.'[5] That is, with Israel *religion* replaced *morality*.

It is true, out of the humble yet divine ground of attention to conduct, of care for what in conduct is right and good, grew morality and religion both; but, from the time when the soul felt the motive of religion, it dropped and could not but drop the other. And the motive of doing right, to a sincere soul, is now really no longer his own welfare, but *to please God*; and it bewilders his consciousness if you tell him that he does right out of *self-love*. So that, as we have said that the first man who, as 'a being of a large discourse, looking before and after', controlled the blind momentary impulses of the instinct of self-preservation, and controlled the blind momentary impulses of the sexual instinct, had *morality* revealed to him; so in like manner we may say, that the first man who was thrilled with gratitude, devotion, and awe, at the sense of joy and peace, not of his own making, which followed the exercise of this self-control, had *religion* revealed to him. And, for us at least, this man was Israel.

---

[1] Prov. xix. 16.   [2] Ps. lxii. 5, 1.
[3] Prov. vi. 2.   [4] Ps. lxiii. 7.   [5] Isa. lviii. 13.

Now here, as we have already pointed out the falseness of the common antithesis between *ethical* and *religious*, let us anticipate the objection that the religion here spoken of is but natural religion, by pointing out the falseness of the common antithesis, also, between *natural* and *revealed*. For that in us which is really natural is, in truth, *revealed*. We awake to the consciousness of it, we are aware of it coming forth in our mind; but we feel that we did not make it, that it is discovered to us, that it is what it is whether we will or no. If we are little concerned about it, we say it is *natural*; if much, we say it is *revealed*. But the difference between the two is not one of kind, only of degree. The real antithesis, to natural and revealed alike, is *invented*, *artificial*. Religion springing out of an experience of the power, the grandeur, the necessity of righteousness, is revealed religion, whether we find it in Sophocles or in Isaiah. 'The will of mortal men did not beget it, neither shall oblivion ever put it to sleep.' A system of theological notions about personality, essence, existence, consubstantiality, is *artificial* religion, and is the proper opposite to *revealed*; since it is a religion which comes forth in no one's consciousness, but is invented by theologians,—able men with uncommon talents for abstruse reasoning. This religion is in no sense revealed, just because it is in no sense natural. And revealed religion is properly so named, just in proportion as it is in a pre-eminent degree natural.

The religion of the Bible, therefore, is well said to be revealed, because the great natural truth, that '*righteousness tendeth to life*',[1] is seized and exhibited there with such incomparable force and efficacy. All, or very nearly all, the nations of mankind have recognised the importance of conduct, and have attributed to it a natural obligation.

[1] Prov. xi. 19.

They, however, looked at *conduct*, not as something full of happiness and joy, but as something one could not manage to do without. But: 'Sion heard of it and *rejoiced*, and the daughters of Judah were *glad*, because of thy judgments, O Eternal!'[1] Happiness is our being's end aim, and no one has ever come near Israel in feeling, and in making others feel, that *to righteousness belongs happiness*! The prodigies and the marvellous of Bible-religion are common to it with all religions; the love of righteousness, in this eminency, is its own.

5

The real germ of religious consciousness, therefore, out of which sprang Israel's name for God, to which the records of his history adapted themselves, and which came to be clothed upon, in time, with a mighty growth of poetry and tradition, was a consciousness of *the not ourselves which makes for righteousness*. And the way to convince oneself of this is by studying the Bible with a fair mind, and with the tact which letters, surely, alone can give. For the thing turns upon understanding the manner in which men have thought, their way of using words, and what they mean by them. And by knowing letters, by becoming conversant with the best that has been thought and said in the world, we become acquainted not only with the history, but also with the scope and powers, of the instruments which men employ in thinking and speaking. And this is just what is sought for.

And with the sort of experience thus gained of the history of the human spirit, objections, as we have said, will be found not so much to be refuted by reasoning as to fall away of themselves. It is objected: 'Why, if the Hebrews of the Bible had thus eminently the sense for

[1] Ps. xcvii. 8.

righteousness, does it not equally distinguish the Jews now?' But does not experience show us, how entirely a change of circumstances may change a people's character; and have the modern Jews lost more of what distinguished their ancestors, or even so much, as the modern Greeks of what distinguished theirs? Where is now, among the Greeks, the dignity of life of Pericles, the dignity of thought and of art of Phidias and Plato? It is objected, that the Jews' God was not the enduring power that makes for righteousness, but only their tribal God, who gave them the victory in the battle and plagued them that hated them. But how, then, comes their literature to be full of such things as 'Shew me thy ways, O Eternal, and teach me thy paths; let *integrity and uprightness* preserve me, for I put my trust in thee! if I incline unto *wickedness* with my heart, the Eternal will not hear me.'[1] From the sense that with men thus guided and going right in goodness it could not but be well, that their leaf could not wither and that whatsoever they did must prosper,[2] would naturally come the sense that in their wars with an enemy the enemy should be put to confusion and *they* should triumph. But how, out of the mere sense that their enemy should be put to confusion and *they* should triumph, could the desire for goodness come?

It is objected, again, that their 'law of the Lord' was a positive traditional code to the Hebrews, standing as a mechanical rule which held them in awe; that their 'fear of the Lord' was superstitious dread of an assumed magnified and non-natural man. But why, then, are they always saying: '*Teach* me thy statutes, *Teach* me thy way, *Show* thou me the way that I shall walk in, *Open mine eyes*, *Make me to understand* wisdom *secretly!*'[3] if all the law they

---

[1] Ps. xxv. 4, 21; lxvi. 18.   [2] Ps. i. 3.
[3] Ps. cxix. 12; lxxxvi. 11; cxliii. 8; cxix. 18; li. 6.

were thinking of stood, stark and written, before their eyes already? And what could they mean by: 'I will *love* thee, O Eternal, my strength!'[1] if the fear they meant was not the awe-filled observance from deep attachment, but a servile terror? It is objected, that their conception of righteousness was a narrow and rigid one, centring mainly in what they called *judgment*: 'Hate the evil and love the good, and establish *judgment* in the gate!'[2] so that 'evil', for them, did not take in all faults, whatever of heart and conduct, but meant chiefly oppression, graspingness, a violent, mendacious tongue, insolent and riotous excess. True; their conception of righteousness *was* much of this kind, and it was narrow. But whoever sincerely attends to *conduct*, along however limited a line, is on his way to bring under the eye of conscience all conduct whatever; and already, in the Old Testament, the somewhat monotonous inculcation of the social virtues of judgment and justice is continually broken through by deeper movements of personal religion. Every time that the words *contrition* or *humility* drop from the lips of prophet or psalmist, Christianity appears.

It is objected, finally, that even their own narrow conception of righteousness this people could not follow, but were perpetually oppressive, grasping, slanderous, sensual. Why, the very interest and importance of their witness to righteousness lies in their having felt so deeply the necessity of what they were so little able to accomplish! They had the strongest impulses in the world to violence and excess, the keenest pleasure in gratifying these impulses. And yet they had such a sense of the natural necessary connexion between conduct and happiness, that they kept always saying, in spite of themselves: *To him that ordereth his conversation right shall be shown the salvation of God!*[3]

[1] Ps. xviii. 1.   [2] Amos v. 15.   [3] Ps. l. 23.

Now manifestly this sense of theirs has a double force for the rest of mankind,—an evidential force and a practical force. Its evidential force is in keeping before men's view, by the example of the signal apparition, in one branch of our race, of the sense for conduct and righteousness, the reality and naturalness of that sense. Clearly, unless a sense or endowment of human nature, however in itself real and beneficent, has some signal representative among mankind, it tends to be pressed upon by other senses and endowments, to suffer from its own want of energy, and to be more and more pushed out of sight. Anyone, for instance, who will go to the Potteries, and will look at the tawdry, glaring, ill-proportioned ware which is being made there for certain American and colonial markets, will easily convince himself how, in our people and kindred, the sense for the arts of design, though it is certainly planted in human nature, might dwindle and sink to almost nothing, if it were not for the witness borne to this sense, and the protest offered against its extinction, by the brilliant æsthetic endowment and artistic work of ancient Greece. And one cannot look out over the world without seeing that the same sort of thing might very well befall conduct, too, if it were not for the signal witness borne by Israel.

Then there is the practical force of their example; and this is even more important. Everyone is aware how those who want to cultivate any sense or endowment in themselves must be habitually conversant with the works of people who have been eminent for that sense, must study them, catch inspiration from them. Only in this way, indeed, can progress be made. And as long as the world lasts, all who want to make progress in righteousness will come to Israel for inspiration, as to the people who have had the sense for righteousness most glowing and strongest;

and in hearing and reading the words Israel has uttered for us, carers for conduct will find a glow and a force they could find nowhere else. As well imagine a man with a sense for sculpture not cultivating it by the help of the remains of Greek art, or a man with a sense for poetry not cultivating it by the help of Homer and Shakespeare, as a man with a sense for conduct not cultivating it by the help of the Bible! And this sense, in the satisfying of which we come naturally to the Bible, is a sense which the generality of men have far more decidedly than they have the sense for art or for science. At any rate, whether this or that man has it decidedly or not, it is the sense which has to do with three-fourths of human life.

This does truly constitute for Israel a most extraordinary distinction. In spite of all which in them and in their character is unattractive, nay, repellent,—in spite of their shortcomings even in righteousness itself and their insignificance in everything else,—this petty, unsuccessful, unamiable people, without politics, without science, without art, without charm, deserve their great place in the world's regard, and are likely to have it more, as the world goes on, rather than less. It is secured to them by the facts of human nature, and by the unalterable constitution of things. 'God hath given commandment to bless, and he hath blessed, and we cannot reverse it; he hath not seen iniquity in Jacob, and he hath not seen perverseness in Israel; the Eternal, his God, is with him!'[1]

Anyone does a good deed who removes stumblingblocks out of the way of our feeling and profiting by the witness left by this people. And so, instead of making our Hebrew speakers mean, in their use of the word God, a scientific affirmation which never entered into their heads,

[1] Num. xxiii. 20, 21.

and about which many will dispute, let us content ourselves with making them mean, as a matter of scientific
fact and experience, what they really did mean as such,
and what is unchallengeable. Let us put into their
'Eternal' and 'God' no more science than they did:—*the
enduring power, not ourselves, which makes for righteousness.*
They meant more by these names, but they meant this;
and this they grasped fully. And the sense which this will
give us for their words is at least solid; so that we may
find it of use as a guide to steady us, and to give us a
constant clue in following what they say.

And is it so unworthy? It is true, unless we can fill it
with as much feeling as they did, the mere possessing it
will not carry us far. But matters are not at all mended
by taking their language of approximate figure and turning it into the language of scientific definition; or by
crediting them with our own dubious science, deduced
from metaphysical ideas which they never had. A better
way than this, surely, is to take their fact of experience,
to keep it steadily for our basis in using their language,
and to see whether from using their language with the
ground of this real and firm sense to it, as they themselves
did, somewhat of their feeling, too, may not grow upon
us. At least we shall know what we are saying; and that
what we are saying is true, however inadequate.

But is this confessed inadequateness of our speech, concerning that which we will not call by the negative name
of the unknown and unknowable, but rather by the name
of the unexplored and inexpressible, and of which the
Hebrews themselves said: *It is more high than heaven, what
canst thou do? deeper than hell, what canst thou know?*[1]—is this
reservedness of affirmation about God less worthy of
him, than the astounding particularity and licence of

[1] Job xi. 7.

affirmation of our dogmatists, as if he were a man in the next street? Nay, and nearly all the difficulties which torment theology,—as the reconciling God's justice with his mercy, and so on,—come from this licence and particularity; theologians having precisely, as it would often seem, built up a wall first, in order afterwards to run their own heads against it.

This, we say, is what comes of too much talent for abstract reasoning. One cannot help seeing the theory of causation and such things, when one should only see a far simpler matter: the power, the grandeur, the necessity of righteousness. To be sure, a perception of these is at the bottom of popular religion, underneath all the extravagances theologians have taught people to utter, and makes the whole value of it. For the sake of this true practical perception one might be quite content to leave at rest a matter where practice, after all, is everything, and theory nothing. Only, when religion is called in question because of the extravagances of theology being passed off as religion, one disengages and helps religion by showing their utter delusiveness. They arose out of the talents of able men for reasoning, and their want (not through lack of talent, for the thing needs none; it needs only time, trouble, good fortune, and a fair mind; but through their being taken up with their reasoning power), their want of literary experience. By a sad mishap for them, the sphere where they show their talents is one for literary experience rather than for reasoning. This mishap has at the very outset,—in the dealings of theologians with that starting-point in our religion, the experience of Israel as set forth in the Old Testament,—been the cause, we have seen, of great confusion. Naturally, as we shall hereafter see, the confusion becomes worse confounded as they proceed.

THE GOD OF METAPHYSICS

(1874)
See Contents, p. v

THERE remain the grounds for asserting God to be a person who thinks and loves which are supplied by metaphysics.

Continuo auditæ voces, vagitus et ingens.

At the mention of that name *metaphysics*, lo! essence, existence, substance, finite and infinite, cause and succession, something and nothing, begin to weave their eternal dance before us; with the confused murmur of their combinations filling all the region governed by *her*, who, far more indisputably than her late-born rival, political economy, has earned the title of the Dismal Science. Yet even into this region we ask the reader of *Literature and Dogma*, if he does not disdain an unsophisticated companion, to enter with us. And here, possibly, we may after all find reason to retract, and to own that the theologians are right. For metaphysics we know from the very name to be the science of things which come after natural things. Now, the things which come after natural things are things not natural. Clearly, therefore, if any science is likely to be able to demonstrate to us the magnified and non-natural man, it must be the science of non-naturals.

2

Professor Huxley's interesting discourse at Belfast drew attention to a personage who once was in the thoughts of everybody who tried to think,—René Descartes. But in this great man there were, in truth, two men. One was the anatomist, the physicist, the mechanical philosopher who exclaimed: 'Give me matter and motion, and I will make the world!' and of whom Pascal said that the only God he admitted was a God who was useless. This is the Descartes on whom Professor Huxley has asked us to turn once more our eyes; and no man could ask it better or more persuasively.

But there is another Descartes who had of late years been much more known, both in his own country and out of it, than Descartes the mechanical philosopher, and that is the Descartes who is said to have founded the independence of modern philosophy and to have founded its spiritualism. He began with universal doubt, with the rejection of all authority, with the resolve to admit nothing to be true which he could not clearly see to be true. He ended with declaring that the demonstration of God and the soul was more completely made out than that of any other truth whatever; nay, that the certitude and truth of every science depended solely on our knowledge of the true God.[1]

Here we have the Descartes who is commonly said to have founded modern philosophy. And who, in this our day of unsettlement and of impatience with authority, convention, and routine, who, in this our day of new departures, can fail to be attracted by the author of the 'Méthode', and by his promises? '*Je n'admets rien qui ne soit nécessairement vrai*; I admit nothing which is not necessarily true.' '*Je m'éloigne de tout ce en quoi je pourrais imaginer le moindre doute*; I put aside everything about which I can imagine there being the smallest doubt.' What

---

[1] Je reconnais très clairement que la certitude et la vérité de toute science dépendent de la seule connaissance du vrai Dieu.

could we, who demand that the propositions we accept shall be propositions we can verify, ask more? *Il n'y a que les choses que je conçois clairement et distinctement qui aient la force de me persuader entièrement; je ne puis me tromper dans les jugements dont je connais clairement les raisons*; Only those things which I conceive clearly and distinctly have the power thoroughly to persuade me; I cannot be mistaken in those judgements of which I clearly know the reasons.' What can be better? We have really no other ground for the certainty of our convictions than this clearness.

The rule of Descartes, therefore, not to receive anything as true without having clearly known it for such, is for us unchallengeable. How vain and dangerous did we find Butler's proposal that we should take as the foundation of our religion something for which we had a low degree of probability! In this direction, assuredly, Descartes does not err. 'Inasmuch as my reason convinces me', says he, 'that I ought to be as careful to withhold my belief from things not quite certain and indubitable as from those which I plainly see to be false, it will be a sufficient ground to me for rejecting all my old opinions if I find in them all some opening for doubt.' Certainly this is caution enough; to many it will even seem excess of caution.

It is true, the doubts which troubled Descartes and which have troubled so many philosophers,—doubts, whether this world in which we live, the objects which strike our senses, the things which we see and handle, have any real existence,—are not exactly the doubts by which we ourselves have been most plagued. Indeed, to speak quite frankly, these are doubts by which we have never been tormented at all. Our trouble has rather been with doubts whether things which people assured us really existed or had really happened, but of which we had no experience ourselves and could not satisfy ourselves that anyone else had had experience either, were really as those people told us. Descartes could look out of his window at Amsterdam, and see a public place filled with men and women, and say to himself that he had yet no right to be certain they were men and women, because they might, after all, be mere lay figures dressed up in hats and cloaks. This would never have occurred, perhaps, to the generality of mankind; to us, at any rate, it never would have occurred. But if this sort of scrupulosity led Descartes to establish his admirable rules: 'I admit nothing which is not necessarily true'; 'Only those things which I conceive clearly and distinctly have the power to convince me'; we cannot regret that he was thus scrupulous. Men, all of them, as many as have doubts of any kind and want certainty, find their need served when a great man sets out with these stringent rules to discover what is really certain and verifiable. And we ourselves accordingly, plain unphilosophical people as we are, did betake ourselves once to Descartes with great zeal, and we were thus led to an experience which we have never forgotten. And perhaps it may be of use to other plain people, for the purpose of the enquiry which at present occupies us,—the enquiry whether the solid and necessary ground of religion is the assurance that God is a person who thinks and loves,—to follow over again in our company the experience which then befell us.

Everyone knows that Descartes, looking about him, like Archimedes, for a firm ground whereon he might take his stand and begin to operate, for one single thing which was clearly certain and indubitable, found it in the famous '*Cogito, ergo sum*; I think, therefore I am'. If I think, said he, I am, I exist; my very doubting proves that I, who doubt, am. 'After thinking it well over and examining it on all sides, to this conclusion I cannot but come; I cannot but consider it settled that this proposition, *I am. I exist*, is necessarily true every time that I pronounce it or that I conceive it in my mind.' The discovery of this axiom appears to have filled Descartes with a profound sense of certitude and of satisfaction. And the axiom has been hailed with general approval and adopted with general consent. Locke repeats it as self-evident, without taking the trouble to assign to Descartes the authorship of it: 'If I doubt of all other things, that very doubt makes me perceive my own existence and will not suffer me to doubt of that.' Thinker after thinker has paid his tribute of admiration to the axiom; it is called the foundation of modern philosophy.

Now we shall confess without shame,—for to the prick of shame in these matters, after all the tauntings and mockings we have had to undergo, we are by this time quite dead,—we shall confess that from this fundamental axiom of Descartes we were never able to derive that light and satisfaction which others derived from it. And for the following reason. The philosopher omits to tell us what he exactly means by to *be*, to *exist*. These terms stand for the most plain, positive, fundamental of certainties, which is established for us by the fact that we think. Now what to *think* means we all know; but even if we did not, Descartes tells us. 'A thing which thinks', says he, 'is a thing which doubts, which understands, which conceives, which affirms, which denies, which wishes, which declines, which imagines also, and which feels.' So far so good. But Descartes does not tell us what those other terms *be* and *exist* mean, which express that fundamental certainty established for us by the fact of our thinking; and this we do not so clearly know of ourselves without being told. Philosophers know, of course, for they are always using the terms. And perhaps this is why Descartes does not trouble himself to explain his terms, I *am*, I *exist*, because to him they carry an even more clear and well-defined sense than the term, I *think*. But to us they do not; and we suspect that the majority of plain people, if they consented to examine their minds, would find themselves to be in like case with us.

To get a clear and well-defined sense for the terms, I *am*, I *exist*, in the connexion where Descartes uses them, we are obliged to translate them at a venture into something of this kind: 'I feel that I am alive.' And then we get the proposition: 'I think, therefore I feel that I am alive.' This asserts our consciousness to depend upon our thinking rather than upon anything else which we do. The assertion is clear, it is intelligible, it seems true; and perhaps it is what Descartes meant to convey. Still, it is disappointing to a plain man, who has been attracted to Descartes by his promises of perfect clearness and distinctness, to find that his fundamental proposition, his first great certainty, is something which we cannot grasp as it stands, but that we have to translate it into other words in order to be able to grasp it.

Perhaps, too, this translation of ours does not, after all, represent what Descartes himself meant by 'I am, I exist'. Perhaps he really did mean something more by the words, something that we fail to grasp. We say so, because we find him, like philosophers in general, often speaking of essence, existence, and substance, and in speaking of them he lays down as certain and evident many propositions which we cannot follow. For instance, he says: 'We have the idea of an infinite substance, eternal, all-knowing, all-powerful, the creator of all things, and with every possible perfection.' Again, he says: 'The ideas which represent substances to us are undoubtedly something more, and contain in themselves, so to speak, more objective reality,—that is to say, they partake by representation in more degrees of being or perfection,—than those which represent to us modes or accidents only.' 'Undoubtedly', says he, this is so; he introduces it, too, with saying: 'It is evident.' So our guide, who admits nothing which is not necessarily true, and puts aside everything about which he can imagine there being the smallest doubt, lays down that we have the idea of an *infinite substance*; and that of *substances* we have ideas distinguished from ideas of modes or accidents by their possessing more *being*, and this is equivalent to possessing more perfection. For when we assert that one thing is more *perfect* than another, this means, Descartes informs us, that it has more reality, more *being*.

All this, I say, our guide finds certain and not admitting of the least doubt. It is part of the things which we conceive with clearness and distinctness, and of which, therefore, we can be persuaded thoroughly. Man is a finite substance, that is, he has but a limited degree of being, or perfection. God is an infinite substance, that is, he has an unlimited degree of being, or perfection. Existence is a perfection, therefore God exists; thinking and loving are perfections, therefore God thinks and loves. In short, we have God, a perfect and infinite Being, eternal, all-knowing, all-powerful, the creator of all things, and having every perfection we can think of for him. And all this turns upon the words *is*, *being*. Infinite being, necessary being, being in itself, as opposed to our own finite, contingent, dependent being, is something, says Descartes, that we clearly conceive. Now something cannot come from nothing, and from us this infinite being could never have come; therefore, it exists in itself, and is what is meant by God.

Not Descartes only, but every philosopher who attempts a metaphysical demonstration of God, will be found to proceed in this fashion, and to appeal at last to our conception of *being, existing*. Clarke starts with the proposition that something must have existed from eternity, and so arrives at a self-existent cause, which must be an intelligent *Being*; in other words, at God as a person who thinks and loves. Locke lays it down that 'we know there is some real being, and that nonentity cannot produce any real being', and so bring us to an eternal, powerful, knowing *Being*; in other words, God as a person who thinks and loves. Of the God thus arrived at, Locke, like Descartes, says that 'the evidence is, if I mistake not, equal to mathematical certainty'. St. Anselm begins with an essential substantial good and great, whereby, he says, it is absolutely certain, and whoever likes can perceive it, that all the multifarious great and good things in the world get their goodness and greatness; and thus again we come to a one *Being* essentially great and good, or Divine Person who thinks and loves.

Now here it is, we suppose, that one's want of talent for abstract reasoning makes itself so lamentably felt. For to us these propositions, which we are told are so perfectly certain, and he who will may perceive their truth,—the propositions that we have the idea of an infinite substance, that there is an essential substantial good and great, that there is some real being, that a self-existent cause there must have been from eternity, that substances are distinguished in themselves and in our ideas of them from modes or accidents by their possessing more being,—have absolutely no force at all, we simply cannot follow their meaning. And so far as Descartes is concerned, this, when we first became aware of it, was a bitter disappointment to us. For he had seemed to promise something which even *we* could understand, when he said that he put aside everything about which he could imagine there being the smallest doubt, and that the proof of things to us was in the perfect clearness and distinctness with which we conceived them.

However, men of philosophical talents will remind us of the truths of mathematics, and tell us that the three angles of a triangle are undoubtedly equal to two right angles, yet very likely from want of skill or practice in abstract reasoning we cannot see the force of *that* proposition, and it may simply have no meaning for us. And let us suppose this may be so. But then the proposition in question is a deduction from certain elementary truths, and the deduction is too long or too hard for us to follow, or, at any rate, we may have not followed it or we may have forgotten it, and therefore we do not feel the force of the proposition. But the elementary assertions in geometry even we can apprehend; such as the assertion that two straight lines cannot enclose a space, or that things which are equal to the same are equal to each other. And we had hoped that Descartes, after his grand promises of clearness and certainty, would at least have set out with assertions of this kind, or else with facts of the plainest experience; that he would have started with something we might apprehend as we apprehend that three and two make five, or that fire burns. Instead of this, he starts with propositions about *being*, and does not tell us what *being* is. At one time he gives us hopes we may get to know it, for he says that to possess more being is to possess more perfection; and what men commonly mean when they talk of perfection, we think we can discover. But then we find that with Descartes to possess more perfection means to possess, not what men commonly call by that name, but to possess more being. And this seems to be merely going round in a circle, and we have to confess ourselves fairly puzzled and beaten.

So that when even Fénelon says, that most attractive of theologians: 'It is certain that I conceive a Being, infinite, and infinitely perfect',—that is to say, infinitely *being*, we have to own with sorrow and shame that we cannot conceive this at all, for want of knowing what *being* is. Yet it is, we repeat, on the clearness and certainty of our conceptions of *being*, that the demonstration of God,—the most sure, as philosophers say, of all demonstrations, and on which all others depend,—is founded. The truth of all that people tell us about God, turns upon this question what *being* is. Philosophy is full of the word, and some philosophies are concerned with hardly anything else. The scholastic philosophy, for instance, was one long debate about *being* and its conditions. Great philosophers, again, have established certain heads, or 'categories' as they call them, which are the final constitutive conditions of things, into which all things may at last be run up; and at the very top of these categories stands *essence* or *being*.

Other metaphysical terms do not give us the same difficulty. Substance, for example, which is the Latin translation of essence or being, merely means *being* in so far as *being* is taken to be the subject of all modes and accidents, that which stands under them and supplies the basis for them. Perhaps *being* does really do this, but we want first to know what *being* is. Spirit, which they oppose to matter, means literally, we know, only breath, but people use it for a *being* which is impalpable to touch as breath is. Perhaps this may be right, but we want first to know what *being* is. Existence, again, means a standing or stepping forth, and we are told that God's essence involves existence, that is, that God's *being* necessarily steps forth, comes forth. Perhaps it does, but we require first to know what *being* is.

Till we know this, we know neither what to affirm nor what to refuse to affirm. We refused to affirm that God is a person who thinks and loves, because we had no experience at all of thinking and loving except as attached to a certain bodily organisation. But perhaps they are not attached to this, but to *being*, and we ourselves have them, not because we have a bodily organisation, but because we partake of *being*. Supreme *being*, therefore, *being* in itself, which is God, must think and love more than any of us. Angels, too, there may be, whole hierarchies of them, thinking and loving, and having their basis in *being*. All this may be so; only we cannot possibly verify any of it until we know what *being* is; and we want to rest religion upon something which we can verify. And we thought that Descartes, with his splendid promises, was going to help us here; but just at the very pinch of the matter he fails us.

After all, plain, simple people are the great majority of the human race. And we are sure, as we have said, that hundreds and thousands of people, if their attention were drawn to the matter, would acknowledge that they shared our slowness to see at once what *being* is, and, when they found how much depended on seeing it, would gladly accompany us in the search for some one who could give us help. For on this we ourselves, at any rate, were bent:—to discover some one who could tell us what *being* is. And such a kind soul we did at last find. In these days we need hardly add, that he was a German professor.

3

But not a professor of logic and metaphysics. No, not Hegel, not one of those great men, those masters of abstruse reasoning, who discourse of being and non-being, essence and existence, subject and object, in a style to which that of Descartes is merely child's play. These sages only bewildered us more than we were bewildered already. For they were so far advanced in their speculations about being, that they were altogether above entertaining such a tyro's question as what *being* really is.

No, our professor was a mere professor of words, not of ontology. We bethought ourselves of our old resource, following the history of the human spirit, tracking its course, trying to make out how men have used words and what they meant by them. Perhaps in the word *being* itself, said we to ourselves, there may be something to tell us what it at first meant and how men came to use it as they do. *Abstracta ex concretis*, say the etymologists; the abstract has been formed out of the concrete. Perhaps this abstract *being*, also, has been formed out of some concrete, and if we knew out of what, we might possibly trace how it has come to be used as it has. Or has indeed the mystic vocable no natural history of this sort, but has dropped out of heaven, and all one can say of it is that it means *being*, something which the philosophers understand but we never shall, and which explains and demonstrates all sorts of hard problems, but to philosophers only, and not to the common herd of mankind? Let us enquire, at any rate.

So, then, the natural history of the word was what we wanted. With a proper respect for our Aryan forefathers, first we looked in Sanscrit dictionaries for information. But here, probably from our own ignorance and inexperience in the Sanscrit language, we failed to find what we sought. By a happy chance, however, it one day occurred to us to turn for aid to a book about the Greek language, a language where we were not quite so helpless as in Sanscrit,—to the 'Principles of Greek Etymology', by Dr. George Curtius, of Leipsic.[1] He it was who succoured a poor soul whom the philosophers had driven well-nigh to despair, and he deserves, and shall have, our lasting gratitude.

In the book of Dr. Curtius we looked out the Greek verb *eimi, eis, esti*, the verb which has the same source as the English verb *is*. Shall we ever forget the emotion with which we read what follows: 'That the meaning, addressed to the senses, of this very old verb substantive was *breathe*, is made all but certain by the Sanscrit *as-u-s*, life-breath, *asu-ra-s*, living, and the Sanscrit *âs*, mouth, parallel with the Latin *os*. The Hebrew verb substantive *haja* or *hawa* has, according to M. Renan (*De l'Origine de Langage*, 4th ed., p. 129), the same original signification. The three main meanings succeed one another in the following order: *breathe, live, be*.' Here was some light at last! We get then, for the English *is*,—the French and Latin *est*, the Greek *estin* or *esti*,—we get an Indo-European root *as*, breathe.

To get even thus much was pleasant, but what was our joy to find ourselves put by Dr. Curtius, in some words following those we have quoted, on the trace of a meaning for the mysterious term *being* itself? Dr. Curtius spoke of a root synonymous with *as*, the root *bhu*, in Greek φυ, and referred his readers to No. 417. To No. 417 we impatiently turned. We found there the account of the Greek verb φύω, φύομαι, I beget, I grow. This word is familiar to us all in our own words *future* and *physics*, in the French *fus*, in the Latin *fui*. All these are from an Indo-European root *bhu*, 'be', which had primarily that sense of 'grow',

[1] *Grundzüge der griechischen Etymologie*, von Georg Curtius; 3rd ed., Leipzig, 1869.

which its Greek derivative has kept. 'The notion *be* attaches to this root,' says Dr. Curtius, 'evidently on the foundation only of the more primitive *grow*.' If the root *as*, breathe, gives us then our *is*, *essence*, the root *bhu*, grow, gives us our *be*, *being*. This was indeed a discovery. *Is*, *essence* and *entity*, *be* and *being*, here we have the source of them all! as in another Indo-European root, *sta*, stand, we have, as everybody knows, the source of our words *existence*, *substance*. Our composite verb substantive in English, like the verb substantive in Latin, employs both the root *as* and the root *bhu*; we have *is* and *be*, as the Latin has *est* and *fui*. The French verb substantive manages to employ,—so M. Littré in his admirable new dictionary points out,—the roots *as*, *bhu*, and *sta*, all three.

Now then it remained for us to ask, how these harmless concretes, *breathe*, *grow*, and *stand*, could ever have risen into those terrible abstracts, *is*, *be*, and *exist*, which had given us so much torment. And really, by attending to the natural course followed by the human mind, to men's ways of using words and arriving at thoughts, this was not so very hard to make out. Only, when once it was made out, it proved fatal to the wonderful performances of the metaphysicians upon their theme of *being*. However, we must not anticipate.

Men took these three simple names of the foremost and most elementary activities in that which they knew best and were chiefly concerned with,—in themselves,—they took *breathing*, *growing*, *standing forth*, to describe *all* activities which were remarked by their senses or by their minds. So arose the verb substantive. Children, we can observe, do not connect their notions at all by the verb, the word expressing activity. They say, 'horse, black', and there they leave it. When man's mind advanced beyond this simple stage, and he wanted to connect his notions by representing one notion as affecting him through its appearing or operating in conjunction with another notion, then he took a figure from the activity that lay nearest to him and said: 'The horse breathes (is) black.' When he got to the use of abstract nouns his verb still remained the same. He said: 'Virtue breathes (is) fair; Valour growing (being) praiseworthy.' Soon the sense of the old concrete meaning faded away in the new employment of the word. That slight parcel of significance which was required had been taken, and now this minimum alone remained, and the rest was left unregarded and died out of men's thoughts.

We may make this clearer to ourselves by observing what has happened in the French and Dutch words for our common word *but*. *But* is in French *mais*, the Latin *magis*, our word *more*; in Dutch it is *maar*, our word *more* itself. *Mais* and *maar* were originally used, no doubt, with the sense of their being a check, or stop, given to something that had been said before, by the *addition* to it of something fresh. The primitive sense of addition faded away, the sense of check remained alone. And so it was with *as* and *bhu*, the primitive *breathe* and *grow*. Whatever affected us by appearing to us, or by acting on us, was at first said by a figure to breathe and grow. The figure was forgotten; and now *as* and *bhu* no longer raised the idea of breathing and growing, but merely of that appearance or operation,—a kind of shadow of breathing and growing,—which these words *as* and *bhu* had at first been employed to convey. And for breathing and growing other words than *as* and *bhu* were now found, just as, in French, *mais* now no longer means *more*, but for *more* another word has been found: the word *plus*. Sometimes, however, as in the case of the Greek verb γίγνομαι, ἐγενόμην, we see the same word continuing to be used both in its old full sense and in its new shrunk sense; γενέσθαι may mean both *to be born* and *to be*. But the user employed it, probably, in the two different acceptations, as if he had been employing two different words; nor did its use as hardly more than a copula necessarily raise in his mind the thought of its originally fuller significance.

Nor indeed were these primitive verbs, *as* and *bhu*, used only as a copula, to connect, in the manner we have described, the attribute with its subject. They were also used as themselves expressing an attribute of the subject. For when men wanted strongly to affirm that action or operation of things, that image of their own life and activity, which impressed itself upon their mind and affected them, they took these same primitive verbs and used them emphatically. Virtue *is*, they said; Truth does not cease to *be*. Literally: Virtue *breathes*; Truth does not cease to *grow*. A yet more emphatic affirmation of this kind was supplied by the word *exist*. For to exist is literally to step forth, and he who steps forth gives a notable proof of his life and activity. Men said, therefore: Duty *exists*. That is, according to the original figure: Duty steps forth, stands forth.

And the *not ourselves*, mighty for our weal or woe, which so soon by some one or other of its sides attracted the notice of man, this also man connected with whatever attributes he might be led to assign to it, by his universal connective, his now established verbs *as* and *bhu*, his *breathe* and *grow* with their blunted and shadowy sense of breathing and growing. He said: God *breathes* angry; our God *breathes* a jealous God. When he wanted to affirm emphatically that this power acts, makes itself felt, lasts, he said: God *exists*. In other words: God *steps forth*.

Israel conceived God with a solemnity and a seriousness unknown to other nations, as, 'The not ourselves that makes for righteousness.' 'When I speak of this unique God of Israel,' asked Moses, 'how shall I name him?' And the answer came (we will give it in the words of the literal Latin version, printed under the Hebrew in Walton's noble Polyglot Bible): 'Dixit Deus ad Mosen: *Ero qui ero. Et dixit: Sic dices filiis Israel: Ero misit me ad vos.*' '*I will breathe* hath sent me unto you'; or, as the Arabic version well renders this mystic name: *The Eternal, that passeth not.* For that this is the true meaning of the name there can be no doubt:—The *I will go on living, operating, enduring.* 'God here signifies of himself,' says Gesenius, 'not simply that he is *he who is,* for of this everyone must perceive the frigidity, but he signifies emphatically that he is *he who is always the same,* that is, the Immutable, the Eternal.' To the like effect Dr. Kalisch, in his valuable Commentary, after reciting the series of more fanciful and metaphysical interpretations, rests finally in this, the simple and the undoubtedly true one: 'He that changeth not, and that faileth not.'

'*I will breathe* hath sent me unto you!' Still the old sensuous image from the chief and most striking function of human life, transferred to God, taken to describe, in the height and permanency of its beneficent operation, this mighty *not ourselves,* which in its operation we are aware of, but in its nature, no.

And here is, indeed, the grand conclusion to be drawn from this long philological disquisition, from our persistent scrutiny of the primitives *as* and *bhu,* breathe and grow: that by a simple figure they declared a perceived energy and operation, and nothing more. Of a *subject,* as we call him, that performs this operation, of the nature of something outside the range of plants and of animals who do indeed grow and breathe, and from whom the figure in *as* and *bhu* is borrowed, they tell us nothing. But they have been falsely supposed to bring us news about the primal nature of things, to declare a subject in which inhered the energy and the operation we had noticed, to indicate a fontal category or supreme constitutive condition, into which the nature of all things whatsoever might be finally run up.

For the original figure, as we have said, was soon forgotten; and *is* and *be*, mysterious petrifactions, remained in language as if they were autochthons there, and as if no one could go beyond or behind them. Without father, without mother, without descent, as it seemed, they yet were omnipresent in our speech, and indispensable. Allied words in which the figure was manifest, such as existence and substance, were thought to be figures from the world of sense pressed into the service of a metaphysical reality enshrined in *is* and *be*. That imposing phrase of the metaphysicians for summing up the whole system of things, *substance and accident*,—phenomena, and that which stands under phenomena and in which they inhere, —must surely, one would think have provoked question, have aroused misgivings,—people must surely have asked themselves what the *that* which stands under phenomena was,—if the answer had not been ready: *being*. And *being* was supposed to be something absolute, which stood under all things. Yet *being* was itself all the while but a sensuous figure, *growing*, and did not of necessity express anything of a thing's nature, expressed only man's sense of a thing's operation.

But philosophers, ignorant of this, and imagining that they had in *being* a term which expressed the highest and simplest nature of things, stripped off (to use a naked phrase of Descartes), when they wanted to reach the naked truth of a thing, one of the thing's garments after another, they stripped away this and that figure and size for bodies, this and that thought and desire for mind, and so they arrived at the final substances of bodies and of mind, their *being* or *essence*, which for bodies was a substantial essence capable of infinite diversities of figure and size, for mind a substantial essence capable of infinite diversities of thought and desire. And that for bodies and for mind they thus got a highest reality merely negative, a reality in which there was less of reality than in any single body or mind they knew, this they did not heed, because in *being* or *essence* they supposed they had the supreme reality.

Finally, in considering God they were obliged, if they wanted to escape from difficulties, to drop even the one characteristic they had assigned to their substance, that of admitting modes and accidents, and thus to reduce, in fact, their idea of God to nothing at all. And this they themselves were much too acute, many of them, not to perceive; as Erigena, for instance, says: '*Deus non immerito nihilum vocatur*; God may be not improperly called nothing.' But this did not make them hesitate, because they thought they had in pure *being*, or *essence*, the supreme reality, and that this *being* in itself, this *essence* not even serving as substance, was God. And therefore Erigena adds that it is *per excellentiam*, by reason of excellency, that God is not improperly called nothing: '*Deus per excellentiam non immerito nihilum vocatur*.'

To such a degree do words make man, who invents them, their sport! The moment we have an abstract word, a word where we do not apprehend both the concrete sense and the manner of this sense's application, there is danger. The whole value of an abstract term depends on our true and clear conception of that which we have abstracted and now convey by means of this term. *Animal* is a valuable term because we know what breathing, *anima*, is, and we use animal to denote all who have this in common. But the *être* of Descartes is an unprofitable term, because we do not clearly conceive what the term means. And it is, moreover, a dangerous term, because without clearly conceiving what it means, we nevertheless use it freely. When we at last come to examine the term, we find that *être* and *animal* really mean just the same thing: *breather*, that which has vital breath.

How astounding are the consequences if we give to *être* and its cognates this their original sense which we have discovered! *Cogito, ergo sum*, will then be: 'I think, therefore I breathe.' A true deduction certainly; but *Comedo, ergo sum*, 'I eat, therefore I breathe', would be nearly as much to the purpose! Metaphysics, the science treating of *être* and its conditions, will be the science treating of breathing and its conditions. But surely the right science to treat of breathing and its conditions is not metaphysics, but physiology! 'God *is*', will be, God *breathes*; exactly that old anthropomorphic account of him which our dogmatic theology, by declaring him to be without body, parts, or passions, has sought to banish! And even to adore,—like those men of new lights, the French revolutionists, haters of our dogmatic theology,—even to adore, like Robespierre, the *Être Suprême*, will be only, after all, to adore the Supreme Animal! So perfidiously do these words *is* and *be*,—on which we embarked our hopes because we fancied they would bring us to a thinking and a loving, independent of all material organisation, —so perfidiously do they land us in mere creature-worship of the grossest kind. Nay, and perhaps the one man who uses that wonderful asbtract word, *essence*, with propriety, will turn out to be, not the metaphysician or the theologian, but the perfumer. For while nothing but perplexity can come from speaking of the essence or *breathing* of the Divine Nature, there is really much felicity in speaking of the essence or *breathing* of roses.

4

Dismayed, then, at the consequence of a rash use of *being* and *essence*, we determined henceforth always to subject these vocables, when we found them used in a way which caused us any doubt, to a strict examination. Far from remaining, as formerly, in helpless admiration of the philosophers, when upon the foundation of these words they built their wonderful cloud-houses and then laughed at us for not being able to find our way about them, we set ourselves to discover what meaning the words, in men's use of them, really did and could contain. And we found that the great thing to keep steadily in mind is that the words are, as we have shown, figure. Man applied this image of breathing and growing, taken from his own life, to all which he perceived, all from which he felt an effect; and pronounced it all to be living too. The words, therefore, which appear to tell us something about the life and nature of all things do in fact tell us nothing about any life and nature except that which breathing and growing go in some degree to constitute; —the life and nature, let us say, of men, of the lower animals, and of plants. Of life or nature in other things the words tell us nothing, but figuratively invest these things with the characters of animal and vegetable life. But what do they really tell us of these things? Simply that the things have an effect upon us, operate upon us.

The names themselves, then, *being* and *essence*, tell us something of the real constitution of animals and plants, but of nothing else. However, the real constitution of a thing it may happen that we know, although these names convey nothing of it and help us to it not at all. For instance, a chemist knows the constitution, say, of common ether. He knows that common ether is an assemblage of molecules each containing four atoms of carbon, ten of hydrogen, and one of oxygen, arranged in a certain order. This we may, if we please, call the being or essence, the *growing* or *breath*, of common ether. That is to say, to the real constitution of a thing, when we know it, we often apply a figurative name originally suggested by the principal and prominent phenomena of our own constitution.

This in the case of bodies. When we speak of the being or essence of bodies, it may be that we know their real constitution and give these names to it. But far oftener men say that bodies have *being*, assert that bodies *are*, without any knowledge, either actual or implied, of the real constitution of the bodies, but merely meaning that the bodies are seen, heard, touched, tasted, or smelt by us, affect our senses in some way or other. And to bodies, thus acting upon us and affecting us, we attribute being or *growing*, we say that they are or *breathe*, although we may know nothing of their constitution. But we apply to their action a figurative name originally suggested by the principal and prominent activities of our own constitution.

And we proceed just in the same way with what are not bodies. Men come by abstraction to perceive the qualities of courage and self-denial, and then talk of the *being* of the qualities at which they have thus come; they say that courage and duty have *growing* or being, they assert that courage and duty *breathe* or are. They apply to the working of their abstraction figurative names, drawn originally from the principal and prominent workings of their own life.

Or, again, they become aware of a law of nature, as it is called,—of a certain regular order in which it is proved, or thought to be proved, that certain things happen. To this law, to the law, let us suppose, of gravitation, they attribute *being*; they say that the law of gravitation is, exists, *breathes, steps forth*. That is, they give to the regularly ordered operation which they perceive, figurative names borrowed from the principal and prominent functions of their own life.

Or, finally, they become aware of a law of nature which concerns their own life and conduct in the highest degree, —of an eternal not ourselves that makes for righteousness. For this is really a law of nature, collected from experience, just as much as the law of gravitation is; only it is a law of nature which is conceived, however confusedly, by very many more of mankind as affecting them, and much more nearly. But it has its origin in experience, it appeals to experience, and by experience it is, as we believe, verified. Men become aware from experience,— that source of all our knowledge,—they become aware of a law of righteousness. And to this law they attribute *being*. They say that the law of conduct, the eternal not ourselves which makes for righteousness, is, exists,— *breathes, steps forth*. That is to say, they give to the stedfast, unchanging, widely and deeply working operation which they perceive, figurative names borrowed from the principal and prominent operations of their own life.

Being and *essence* men in this way attribute to what they perceive, or think they perceive, to be a law of nature. But often, long before they perceive it as a law of nature, they are conscious of its working; they feel its power by many a sharp lesson. And imagination coming in to help, they make it, as they make everything of which they powerfully feel the effect, into a human agent, at bottom like themselves, however much mightier,—a human agent that feels, thinks, loves, hates. So they made the Sun into a human being; and even the operation of chance, Fortune. And what should sooner or more certainly be thus made into a human being, but far mightier and more lasting than common man, than the operation which affects men so widely and deeply, —for it is engaged with conduct, with at least three-fourths of human life,—the *not ourselves* that makes for righteousness?

Made into a human being this was sure to be, from its immense importance, its perpetual intervention. But this importance does not make the personifying, anthropomorphic process, the less explanation of the attributed human qualities in this case, than it is the explanation of them in others. Yet we will have it, very many of us, that the human qualities are in the one case really there and inherent, but in all the other cases they are the mere work of man's plastic and personifying power. What was the Apollo of the religion of the Greeks? The law of intellectual beauty, the eternal not ourselves that makes for intellectual beauty. By a natural and quite explicable working of the human spirit, a heightened, glorified human being, thinking and loving, came to stand for the operation of this power. Who doubts this? But the thinking and loving Apollo of the Greeks, and every other example of the like kind except one, this natural working of the human spirit is supposed to explain; only the thinking and loving Jehovah of the Hebrews shall not be explained by this working, but a person who thinks and loves he really is!

To return, then, to our much abused primitives. They were supposed to give us for conscious intelligence, for thinking and loving, a basis or subject independent of bodily constitution. They do in fact give us nothing beyond bodily phenomena; but they transfer by a figure the phenomena of our own bodily life to all law and operation. On a fine and subtle scale they still carry on that personifying anthropomorphic process, native in man and ineradicable, which in all the early religions of the world we can see going forward on a scale gross and palpable.

So it appears that even when we talk of the *being* of things, we use a fluid and literary expression, not a rigid and scientific one.

5

Armed with this key of the real signification of our two poor little words, *is* and *be*, let us next boldly carry the war into the enemy's country, and see how many strong fortresses of the metaphysicians, which frown upon us from their heights so defiantly, we can now enter and rifle. For *is* and *be*, we have learnt, simply mean, in reality, *breathe* and *grow*, while in mankind's use of them they simply mean *operate*, or *appear to man to operate*. But when the metaphysicians start with their at least certainly knowing that *something is*, they always have in their minds: 'Something thinks which neither breathes nor grows, and we know of a subject for thinking which neither breathes nor grows, and that subject is *being, être*.' They are unaware that *being, être*, are two words which in reality simply mean breathing and growing. And then, with two supposed data of a cogitative substance and an incogitative substance, the metaphysicians argue away about the necessary mutual relations of these two in the production of things, and form all manner of fine conclusions. But all the knowledge they do really set out with in their *something is* amounts to this: 'We are aware of *operation*.' And this neither tells them anything about the nature and origin of things, nor enables them to conclude anything.

Now, if we keep this in mind, we shall see the fallacy of many reasonings we meet with. The *Edinburgh Review* says: 'All existing things must be persons or things; persons are superior to things; do you mean to call God a thing?' But he who pronounces that God must be a person or a thing, and that God must be a person because persons are superior to things, talks as idly as one who should insist upon it that the law of gravitation must be either a person or a thing, and should lay down which of the two it must be. Because it is a law, is it to be pronounced a thing and not a person, and therefore inferior to persons? and are we quite sure that a bad critic, suppose, is superior to the law of gravitation? The truth is, we are attempting an exhaustive division into things and persons, and attempting to affirm that the object of our thought is one or the other, when we have no means for doing anything of the kind, when all we can really say of our object of thought is, that it *operates*.

Or to take that favourite and famous demonstration of Anselm and Descartes, that if we have the idea of a perfect being, or God,—that is to say, of an infinite substance, eternal, all-knowing, all-powerful, the creator of all things, and with every possible perfection,—then this perfect being must exist. Existence, they argue, is a perfection, and besides, our imperfect finite being could never have given to itself the idea of a perfect infinite being. But we have this idea, they say, quite clearly and distinctly, and therefore there must exist some other being besides ourselves from whom we must have received it. All this, again, tumbles to pieces like a house of cards the moment we press it. The ambiguity lies in the words *perfect being, infinite substance*. Of a *not ourselves* we are clearly aware;—but a clear idea of an infinite substance, a perfect being, knowing and thinking and yet not breathing and growing? And this idea we could not have given to ourselves, because it is a *clear idea* of an infinite substance, full of perfection; and we are a finite substance, full of imperfection? But the idea which men thus describe is not a clear idea, and it is an idea which, in the only state wherein they really have it, they may perfectly well have given to themselves. For it is an idea of a man hugely magnified and improved.

The less and more in ourselves of whatever we account good, gives us a notion of what we call perfection in it. We have degrees of pleasure, and we talk of perfect, infinite pleasure; we have some rest, and we talk of perfect, infinite rest; we have some knowledge, and we talk of perfect, infinite knowledge; we have some power, and we talk of perfect, infinite power. What we mean is a great deal of pleasure, rest, knowledge, power; as much of them as we can imagine, and without the many lets and hindrances to them which we now experience. Our idea of a perfect being, all-knowing, all-powerful, is just like that idea of a myriagon, of which Descartes himself speaks somewhere. Of a pentagon, or five-sided figure, we have a distinct idea. And we talk of our idea of a myriagon, or ten-thousand-sided figure, too; but it is not a clear idea, it is an idea of something very big, but confused. Such is our idea of an infinite substance, all-knowing,

all-powerful. Of a bounded man, with some knowledge and some power, we have a distinct idea; of an
unbounded man, with all knowledge and all power, our
idea is not clear; we have an idea of something very wise
and great, but a confused idea. And even granting that
clear ideas prove themselves, this alleged clear and distinct idea of an infinite substance, all-knowing and all-
powerful, is one of those cases where an idea is fancied to
be clear and distinct when it is not.

But people still insist that our truly perfect ideas, at
any rate, must have being quite independently of us and
our experience, and must inhere, therefore, in a source, a
subject, an infinite substance, which is God. For we have,
say they, the idea of a perfect circle; yet this idea cannot
be given us by experience, because in nature there is no
such thing as a perfect circle. We have the idea of a perfect good; yet this idea cannot be given us by experience,
because in nature there is no such thing as a perfect good.
But let us ask ourselves whether even the circle and the
triangle were first, probably, pure conceptions in the
human mind, and then applied to nature; or whether
these forms were not first observed in nature, and then
refined into pure conceptions? And was perfect good, in
like manner, or perfect beauty, first a pure conception
in the human mind, and then applied to things in nature?
or were things more or less good and beautiful first
observed in experience, and goodness and beauty then
refined into pure conceptions? Because, in that case, our
ideas of a perfect circle and a perfect good are simply the
imagination of a still rounder circle and a still better
good than any which we have yet found in experience.
But experience gave us the ideas, and we have no need
to invent something out of experience as the source of
them.

Finally, let us take the grand argument from design. Design, people say, implies a designer. The ambiguity lies in the little termination *er*, by which we mean a *being* who designed. We talk of a being, an *être*, and we imagine that the word gives us conscious intelligence, thinking and loving, without bodily organisation; but it does not. It gives us one of two things only;—either it gives us breathing and growing, or it gives us effect and operation. Design implies a designer? Human design does; it implies the presence of a being who breathes and thinks. So does that of the lower animals, who, like man himself, breathe, and may be said to think. A very numerous class of works we know, which man and the lower animals make for their own purposes. When we see a watch or a honeycomb we say: It works harmoniously and well, and a man or a bee made it. But a yet more numerous class of works we know, which neither man nor the lower animals have made for their own purposes. When we see the ear, or see a bud, do we say: It works harmoniously and well, and a man or one of the lower animals made it? No; but we say: It works harmoniously and well, and an infinite eternal substance, an all-thinking and all-powerful being, the creator of all things, made it. Why? Because it works harmoniously and well. But its working harmoniously and well does not prove all this; it only proves that it works harmoniously and well. The well and harmonious working of the watch or the honeycomb is not what proves to us that a man or a bee made them; what proves this to us is, that we know from experience that men make watches and bees make honeycombs. But we do not know from experience that an infinite substance, all-thinking and all-powerful, the creator of all things, makes ears and buds. We know nothing about the matter, it is altogether beyond us. When, therefore, we are speaking exactly, and not poetically and figuratively, of the ear or of a bud, which we see working harmoniously and well, all we have a right to say is: It works harmoniously and well.

6

We besought those who could receive neither the miracles of popular theology nor the metaphysics of learned theology, not to fling away the Bible on that account, but to try how the Bible went if they took it without either the one or the other, and studied it without taking anything for granted but what they could verify. But such indignant and strenuous objection was made in the religious world to this proposal, and in particular it was so emphatically asserted that the only possible basis for religion is to believe that God is a person who thinks and loves, that the readers of *Literature and Dogma* who had taken our advice and had begun to find profit from it, might well be supposed to feel alarm and to hesitate, and to ask whether, after all, they were doing well in following our recommendation. So we have had to look again at the reasons for laying down as the foundation of religion the belief that God is a person who thinks and loves. And we found reasons of two kinds alleged: reasons drawn from miracles, and reasons drawn from metaphysics. But the reasons from miracles we found, after looking at miracles again, that we could not rely on, that fail us sooner or later they surely must. And now we find the same thing with the reasons drawn from metaphysics.

The reasons drawn from miracles one cannot but dismiss with tenderness, for they belong to a great and splendid whole,—a beautiful and powerful fairy-tale, which was long believed without question, and which has given comfort and joy to thousands. And one abandons them with a kind of unwilling disenchantment, and only because one must.

The reasons drawn from metaphysics one dismisses, on the other hand, with sheer satisfaction. They have convinced no one, they have given rest to no one, they have given joy to no one. People have swallowed them, people have fought over them, people have shown their ingenuity over them; but no one has ever enjoyed them. Nay, no one has ever really understood them. No one has ever fairly grasped the meaning of what he was saying, when he laid down propositions about finite and infinite substance, and about God's essence involving existence. Yet men of splendid ability have dealt in them. But the truth is, the reasons from metaphysics for the Divine Personality got their real nourishment and support out of the reasons from miracles. Through long ages the inexperience, the helplessness, and the agitation of man made the belief in a magnified and non-natural man or men, in etherealised men,—in short, in preternatural personages of some sort or other,—inevitable. And, the preternatural having been supposed to be certainly there, the metaphysics, or science of things coming after natural things and no longer natural, had to come in to account for it. But the miracles proving to be an unsubstantial ground of reliance, the metaphysics will certainly not stand long. Now, an unsubstantial ground of reliance men more and more perceive miracles to be; and the sooner they quite make up their mind about it, the better. But if it is vain to tamper with one's understanding, to resist one's widening experience, and to try to think that from miracles once can get ground for asserting God to be a person who thinks and loves, still more vain is it to try to think one can get ground for this from metaphysics.

And perhaps we may have been enabled to make this clear to ourselves and others, because we, having no talent for abstruse reasoning and being known to have none, were not ashamed, when we were confronted by propositions about essence and existence, and about infinite substance having undoubtedly more objective reality than finite substance, we were not ashamed, I say, instead of assenting with a solemn face to what we did not understand, to own that we did not understand it, and to seek humbly for the meaning of the little words at the bottom of it all; and so the futility of all the grand superstructure was revealed to us. If the German philosopher, who writes to us from Texas reproaching us with wasting our time over the Bible and Christianity, 'which are certainly', says he, 'disappearing from heart and mind of the cultured world', and calling us to the study of the great Hartmann, will allow us to quote the Bible yet once more, we should be disposed to say that here is a good exemplification of that text: '*Mansueti delectabuntur*; The meek-spirited shall be refreshed.'

But to our reader and to ourselves we say once again, as to the metaphysics of current theology, what we said as to its miracles. When we have made out their untrustworthiness, we have as yet achieved nothing, except to get rid of an unsafe stay which would inevitably have sooner or later broken down with us. But to use the Bible, to enjoy the Bible, remains. We cannot use it, we cannot enjoy it, more and more of us, if its use and enjoyment require us first to take for granted something which cannot possibly be verified. Whether we will or not, this is so; and more and more will mankind, the religious among them as well as the profane, find themselves in this case. 'In good truth,' said Pascal to the Jesuits, 'the world is getting mistrustful, and no longer believes things unless they are evident to it.' In the seventeenth century, when Pascal said this, it had already begun to be true; it is getting more widely true every day. Therefore we urge all whom the current theology, both popular and learned, dissatisfies (for with those whom it does not dissatisfy we do not meddle), we urge them to take as their foundation in reading the Bible this account of God, which can be verified: 'God is the eternal power, not ourselves, which makes for righteousness', instead of this other: 'God is a person who thinks and loves', which cannot. We advise them to eschew as much as possible, in speaking about God, the use of the word *Being*, which even strict thinkers are so apt to use continually without asking themselves what it really means. The word is bad, because it has a false air of conveying some real but abstruse knowledge about God's nature, while it does not, but is merely a figure. *Power* is a better word, because it pretends to assert of God nothing more than effect on us, operation. With much of the current theology our unpretending account of God will indeed make havoc; but it will enable a man, we believe, to use and enjoy the Bible in security. Only he must always remember that the language of the Bible is to be treated as the language of letters, not science, language approximative and full of figure, not language exact.

Many excellent people are crying out everyday that all is lost in religion unless we can affirm that God is a person who thinks and loves. We say, that unless we can verify this, it is impossible to build religion successfully upon it; and it cannot be verified. Even if it could be shown that there is a low degree of probability for it, we say that it is a grave and fatal error to imagine that religion can be built on what has a low degree of probability. However, we do not think it can be said that there is even a low degree of probability for the assertion that God is a person who thinks and loves, properly and naturally though we may make him such in the language of feeling; the assertion deals with what is so utterly beyond us. But we maintain, that, starting from what may be verified about God,—that he is the Eternal which makes for righteousness,—and reading the Bible with this idea to govern us, we have here the elements for a religion more serious, potent, awe-inspiring, and profound, than any which the world has yet seen. True, it will not be just the same religion which prevails now; but who supposes that the religion now current can go on always, or ought to go on? Nay, and even of that much-decried idea of God as *the stream of tendency by which all things seek to fulfil the law of their being*, it may be said with confidence that it has in it the elements of a religion new, indeed, but in the highest degree hopeful, solemn, and profound. But our present business is not with this. Our present business is with the religion of the Bible; to show a new aspect of this, wherein it shall appear true, winning, and commanding.

And if our reader has for a time to lose sight of this aspect amid negations and conflicts,—necessary negations, conflicts without which the ground for a better religion cannot be won,—still, by these waters of Babylon, let him remember Sion! After a course of Liberal philosophers proposing to replace the obsolete Bible by the enouncement in modern and congenial language of new doctrines which will satisfy at once our reason and imagination, and after reading these philosophers' grand conclusion that there is little indeed in the history and achievement of Christianity to support the claim made on its behalf to the character of a scheme divinely revealed for the salvation of the human race, a man may of a truth well say: '*My soul hath dwelt among them that are enemies unto peace!*' and may with longing remember Sion. But we will not quarrel with him if he says and does the same thing after reading us, too, when we have kept him so long at the joyless task of learning what not to believe. But happily this part of our business is now over. In what follows, we have to defend ourselves, and secure him, against the Liberal philosophers who accuse us of teaching him to believe too much.

PRINTED IN GREAT BRITAIN
AT THE UNIVERSITY PRESS, OXFORD
BY VIVIAN RIDLER
PRINTER TO THE UNIVERSITY